ARROW TALK

ARROW
TALK

Transaction, Transition,
and Contradiction in
New Guinea Highlands History

Andrew Strathern and
Pamela J. Stewart

The Kent State University Press ▸ *Kent, Ohio, and London*

© 2000 by The Kent State University Press, Kent, Ohio 44242

All rights reserved

Library of Congress Catalog Card Number 99-048675

ISBN 0-87338-661-2

Manufactured in the United States of America

07   06   05   04   03   02   01   00   5   4   3   2   1

Library of Congress Cataloging-in Publication Data

Strathern, Andrew.

Arrow talk : transaction, transition, and contradiction in New Guinea highlands history /
Andrew Strathern and Pamela J. Stewart.

p.   cm.

Includes bibliographical references and index.

ISBN 0-87338-661-2 (pbk. : alk. paper) ∞

1. Melpa (Papua New Guinea people)—Commerce.   2. Melpa (Papua New Guinea
people)—Politics and government.   3. Speeches, addresses, etc., Melpha.   4. Political
oratory—Papua New Guinea—Western Highlands Province.   5. Ceremonial
exchange—Papua New Guinea—Western Highlands Province.   6. Social change—Papua
New Guinea—Western Highlands Province.   7. Western Highlands Province (Papua New
Guinea)—Social life and customs.   I. Stewart, Pamela J.   II. Title.

DU740.42.S768   2000

306'.09956'5—dc21   99-048675

British Library Cataloging-in-Publication data are available.

▸ ▸ ▸ FOR ▸ ▸ ▸

"Strawberry Fields Forever"

▶ ▶ ▶ CONTENTS ▶ ▶ ▶

The Highlands of Papua New Guinea, first introduced to direct colonial influences in the 1930s, have since then been the scene both of a remarkably rapid set of introduced changes and a complex array of responses to these. As an ethnographic "region," the Highlands became well known in anthropological discussions from the 1960s onward, with successive waves of interest in descent theory and affiliation, ceremonial exchange and leadership, gender relations, entrepreneurship in business and politics, concepts of personhood, and most recently, the idea of the body and embodiment theory. A notable range of monographs, collections, and articles has been generated from these studies, and the region continues to attract a stream of discursive and reflective analytical writings. While a growing number of these studies take into account anthropology's increasing general engagement with questions of history, there are still not many full-length discussions of historical issues for particular peoples that extend through from precolonial times to the present (that is, the end of the twentieth century), a span of some seventy years. This book makes a contribution to the project of writing the anthropological history of the Highlands, focusing on one area, Mount Hagen, which has been studied successively since the 1930s by Lutheran and Catholic missionary scholars and by several anthropologists. The emphasis of the book is on the classic themes that have preoccupied ethnographers in theoretical and empirical terms, but the aim here is to bend these themes to the purposes of creating an historical account, situating the area both by way of detailed local ethnography and in relation to the wider influences unleashed by colonialism and subsequent political independence since 1975.

The book draws in part on some earlier studies, co-authored by us, done with this same overall project in mind, and we are grateful to the following organizations for permission to incorporate sections of materials that have been previously published into the present text: University of Pittsburgh Press for chapter 3, first printed in *"Money and Modernity,"* ed. D. Akin and J. Robbins, ASAO Monograph no. 17, 1999, and for chapter 4, part of which was first printed in the introduction to "Identity Work," ed. Pamela J. Stewart and Andrew Strathern, ASAO Monograph no. 18, 2000; the journal *Social Analysis* for chapter 11, first printed in that journal no. 42(2): 132–148, 1998; and the journal *Pacific Studies* for chapter 10, first printed in that journal no. 21(1), 1998.

We would also like to thank John Terrell and Rob Welsch for initially stimulating us to write on the topic of chapter 2 and for their insightful perspective on it. We thank Richard Feinberg for his valued comments on our manuscript.

The title of this book was originally proposed in conjunction with a grant application to the Harry Frank Guggenheim Foundation for work carried out in 1991 and 1994. Grateful thanks are made to the Foundation for its support, which was instrumental in facilitating the development of a continuous historical perspective on the Mount Hagen and Duna areas of the Highlands during the last decade. The Duna materials that we have collected will be presented in a subsequent publication.

Grateful acknowledgment is also made to the following agencies for support of fieldwork since 1991: the National Science Foundation (grant no. BNS 9006000) and the Wenner-Gren Foundation (grants nos. 5375 and 5600). Thanks also go to the Office of the Dean, Faculty of Arts and Sciences, University of Pittsburgh, and to the Pitcairn-Crabbe Fund, Department of Religious Studies, University of Pittsburgh, for ongoing help since 1987; to the School of Anthropology and Archaeology, James Cook University of North Queensland, Australia, for assistance in 1997 and 1998; and to the American Philosophical Society for support in 1994 and 1998. We acknowledge also with gratitude permissions gained through the National Research Institute and the Department of the Western Highlands Province in Papua New Guinea to carry out continuing field investigations. Where appropriate, abbreviations and/or pseudonyms have been used. Our sincere thanks also to many individuals in the Hagen community for working collaboratively with us during this time and in some instances helping us to escape physical danger in the increasingly violent atmosphere of Papua New Guinea today, including Ru-Kundil, Ongka-Kaepa, Yara-Ongka, Pik-Ruin, Tom-Kapi and his wife, Anna, and their sons, Mande-Kele, Elizabeth-Mambokla, Reiya-El and his wife, Ka, Puklum-El (John Keni), Emmanuel-Reiya, and Nikint-Reiya. We also thank others not named here who extended kindness to us during our sometimes difficult fieldwork experiences. What we have learned from them has made its way into much of our text, along with our own compilations, reflections, and analyses.

The love and respect that we share with each other is the strength of our collaboration and the spark of a unique chemistry. The order of our names on this book does not reflect relative contributions of work or ideas, since we both fully collaborated on all aspects of this project.

► ► ► INTRODUCTION ► ► ►

ONE

"Arrow Talk" (*el ik*) is a genre of political oratory among the Melpa-speaking people of Mount Hagen in the Western Highlands Province of Papua New Guinea. It is practiced at the end of political events to express how history has crystallized into a state of transactional play between participants in the exchanges that constitute the event, including a sense of the event as a transition between other events and any suggestions of contradictions involved in these transitions. The term *arrow talk* thus forms an apt signpost to the analytical themes of this book, which analyzes a series of historical shifts of ideology and practice in the Highlands societies of New Guinea, often described as exchange-oriented, particularly the Hagen area. The themes of transaction, transition, and contradiction engage with a variety of the issues that have emerged from the cumulative literature on these Highland areas of New Guinea (primarily but not exclusively Papua New Guinea). *Transaction* refers to the debates about the character of exchange and its role in historical terms. *Transition* points to discussions about putative directions of change that are in turn tied up with the evaluation of the significance of exchange itself. *Contradiction* refers to the theory that dialectical processes are at work in the production of history and identity over time.

The book is accordingly divided into four parts. In the first part, on transaction, we review some theories of exchange that have been used to explain Highlands societies, employing the notion of the egalitarian society on which approaches to competitive exchange have been made. Transactional theories of exchange used ideas of competition, individual action, and maximization to explain the processes of competition in behavioral terms. Such theories were also opposed to Marxist forms of theorizing, which tended rather to emphasize domination, exploitation, and inequality, including gender inequality, and the structural frameworks underpinning these societal characteristics. Transactional theory also depends on a particular view of individual action which tends to be opposed to the viewpoints expressed in the ethnography of the 1980s and 1990s on social personhood and agency seen in terms of the Melanesian "dividual" rather than the individual. These latter-day approaches all stem from the relativist concerns of anthropology that followed from a turn toward the interpretation of meanings in people's own terms seen in contradistinction to the understanding of processes of social life as the product of strategic transactions between individuals. The Melanesian "dividual" was a construct designed in model terms to contrast with the construct of the "individual" implied in transactional approaches, stressing the relational aspects of personhood and the idea of the person as the site of social relations rather than an originator of them (see generally M. Strathern 1988, although this author's actual formulation was simply that persons are as dividually as they are individually constructed, 1988: 13). Such reinterpretations of personhood belong in general to the trend known as Interpretivism in anthropological analysis. In our view, there is partial merit in all three of these approaches (Transactionalism, Marxism, and Interpretivism), but we wish to introduce a new term, the "relational-individual," in order to mediate the differences between the approaches in their treatment of social personhood. We concentrate on this point rather than reviewing these theories generally.

The second part of the book, on transition, gives the bulk of the historical information necessary to discuss the main processes of change and of historical movement from the 1960s, a starting point for much of the fieldwork in the New Guinea Highlands through to the 1990s. Major themes to be traced here are political and legal changes, economic changes, and changes in exchange practices generally. Overall the narrative traces the gradual commodification of social relations and values over time, alterations in the division of labor, the creation of new forms of political power, the strengths and weaknesses of the state, and the changeover from colonial administration to postcolonial democratic governance, and in particular the florescence and decline of practices of competitive exchange, their deflection into practices of simple compensation, the escalating problems of violence and predation in social relations, and the emergence of pervasive difficulties at the local level owing to land shortages, cash cropping, population shifts, unstable political competition, and the loss of articulating frameworks of behavior such as were provided by the *moka* system in Hagen. These changes are discussed also in terms of contemporary debates about globalization, localization, and the emergence of new senses of identity.

The third part of the book, on contradiction, pursues these issues into the time of the millennium. The tensions in society caused by the introduction of

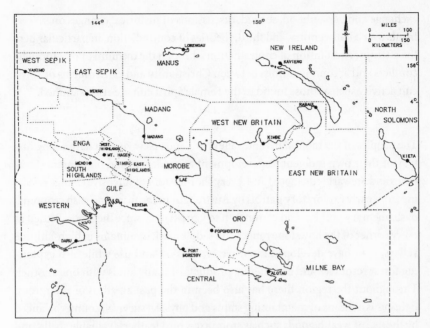

▸▸▸ *The provinces of Papua New Guinea, with some locations, including Mount Hagen.*

capitalism and democracy into local societies based on competitive egalitarianism have led to major contradictions in social life, related to the development of patterns of inequality analogous to those of social class. The experience of these contradictions has in turn led to the appropriation of forms of Christian worship and rhetoric as attempts to create peaceful resolution of conflicts, to reorder gender relations, and to produce a new sense of history. This appropriation is in turn greatly complicated by the parallel progression of "end times" or millennial rhetoric regarding the impending end of the world. Christian rhetoric is therefore the "arrow talk" of the future but itself leads to another contradiction, that between the production of history and the sense that history will soon come to an end (see, e.g., Stewart and Strathern 1998a. We do not discuss this last contradiction at length in the present work).

The fourth part of the book presents some summations and conclusions. Chapter 11 provides a conspectus of political and economic influences that have contributed to the transformation of ideas of personhood. Chapter 12 continues that theme, examining the specific importance of Christian ideas and alterations in patterns of exchange.

The book thus makes a contribution to three major strands of contemporary and past writing in the anthropology of New Guinea: first, theories of exchange and personhood, second, discussions of historical changes on several fronts over a half-century, and third, theories of contradiction, in particular here the attempted resolution of contradictions through the medium of religion. The conflicts and accommodations between Christianity and earlier forms of spirit cult activity such as those found in the Female Spirit cult are also examined.

Two

The peoples of the mountains and valleys of Papua New Guinea have a long history of their own indigenous development as gardeners and pig-rearers (Strathern and Stewart [eds.] 1998) and a very short history of intensive change resulting from early exploratory patrols by Australians in the 1930s and cash cropping, parliamentary politics, and conversion to Christianity since the 1960s. Settled in every corner of the limestone ranges and saddle-back mountains in high-altitude valleys, they have developed intensive systems of land use while also exploiting forest resources and exchanging products of many kinds with one another. Throughout the region there has also been in the past an ethos of intergroup fighting as a means of maintaining status and physical survival, counterbalanced by the use of wealth goods such as stone axes, bird feathers, valuable shells, and pigs in exchanges connected with marriage alliances and payments for deaths in warfare designed to create arenas of peaceful cooperation.

These conditions of life, elaborated in different ways over centuries, in processes of change influenced by the introduction of crops such as Colocasia taro and sweet potato and the progressive colonization of forest lands for agricultural use, have firmly shaped the main emphases of life in the Highlands: a concern for health, fertility, and reproduction; an emphasis on the use of ties of kinship and marriage in a mixture of competitive and collaborative struggles for survival and prestige; and a combination of strongly expressed sentiments of collectivity juxtaposed with an insistence on individual aims in circumstances of conflict. Resourceful in their responses to colonial control, these people even at first resisted the departure of the white Australians at the time of Papua New Guinea's independence in 1975 because they saw the foreigners as sources of much valued wealth (originally in shells, subsequently in money). Their own leaders are strategists who manipulate codes of behavior and cultural values in pursuit of a roster of aims. Quick to take offense and to suspect others, they are also adept at self-defense and in the verbal arts of self-presentation generally.

It is one of the arguments of this book that in trying to understand patterns of change and topics such as the definition of personhood in these societies, it is important to bear in mind this aspect of rhetorical discourse in the presentation of the self and to recognize, with Erving Goffman, that such presentations are made in the contexts of everyday life as well as on ceremonial occasions (Goffman 1959). Attention to this point therefore forms one of the threads running through this book and holding it together. Rhetoric is used to mediate between the often contradictory action patterns of expressing and recognizing relationships and pressing individual claims. Such pressures are, indeed, exercised in the idioms of kinship or friendship themselves, yet we must understand that individual calculations are also at work.

This discourse of recognizing and making claims is inflected in many ways. It may take the form of appealing to an idea of common descent or a denial of such ties; of denying inequality of status between people or asserting it; of playing on dimensions of perceived gender differences which are related to relative claims of authority and influence between the genders. The rhetorics of both politics and religion are inflected in gendered terms because links through females are fundamental to exchange ties and women's agency affects the operation of these ties in powerful ways that are at times denied, at times acknowledged by men; and the traditional religion takes cognizance of all this in the image of the Female Spirit and her cult, practiced until the 1980s and succeeded by a wave of influence of charismatic Christian sects in which women also play important roles.

The book overall is a set of historical reflections on the state of society in Hagen since early colonial times (and bearing in mind the long prehistory of change in the Highlands region as a whole). The Mount Hagen area received early attention in the work of comparative analysts of the Highlands societies partly because of the existence of ethnographies by the missionary anthropologists Georg Vicedom (Vicedom and Tischner 1943–48) and Hermann Strauss (Strauss and Tischner 1962). Vicedom's work was picked on because of his portraits of a society with chieflike leaders, made up of different ethnic strata, and possessing "slaves" at the bottom rung of the social ladder. In spite of Strauss's early disagreement with Vicedom on this and other points, Vicedom's views entered the literature as a kind of benchmark against which to test theories of evolutionary change in the Highlands (see Feil 1987). Our purpose here is different. We are not much concerned with typological questions (such as whether leaders are best seen in some objective way as "chiefs" or as "big-men") or with matters of social class and stratification in the past (i.e., whether Hagen was a "class society"), although there is merit in considering at least the rhetorical antecedents to today's incipient class structures. Rather, our focus is processual and historical. Our work in this vein, combining the perspectives of interpretive anthropology and political economy in the manner advocated by George Marcus and Michael Fischer (1986), joins a body of work by other writers which has transformed the anthropology of the Pacific from a focus on the synchronic to a concern with the diachronic (e.g., Brown 1978, 1995; J. and A. Carrier 1991; Errington and Gewertz 1995; Finney 1973; Gewertz and Errington 1999; Lattas 1998; Lederman 1986; Keesing 1992; Knauft 1999; Jolly and Keesing 1992; LiPuma n.d.; Salisbury 1962; Sillitoe 1996; Thomas 1989, 1991; Wiessner and Tumu 1998). These authors represent a variety of styles and theoretical positions, but they have shared an interest in developing an historical anthropology capable of dealing with both local and global events and in particular with the co-presence of the global and the local in particular sequences of events.

THREE

Transaction is chosen as the focus of the first part of the book. Theories of exchange have often been taken as central to the analysis of Melanesian societies generally and Highlands societies in particular, ever since the work of Bronislaw Malinowski (1922) and Marcel Mauss (1925 [1967]). Exchange is a very general term, and transaction may be held to have special connotations that narrow its meaning down. Indeed, we use the term *transaction* to signal the idea that exchanges in which specific kinds of balanced reciprocity are sought are our focus of interest. Beyond this, in Hagen at any rate, there is a pervasive tendency to make calculations about the size of gifts or payments, to argue about this, and to seek either to give or to receive a prestigious number of items. Hence the further sense of transaction comes into play, derived from transactionalist theory, which takes into account the strategizing behavior of those who make the exchange. And strategizing is in turn often expressed in verbal rhetoric. In Hagen requests for a higher level of giving are categorized as *pek rui*, "to scrape," in the same way as a scraper is used to peel tubers, revealing their inner flesh. "To scrape" is a recognized and expected routine of behavior evoking either compliance or resistance and depending on ideas of shame and honor. It also implies the agency of the scraper and the pain felt by the one scraped. Nuanced shaming thus becomes a part of the art of transacting. In turn, it becomes a part of the definitions of personhood that have currency; it enters into the jockeying of trade partners and their invocations of mutual friendship and into the history of changes in forms of wealth used over time. All these processes have contributed to the construction of the person in Hagen as a relational-individual, a state of being that cannot be described either simply as "relational" or as "individual" but is the product of a ceaseless dialectic or interplay between relationality and individuality, neither being prior to nor ascendant over the other. That this is so can be seen from the fact that the code in which rhetorical claims are put forward uses relationality as its basis. This is not necessarily a matter of a scheming individual hiding behind a screen of relational rhetoric, although this can certainly be the case. People think in relational terms about themselves. But they also behave in ways designed to advance their own interests at the expense of, regardless of, or making use of, others, and they make their own decisions to do this. In this sense, individuality is just as much ingrained in people as relationality. We argue that this is not just a modern or postcolonial phenomenon, although social relations that are commodified are inflected further and further toward forms of individuality that begin to deny, and not just use, the codes of relationality. Today's individual may be different from yesterday's, but there is a thread that binds them together—the pursuit of interests. Such an emphasis on transactions and the individual in no way denies or replaces emphases on relationality or on the collective group level or the pursuit of meanings. It simply adds a further dimension to all of these.

Transition is a term we use in an empirical sense to cover the major scope of changes that have led to alterations in ideas of personhood and in social relations over the last half-century or so. We pay attention in this part of the book to the perceptions and evaluations people themselves have made on processes of change, in which they express their aims, suspicions, dissatisfactions, and distrusts as well as their occasional pride in achievements. Rhetoric is employed both to reveal and to conceal these feelings. A major part of people's expressions is also organized around a perceived dialectic between "law," that is, introduced ways of behaving founded on new ideas of order and connected with notions of government, control, Christianity, business, and the like; and "custom," seen as the realm of the indigenous, the original, the locally based, that which is internal to social concerns of kinship or ritual. The dialectic between law and custom forms a major strand of people's ways of cognizing and arguing about the historical changes in their lives, especially in contexts of disputes and conflicts that are such an enduringly pervasive part of Hageners' life ways. Since "law" is linked to disputing, it is not hard to see why arguments about it have become central to people's changing ways of conducting themselves in disputes.

Contradiction, as the title of the third part of the book, builds on this example of a law/custom dialectic to develop a wider, more systemic picture of how contradictory principles and patterns play themselves out in social behavior. In the preceding parts we have identified potentially contradictory elements in the relational versus individual aspects of personhood and in the distinction between law and custom. In this third part we look at how these and other contradictions have been mediated in practice. First, we look at the history of compensation practices, the contradictory pulls of aggression and peacemaking that found their resolution in the moka system of exchange, and the limits of the development of the moka historically. We speak also in this chapter of the rhetorically employed concepts of honor and shame embedded in people's attempts to express their agency and to influence one another. The next chapter also explores these themes, retracing aspects of the history of exchange in the context of colonial control. We then show how the motif of confession, altered in today's Christian contexts, has been and is a major way of mediating contradictions and bringing disputes to resolution.

Two chapters offer conclusions (Part 4). Chapter 11, on money, politics, and persons, draws together many of the themes in Parts 2 and 3, paying considerable attention to the contexts of the nation and the state and the specific ways in which national politics have influenced the local levels, along with capitalist-style business. The chapter shows the relational-individual now operating in new arenas. The final chapter gives a further overview, in particular looking at the extent to which Christianity represents radical change ("revolution") in Hagen society and achieves radical answers ("resolutions") to problems of contradiction and change. This chapter therefore draws together the three main threads of the study as whole, arguing that new forms of transactions envisaged in Christian practice and discussed in Part 3 are to be seen as the outcome of the transitional processes outlined in Part 2. Christian personhood in some senses represents a radical break with the past, yet the actual practices of people indicate that they continue to operate with relational-indivual ideas also embedded in the forms of transaction examined in Part 1. At the same time, their consciousness of change in terms of differences between the generations has become sharper at the turn of the century than it was twenty years before. Older leaders recognize that younger people do not necessarily listen to them and that young men, in particular, are prepared to exercise violence, not just against outsiders, but within their own groups. This is part of an ongoing and developing tension between the generations.

As can be seen from this summary, the book is by no means a straightforward chronological account. Instead, its focus is thematic. While it is cast entirely in terms of the understanding of history as change and as continuity, the account starts, restarts, and returns to points in time repeatedly throughout. It does not therefore have to be read in a linear fashion from this point of view. But its portraits and arguments are designed to be cumulative, as well as overlapping, and the above has been intended as a road map to the way that the argument proceeds in both linear and recursive modes.

► ► ► PART ONE ► ► ►

TRANSACTION

Theories of exchange and transaction took up a good part of the analytical efforts of anthropologists working in the New Guinea Highlands in the 1960s and 1970s. Since then, there have been attempts to re-evaluate that overall emphasis and to make more complex the taxonomies of political and personal power that we construct as analytical devices in our ethnographies. In this first part of the present book, we review some of the history of theorizing about exchange in Highlands societies, centering our discussion on concepts of personhood and on the meaning attributed to activities such as "trade" and the historically altering constellations of wealth items. We arrive at the concept of the "relational-individual" as a portmanteau term encompassing the complexities of personhood and agency.

ONE

Transaction and Personhood

Marshall Sahlins set an initial tone in studies of Melanesian big-manship by arguing that there was a crucial difference between chiefs and "big-men" as leaders in Pacific societies, Polynesia the home of the former and Melanesia of the latter. This typological distinction broke down through negative cases: chiefs in Melanesia and big-men in Polynesia (Sahlins 1963; Hau'ofa 1975). Later, it was proposed that Melanesia be divided into big-men versus great-men societies (Godelier 1982, 1986), a distinction that has since been expanded (Lemonnier 1986, 1991) and critically reconsidered (A. J. Strathern 1993a). Here, we are concerned largely with the case of big-manship in Mount Hagen. Sahlins's second trend-setting characterization was his description of the typical personality profile of the Melanesian big-man as a rugged, free-booting individualist entrepreneur. This portrait also later came to be seen as problematic, since it was argued that it was influenced by a projection of Western economic models onto Melanesian phenomena. Sahlins's picture came to be dubbed as a product of ethnocentricity.

The idea of the big-man as an entrepreneur is central to the issue here, along with the particular image of individualism that goes with it. The big-man as entrepreneur is both a personality type and a type of social personhood. This view of big-manship was also related to two trends of thought in social and cultural anthropology in the 1960s: transactionalism and methodological individualism. The latter stressed that we must concentrate on individuals and their actions in order to understand social processes, while the former argued that these actions are in fact transactions, exchanges with others in which individuals attempt to secure, and perhaps maximize, gains for themselves. The work of Fredrik Barth (e.g., 1966) was particularly influential in giving force to these trends, although Barth's overall social theory is not to be equated with either of them. Barth argued that we need generative models of how social processes and institutions work and that processes are generated through transactional exchanges of value between actors. He added to this a theory of the entrepreneur: entrepreneurs create new values out of transactions between spheres of exchange that were formerly separate, taking risks in the process of doing so.

These discussions by Sahlins and Barth were largely conducted on different ethnographic terrains, but Barth's ideas of the entrepreneur can certainly be fed into Sahlins's picture of the big-man. Both theorists, in turn, were surely cognizant of the long-standing debate in economic anthropology between formalists and substantivists. Formalists argued, like transactionalists, that individuals act to maximize gains, they "economize" in this sense; substantivists argued that people's "economic" actions are roles set into social matrices governed by cultural values and that these values set the terms for people's actions. Substantivists were concentrating on frameworks for action, formalists on particular actions themselves, operating within or outside of such frameworks. A full analysis requires both perspectives (see A. J. Strathern 1971:xii). Nevertheless, the argument went deeper at the individual level: effectively, substantivists argued that formalist arguments were ethnocentric in the same way that Sahlins's depiction of the big-man was labeled as ethnocentric. In the substantivist view, individuals did not maximize; instead they enacted social roles and values, and the economy was always seen as embedded in wider social contexts.

As with so many debates in the social sciences, truth lies in a middle pathway incorporating elements of two extremes, but this is not how things generally proceed. Instead, one viewpoint tends to prevail over the other, at least for a while, until both are superseded by some new trend. In the 1960s anthropologists interested in social change were attracted to the idea of entrepreneurship implicit in the work of both Sahlins and Barth. Ben Finney, for example, in his work on early coffee growers in the Eastern Highlands of Papua New Guinea, propounded two points: first, that big-men were quick to seize on business opportunities because of their preexisting entrepreneurial propensities, and second, that the Highlands societies as a whole were preadapted to capitalist development (Finney 1973). Finney's argument was a very valuable contribution at the time. It demolished in advance any myth of the "primitive," communalistic society incapable of adapting to the "modern" world. Rather, it presented Highlanders as innovators, eager for change. The difficulties that have subsequently been identified in this argument are also twofold: first, the big-men who became entrepreneurs were not necessarily typical of their society and they twisted indigenous usages in pursuit of their own ends; and second, though Highlanders may have been ready for change, they were not simply preadapted to all the implications of capitalism because these can be deleterious, even though in other ways beneficial (see Finney 1993). Realization of these unfavorable consequences then leads people to resist, rather than support, certain further structural changes, such as alterations in rules of land tenure in the direction of private freehold ownership.

Nevertheless, it would be hard to deny that Highlanders were indeed keen on gaining benefits from and through the world of the whites and quickly sought ways to do so, as they still do. The basic portrait of the entrepreneurial tendencies of big-men in colonial through to postcolonial times therefore stands. It is, however, significantly modified by pointing out that entrepreneurial values are set into the total matrix of values surrounding transactions (A. J. Strathern 1972a) and that the ambitious behavior of individuals often meets resistance and even threats of violence when this total matrix is perceived as being violated. In Hagen, the "new big-men" of the 1970s, then younger men who were establishing businesses buying coffee, running trucks, and opening trade stores, frequently spoke of their fear that outside groups were secretly channeling lethal sorcery-stuff into their area along covert kin lines, to enable jealous intermediate relatives to kill them.

Although the jealousy of rivals was well understood by the first generation of entrepreneurs in Hagen and conceptualized in terms of sorcery fears, they also, like the traditional big-men before them, knew very well that their success depended on the support of their own domestic groups, especially on the work and social support of their wives, who weeded coffee plots, picked the berries, and dried them in the sun before sale. This gendered element of the society tended to be left out of the earlier transactional models, but it is vital to include it in any latter-day synthesis. The division of labor, the sharing of proceeds from cash cropping, the extraction of money for contributions to compensation payments, and the claims of women on consumption goods as well as their growing importance in the 1990s in Christian church activities are all vital matters that have influenced changing concepts of personhood over time. A gendered perspective brings to the fore both the issue of domination, much debated in the literature, and the factual character of the interdependence and complementarity of gender relations. While Hagen men in the 1960s were prepared to declare that only they were "strong" enough to fight, make speeches, and give pigs away in exchanges, they also admitted that only women were "strong" enough to bear children, carry loads of food, and rear the pigs in the first place (see also Sillitoe 1985:497–498 on men's and women's views on work among the Wola people).

Although the transactional history of businessmen and politicians in the Highlands has continued amply to show the relevance of the early 1960s writings on the Highlands, fashions in anthropological writings as a whole have appeared to shift away from the transactional viewpoint. This shift has in turn to do with the move to the "interpretive turn" in anthropology, a transition from function to meaning as the focus of interest. Transactionalism dealt with exchanges between actors and their consequences, anticipated or otherwise. Interpretive anthropology, by contrast, deals with the conceptual frameworks in terms of which transactions are placed and the meanings people themselves give to consequences. In the present instance the interpretive turn in Melanesianist anthropology allied itself strongly with the traditions of substantivism in economic anthropology at large. In so doing, it also questioned the idea of the individual, which is central to transactionalism, stressing instead the communal and relational character of action and agency in Melanesian societies and the ethnophilosophies of substance and personhood putatively at the heart of Melanesian cultural forms. The result was a sea change in the overall perception of these societies that over time all but obliterated the traces of the old anthropological accounts centered on notions of the individual and on entrepreneurship. Sahlins's model was not just pushed to one side: it was engulfed in an ocean of altered interpretations, visible only at a distance from above in an altered image of itself.

Our purpose here is not simply to engage in intellectual underwater archaeology or to raise a wreck for inspection. It is, however, to recover what was worthwhile in the earlier viewpoint and to place it in dialectical relationship with contemporary views. The transactionalist view of exchange is sometimes today opposed to the interpretivist view, in spite of the fact that transaction and meaning were long ago brought together (see, for example, Kapferer 1976). It is not therefore a matter of attempting to reinstate an outmoded view, since the transactionalist approach was not so much refuted as engulfed, as we have seen. It is rather a matter of setting the two approaches alongside each other for consideration.

A typical context from the Mount Hagen moka exchange system can be given by way of illustration here. In the moka people try to give as much to their partners in wealth objects as they can. The more they give, the more they maximize their proceeds of prestige. This in turn obviously benefits the partners, who maximize their immediate economic gains. If this transactional sequence were considered purely by itself, it would make no sense in terms of Western conceptual frameworks, unless we knew what can be done with prestige. A person cannot live by prestige alone. In the moka, however, prestige leads to the likelihood of inspiring confidence in people to give to one and hence to finance future transactions; and in any case the recipient partner is expected to make even greater returns later, so there is both a short-term and a long-term advantage in giving generously, unless partners renege on their obligations. In this regard, the moka worked as any financial institution does cross-culturally, on investor trust. The system is also structured in such a way that any attempt to short-circuit it by maximizing gains in the wrong way, that is, by receiving a large gift and *not* repaying it, is penalized by a large drop in prestige and a refusal of others to invest in one again. Cheating occurs but tends more to be eliminated by sheer cultural logic than to be encouraged by individual desires and machinations. In this case, therefore, there is indeed maximization and economizing, but the form of these two activities makes no sense at all unless it is understood in terms of the basic transactional structures and frameworks of understanding. Should these in turn break down, the moka itself would do so. (We explore at length later in this book the real-world history of the moka and how this exchange system has fallen into decline.) A picture of the moka in action requires therefore that we depict individuals, but these are individuals who are themselves constituted, and who creatively and variably constitute themselves, within the relational frameworks outlined above.

The above example shows what we mean by bringing transaction and personhood into articulation with each other. In effect, Sahlins developed a portrait of the Melanesian big-man's "personality" out of a certain idea of transaction itself. But this needs to be complemented by a serious consideration of local ideas of "personhood" which incorporates the frameworks of knowledge and understanding that people bring to their lives. When that is done, evaluative notions such as "the big-man as entrepreneur" can themselves be seen in a more accurate way. We find that the big-man does indeed maximize, but what is maximized and how and why all shift. It is to accommodate this insight that we have developed the concept of the relational-individual which is explored later in the book.

Two further points are worthwhile to make here. We have reviewed the idea of the big-man as entrepreneur. Such a notion tends to apply most aptly to circumstances of wider historical change, when new opportunities, such as growing cash crops, are brought in from outside. So the idea of the big-man as entrepreneur might be considered moot if applied to precolonial times, and this would be another objection to Sahlins's view. That, however, would be incorrect, since Highlands societies have experienced many hundreds, if not thousands, of years of change of various sorts, and big-manship itself is likely to have evolved pari passu with this longer overall history of change. At first, responses to opportunities, such as the arrival of a new crop like the sweet potato, which later became the Highlands staple, no doubt generated experimental activities carrying risks of failure that later settled into more stable adaptations. A surplus of food may have encouraged the use of pigs in exchanges and the "rules" of exchange would be worked out, again in an initial context of risk. The moka system itself, with its

▸▸▸ *A leader orates beside a display of beer cartons, whiskey and gin bottles, money, and pigs' legs and heads, to be given away in an internal compensation payment (Kawelka Kurupbmo, 1970s).*

reliance on investments and their timing, carried intrinsic elements of risk. And the value of human life = wealth must itself have been at some point the creation of an entrepreneurial imagination in the broadest sense. So people as risk-takers are not the products solely of modernity.

We can argue, however, that sharply transitional times, with their swift alterations in demands on people, do lead to the accentuation of two problems: one, the need to improvise within unknown parameters as the factors of change multiply. This has certainly been one of the puzzling challenges for Hagen men and women in the last twenty years or so, and they have become used to what we may call an improvisational mode of response to difficulties (compare Appadurai 1991:200 on contempory life generally). The second problem, related to the first, is that of legitimacy and respect. When change is rapid and there is a large gap between the experiences of different generations, there is also a gap in respect, and respect is needed to sustain certain interpretive frameworks that control actions. Such frameworks appeared to be operating powerfully in the 1960s, even as they were already incorporating many new and significant elements drawn from administrative and mission influences. These frameworks also appeared under greatest challenge in the 1990s, leading to attempts at refurbishing them through the explicit adoption of Christian patterns of rhetoric and symbolism.

The question of how typical big-men are in their own societies has been raised above. In one sense they are clearly not typical because they are in a minority. In another sense, however, they embody core shared values of their society, since they are looked to in order to provide leadership and competitive power in a world of contested negotiations about politics and wealth exchanges. From another perspective, individual big-men may carry their manipulative tendencies too far and cause resentment in others; yet if they do not conduct themselves forcefully and energetically they will cease to be regarded as men of influence. Typicality is not so much at issue here as legitimacy. Further, it is true that not all big-men carry out the same roles. Some are prominent in exchanges, some in speech-making. The most prominent of all hold positions of preeminence in both spheres because persuasive and eloquent speech is one of the means to attract wealth and achieve success in interpersonal and intergroup dealings. Men of lesser status may be seeking in their lifetime to approximate such successes. Others are content to stay as they are or realize they cannot do otherwise; but they are likely to subscribe to the values the big-men stand for and to support particular big-men unless they feel these have cheated or misused them, as can happen. In that case, the egalitarian ethos asserts itself: the big-man is no longer a big-man in their eyes, he is instead a "rubbish-man" (*wuö korpa,* one who seeks wealth and does not find it, or who behaves wrongly to get it).

Women also subscribe to the same overall scales of value and use in their discourse combative ways of evaluating one another's actions that employ the notions of being *nuim* (big, important) and *korpa* (rubbish). They may—and in the past also might—fight each other or dispute with each other using arguments along these lines. We take here an example from the 1980s in which two women disputed over a pig and reproduce some of their statements and interchanges to show what we mean (see A. J. Strathern 1993b:15–42 for more details).

The two women in the dispute were sisters-in-law, the one married to the other's brother. The sister had helped her brother on one occasion with a pig for his bridewealth payment and had received separately a small pig, which she had proceeded to rear. Later the other woman came and seized the pig, and they fought over it, biting and drawing blood in a contest of strength. The transactional state of play between them was disputed. One woman said she had to receive back the pig she had contributed to the bridewealth of her brother, plus a monetary sum of fifty kina she had given previously, before allowing the other to take off the pig that had been seized. The other woman countered that the small pig had been given on condition that it be exchanged in moka for another and the exchange pig would come back to her and her husband. Each woman therefore declared that she was the one in credit with the other and could say with legitimacy "you owe me"; and each manipulated her understanding of the history of dealings between them to promote her own view. Men related to each of the women in a complex network of kin and locality ties and also enmeshed in a historical set of moka payments designed to stabilize land claims and settle issues resulting from deaths intervened to remind both women of these wider contexts and to ask them to settle their dispute peacefully, not violently or in such a way as to worsen local political relations. While the women were locked in an obsessive contest with each other as sisters-in-law, the men made them consider matters from another context of relationality in which each was urged not to disturb the network of relationships around her. The discussion proceeded to the point at which this viewpoint prevailed, but it is important to note that at the outset, and indeed throughout their own angry statements, each woman was concerned both to assert herself as a single, decision-making person and to appropriate claims to legitimacy and correctness through the norms of relationality. As well, each disparaged the other's status in terms of the nuim/korpa ("big"/"rubbish") profile. Some textual excerpts may be cited to illustrate these points.

YA.: I told them that I would make moka first, and after the moka if I had a pig left I would give it to you and my brother, but not yet! I told them already, yet they came today and stole my pig. When the two of them did that I was very angry because the pig was only small when they first gave it to me. I did all the hard work and the pig grew up and now they want to get it. But I won't let them take it without my permission. Also, I was not in my house when they came and stole the pig.

Here the speaker refers to her sister-in-law and her own brother, blaming both for coming to recover the pig. She asserts herself as a legitimate decision maker, explaining that she has a right to be angry and that she personally raised the pig and therefore must be compensated for her incremental work in making it grow. Finally, she declares that the pig cannot be taken against her will and that it should not have been removed from her house without her presence, as this amounted to theft. The sister-in-law later countered that she and her husband had called on Ya. to come up to her house and discuss the pig and that they had not received an exchange pig for it as promised and that she needed it to help pay for her own brother's bridewealth.

The two then proceeded into vituperations.

YA.: You listen, this pig is not yours, you didn't bring any pig when you came to marry my brother! This pig belongs to my brother and I used to feed it and was keeping it for him. You woman! You have nothing in your background, nothing in your possession. You are talking for nothing, forget it!

She demanded further that her sister-in-law, N., should compensate her for biting her and marking her body. N. replied with sarcasm:

N.: "You, I will give it to you, because in this place your name is heard of by many people and your name is higher than any other woman in this world, so I will compensate you, don't worry."

To which Ya. replied that she was making no special claims for herself, she was just an ordinary woman.

Further insults followed:

YA.: "Are you talking about the things which you used to give to your father? Your father is a poor man, he is really poorer than any other man. You go from men to men and never give anything to your family."

N.: "Sorry, you never give anything to your father either. You are just the same as I am!"

YA.: "When you marry some men, you work as their laborer and never get anything out of the hard work. No wonder you go from man to man, because the men you marry use you for nothing and never give any brideprice to your father. Now you are with my brother, he'll do the same to you, when he lifts up something to eat, you look up and down like a dog."

N.: "If you are talking about me, I think you don't know my name, I used to look after many pigs and give them to my father and all my family. I am not like you, working as a laborer for someone and never giving anything to your father."

A local mediator reminded them of their relationship:

MA.: "N. is your brother's wife and both of you are sisters-in-law, so you talk about it and solve the problem among yourselves."

Both, however, repeated their insults and claims of relative status. N. declared that she transacted many pigs in moka and challenged Ya. to declare parity with her. Ya. retorted that N. had married the ex-husband of her sister and added: "I wouldn't marry my sister's divorced husband. My people would criticize me for that."

Finally, some of the men involved said N. could not take the pig away, at least yet, because they held grudges against her father for not meeting his moka debts. They deferred all the specific issues and held onto the pig as surety for their own debts, trying to use it as a lever in a wider set of concerns.

Our purpose here has not been to recount the details or the outcome of this case but to look at some of the terms in which each woman presented her personhood. First, it is obvious how forcefully they did so. Second, it is equally clear that each woman simultaneously praised herself and denigrated the other. Third, each cited normative patterns and claimed to have kept to them. Fourth, the dimensions they invoked were those of sexual behavior, kin ties, participation in exchange, and social status resulting therefrom. How does all this throw light on the question of relationality versus indivduality?

It is apparent from these excerpts that we cannot really separate these two trends in behavior: relational idioms are used to assert individual claims, and these claims in turn belong to relational contexts. At the same time, we gain a picture of determined individual people, battling for their interests as ruggedly as any business person in the marketplace. The issues are largely left undecided, but the episode of open dispute ends with an imposition of wider interests by some of the men involved on Ya.'s side and a substitution of one set of interests for another, subsuming each woman's viewpoint in a wider set of strategic and tactical constraints.

Without claiming that these events exactly duplicate patterns that would have been exhibited in precolonial times or that would occur today in the same local context, we argue that certain core aspects of this case are classic to the so-ciety and are relatively invariant. In the precolonial past, women might not have been able to raise their concerns so forcefully because there were no persons appointed as magistrates and mediators to whom they could take their case; but they could still appeal to their own kin. Today, we would expect that more refer-ence would be made to Christian values. But the core elements involved in this case are each woman's insistence on decision-making rights and the setting of the dispute in a wider context of exchanges. These two elements correspond to the individual and relational poles of personhood, expressed in overwhelmingly transactional contexts and hence showing the connections between transaction and personhood.

As we have briefly sketched here, big-man systems are the products of complex processes of historical change, involving alterations in conditions of production and in the items used in exchanges. The competitive elements in the moka sys-tem possibly grew out of a preexisting nexus of trading relations based on an ethic of "friendship" between partners. In the next chapter we explore this point in more detail and go on to discuss alterations in the supply and type of valuables used in exchanges over time, focusing on the period of time since the 1930s. This longer-term background is necessary to enable us to understand better the con-temporary issues of the 1980s and 1990s.

TWO

▶ ▶ ▶ ▶ ▶

Trade as Transaction
and "Friendship"

The domain of "friendship" influences trade and exchange throughout the Central Highlands of Papua New Guinea. On closer inspection and reconsideration, it turns out to be important as one element that historically has given ideological underpinning and both cultural and personal meaning to trade and exchange transactions themselves.

Our main purpose in this chapter is therefore to reset the basic terms of discussions regarding trade and exchange not by way of opposing them but by linking them through the concept of friendship. This aim, however, requires us to look first at some of the earlier discussions and also to say how we are going to use the term *friendship*. We will do so by referring to the approaches made to "barter" in the edited work by Caroline Humphrey and Stephen Hugh-Jones (1992) and to "friendship" by J. B. Watson (1983).

Humphrey and Hugh-Jones, in the introduction to their volume, recognize the inadvisability of setting up a universal definition or model of barter that does not correspond to reality; and the same can be said for the term *trade*, which in nonmonetary contexts may be seen as closely related to barter. They also point out that barter is a widespread phenomenon and not one that necessarily disappears with monetization. It holds an intermediate place between ceremonial exchange and market exchange as "a mode of exchange in its own right" (1992:7). In it objects are evaluated directly against each other rather than by some external canon such as money, and each transaction has to be seen as "fair" in its own way, by a matching of unlike items. There is a contrast here with some forms of gift or ceremonial exchange in which like items may be exchanged over time (e.g., pigs for pigs). But in other ways there is a similarity, since both gift exchange and barter (trade) involve sociality. The parties may be quits with respect to a specific transaction, but their relationship may be based on a form of ongoing friendship just as with ceremonial exchange. Indeed, the same people may be partners with respect to both forms of transaction. Alfred Gell, in his paper in the volume edited by Humphrey and Hugh-Jones, has further stressed the importance of what he calls commodity exchange (trade) as a basic kind of transaction in Melanesia, arguing that gift exchange grew out of it rather than being a primordial form (Gell 1992:142–168). Here we are not so much concerned with the historical/evolutionary argument as such (since this seems hard to settle), but we agree that gift exchange could more easily have been modeled on commodity exchange if the latter were in fact based on friendship, as it often is. This element also explains how value is calculated: neither simply by reference to an external medium nor by any clear quantifiability of value in other terms but in terms of quality as an expression of relationship. Personhood is involved, but it is personhood *in the framework of friendship* that interests us here. We steer clear, therefore, both of "revised" evolutionary arguments and of "straw man" representations of barter or trade as such contrasted with gift exchange (see also A. J. Strathern 1971:101, in which a series of hypothetical dichotomies is set up but rejected because trade appears in these as the simple opposite of gift exchange).

But if friendship is in focus, what is "friendship"? As with "barter," this is a contestable and ambiguous domain. Watson, in his discussion of Tairora culture, speaks of friendship as an important element in social relations, especially against the backdrop of "fierce and perennial" intergroup warfare (1983:209) and the accompanying lability of group fortunes. Fluctuating relations of hostility and friendship or enmity and amity corresponded to these conditions, and it was harder to keep friends than to make enemies (p. 211). Watson adds that "friendship and enmity have both a collective or group face and a serial or individual one" and individual ties influenced group ones (p. 212). These individual ties in turn were created through immigration and intermarriages. Crosscutting ties made for an inescapable problem "of ambiguous friendship" (p. 214).

Here friendship seems to be equivalent to military alliance and difficult to maintain at that. Watson goes on to argue that "kinship is on balance probably more economical than friendship" (p. 216). Kinship means, in terms reminiscent of Meyer Fortes, amity or "mandatory friendship," whereas friendship outside of kinship is uncertain. If friendship results from marriage and marriage gives rise to kinship, however, it is obvious that in practice the two are intertwined. We shall see this again in a discussion of Melpa affinity and food names (below).

Opposing friendship to kinship tends to peripheralize the former and to give it an exclusive definition. Linking the two or recognizing that they overlap gives us a more inclusive definition. The first definition may correspond to European folk models that oppose kinship to friendship as Watson does. The second, however, may be true to the Melanesian situation, so we adopt it here. Friendship is a state of mutual sociality predicated on goodwill and support that can exist either within or outside of the ambit of kinship and affinity.

Earlier definitional attempts to delimit a sphere of friendship have tended, then, to oppose it to kinship just as trade has been opposed to exchange. Friendship is then seen as operating outside of, beyond, the boundaries of kinship. In practice, however, as we have just seen, it is more productive to look on friendship and kinship as overlapping domains of reference and to recognize that trade and ceremonial exchange fit together in a single overall nexus of activities. Friendship may also exist on different scales, between persons or between collectivities represented by persons, for example. It can be ephemeral or span generations, highly elective or highly constrained by obligation. When we look at these complications, we must recognize that the term *friendship* itself has to be stretched to cover the whole range of semantic senses involved, and certain distinctions need to be made. What is generally important, however, is to understand the idioms in terms of which a global domain of sentiments is constructed that underpins the various contexts of its application.

THE MELPA

Among the Melpa people in Hagen we see that in the Melpa language one term for those who exchange wealth goods is *mel etemen*, "they make wealth." An alternate term for "wealth" here is *monge*, which carries connotations of friendship. Exchanging things in general is a prime context of sociality itself, but exchange partnerships that have continuity in time are constituted by *monge etemen*, "they make 'friendship.'"

Such partnerships in turn are further characterized as producing, and as the products of, *mìn*. Mìn is pork fat, and pieces of pork with fat in them are seen as having *kopong*, "grease," engendering fertility, health, wealth, goodwill, a bright shining skin, a good condition of both person and cosmos. Persons who make mìn in their exchanges are said to give their *noman*, or minds, to each other, and as a result their bodily practices are good. That is, the state of the noman directly influences the bodily state of a person. If the noman is good, the person's skin is healthy and fat, not dull and thin, and the *noman* is good if friends support one, give one food, and so on. "Giving the mind" can thus also stand as proxy to friendship, liking, or loving another person. A big-man or leader is further said to be able to make kopong (*kopong etem*): to create abundance and health around him, quintessentially in the feasts at which pork is cooked in earth ovens (*röng kotemen*). If the vegetable foods are well soaked with fat and there is a pool of liquid fat at the bottom of the oven, this both demonstrates the achievement of fertility and is a prognosis of it for the future.

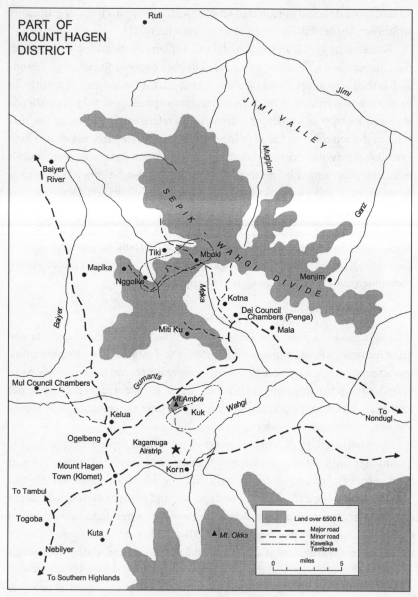

PART OF MOUNT HAGEN DISTRICT

Ruti

JIMI VALLEY

Jimi

Muglpin

Ganz

Baiyer River

SEPIK — WAHGI DIVIDE

Tiki

Mbukl

Maplka

Nggolke

Menjim

Mika

Kotna

Miti Ku

Dei Council Chambers (Penga)

Mala

Baiyer

Gumants

Mul Council Chambers

Mt. Ambra

Wahgi

To Nondugl

Kelua

Kuk

Ogelbeng

Kagamuga Airstrip

Mount Hagen Town (Klomet)

Korn

To Tambul

Togoba

Kuta

Mt. Okka

Nebilyer

To Southern Highlands

	Land over 6500 ft.
– – –	Major road
- - -	Minor road
-·-·-	Kawelka Territories

0   miles   5

▸▸▸ *Part of Mount Hagen District, showing locations of the Kawelka territories at Mbukl and Kuk.*

Mtn and kopong therefore refer to the same substance at different stages of transformation. Mtn grows on a living pig as it matures, shows itself under the skin of the pig when it is slaughtered, and transmutes into kopong, a liquid, flowing substance that can be ingested, rubbed on the skin, and enrich the earth itself. Moreover, kopong acts as a general concept of fertility, prosperity, and well-being. Both breast milk and semen, life-giving fluids, are examples of kopong. The fertility of the earth is kopong, and the cyclicity of life and death associated with the earth is marked by the presence or absence of kopong and its flows between living creatures (plants, animals, humans) and the earth. If kopong, then, is the cosmic equivalent of mtn, we can say that "friendship makes the world go round," in this expanded sense, for the Melpa. Pork sacrifices further tie the living and the dead together: the dead, to whose names slaughtered pigs are dedicated, come and smell the smoke and steam, the people eat the meat and rub fat on their skins, and parts of the grease and the blood go into the earth. Pig sacrifice conjoins elements of the cosmos together through the flow of transformed and relocated substances from the pig's body.

The point here is that these embodied images are appropriated as signs of friendship in exchange between partners who transact pigs, pork, shells, or money, and other goods. These partners may or may not be kin. Monge refers preeminently to gift exchanges in the sphere known as moka relations (marked formally by generosity and competition); but it can also extend to acts of giving and receiving outside of moka that we could call trade provided that these are not seen as just segmented and transitory interactions. Seen as a transitory act without an element of generosity and long-term indebtedness, an immediate exchange of goods is described as *mel rarop rui,* a term that nowadays is translated as "to buy and sell." Trade without friendship thus becomes less productive of sociality. Friends "stick together" (*römb nitimin*) and "go around together" (*rup roromen*) over time, as kin do. The term *römb* is also used in fertility magic in cults where pigs' blood is rubbed onto the earth and said to produce a "sticking" or fertile quality of humans, animals, and plants generally.

MELPA NAMING PRACTICES AND FRIENDSHIP

Another way in which kinship and friendship overlap semantically for the Melpa is in the domain of food names used between kinsfolk and friends (A. J. Strathern 1977a). Foods may be exchanged, or rather shared, in a ritual action by which the persons involved renounce the use of their ordinary name in relation to each other and must reciprocally use only the name of the food that has been shared when establishing the food-name relationship. Indeed, they begin by literally exchanging identities, each declaring that they now take the name of the other (while also abolishing both names between them). The phrase used is *tik wakaka, na,* where the first two words are purely conventional and *na,* meaning I, precedes the name of the other person. This act commemorates and recognizes the act of sharing that binds the two persons together. This frequently occurs when two people are eating food from a common oven or fire—a situation that in itself implies amity—and they decide to share a portion of food so as to establish a food-name relationship, calling each other in future by the name of the shared substance. The breaking of one piece of food into two and its partition between the two persons creates a consubtantiality between them that parallels the consubstantiality of kinship through shared blood and semen, the two substances that come together at the conception of a new human life. The giving and sharing of food is synonymous with sociality and the use of food names is a powerful reminder of a friendship relationship that becomes inscribed into everyday behavioral interactions. In addition to friendship, the symbolism of using food names to refer to persons with whom amicable relations exist is extended to encompass the notion of shared substance and thereby identity. The Melpa consider a good person to be one who shares food, *mok rorom. Mok* is a word that also refers to the manner in which pigs' toes radiate outward from a central zone in the same way that gifts of food should radiate outward to friends from the giver as a source.

Failure to use the food name gives offense and is seen as an unfriendly act that should be rectified by payment of a fine to the offended person. (Note the difference here with ordinary consanguineal kin terms: there are no equivalent sanctions on the use or nonuse of these.) Food names are structurally analogous to reciprocal kin terms. For example, father and son call each other *ta,* mother and son *ma,* brother and sister *aya,* and so on. The food name functions as a marker of relatedness through food.

The food name also operates like the *nuip* (same-name) relationship, which is the sharing of an actual name. This relationship also carries connotations of support and co-identity. Like food names, which are established by choice and should not be abrogated, so may same-name relationships be set up by choice, as when someone names a child with his or her own name so as to establish a permanent co-identity relationship, or when parents name a child after a friend or kinsperson with the same intent, creating a relationship comparable to godparenthood.

Another set of naming practices, one that proclaims both amity and distance, is the use of affinal terms. Affines of various degrees may not use ordinary names. A series of "inside names" is used (*mbi rukrung,* referred to as *mawa ndoromen,* "they make a taboo name," *paka ndok nitimin,* "they cover up and say," or "they make a fork and say," i.e., they make a second name in place of the ordinary one).

The use of these names indicates distancing as well as respect. Whereas food names commemorate a private act of mutuality (i.e., sharing food) and mark it publicly, the use of inside names commemorates a public act of alliance-making through marriage but does not refer to the ordinary names of the persons involved, who are related via the private act of sexual intercourse. The inside name, however, is like a food name in that it constrains its users. If they fail to employ it, this causes displeasure and may cost a fine. The friendship involved is thus a "mandatory alliance." At first chosen, it becomes obligatory, unless it is later broken. The contrast with ordinary consanguineal kin relationships is clear again, since in these no special terms need be used but the relationship cannot in principle be broken.

Friendship and Gender

Friendship is involved in many different spheres of life. It underpins exchange and sociality for the Melpa. It also implies emotions such as *kaemb* ("liver," sympathy), *kond* (sorrow, grief), and *noman ngui* (liking), which motivate people to action. Trading friends are thus only one kind of friend. Friendship also operates selectively between kin and is exercised between women and men equally. Its cross-sex application is differently configured, however, than its within-sex application. Spouses, for example, may be described as "friends" (*min morom*), but such friendship is not constitutive of the spousal relationship. It is an element added in certain instances, as among kin generally. Same-sex kin or friends, however, are expected to "go around together," as we have earlier noted. Here friendship connotes a diffuse, supportive solidarity based on personal congeniality. Kaemb implies sympathy to the living; kond can also mean regret for the dead or sympathy for a bereavement. These emotions are shown in acts of giving or attendance at funerals and of food tabooing after a death in commemoration of the dead person. The grieving person taboos a favorite food in order to show sorrow for the dead. This is also known as mawa ndoromen.

A special type of friendship relationship is established between women through the various contexts of sociality that arise from working together in clusters, such as when women sit with their friends and produce netbags (Stewart and Strathern 1997a) or jointly work in garden spaces that are contiguous with one another, thus providing a special opportunity to share conversation as well as to transmit or trade knowledge about life skills such as child care and food preparation.

Another type of friendship that is unique to females is the relationship between co-wives who share a husband. Although many instances of fighting and jealousy can be documented between women each of whom wants to maximize

▸▸▸ *A woman with her young son at an informal rural market in a government school area, selling lengths of sugarcane (Kawelka Kundmbo, 1970s).*

the amount of goods obtained from, as well as in some instances the attention of, their husbands, other emotions of a friendly or sisterly type are shared between women placed in these similar circumstances not of their own making. The co-identity of women in this position results both in their enmity and in their "mandatory friendship."

MELPA TRADE AND GIFT EXCHANGE:
SOME ELEMENTS OF HISTORY

We have taken our discussion to its broadest point now with regard to friendship generally. Friendship can be either with kin or nonkin, can be either freely chosen or obligatory, and can exist in a variety of within-sex and between-sex contexts. The aim has been to indicate that friendship between trade partners is one variety of this wider class of relationships, and it is what creates trust and continuity between them. It is necessary now to return to the question of exchange itself and to how moka gift exchanges and trade can be seen as intertwined and related through ideas of friendship.

Moka has been extensively described elsewhere (e.g., A. J. Strathern 1971). Here we are more concerned with some of its cultural meanings and its historical and geographical background. Moka is a form of exchange defined in strict

‣‣‣ *Relatives of a dead person beginning to count up a display of money paid as a compensation (Dei Council, 1970s).*

terms by the presence of increment. Merely repaying a debt by an equivalent exchange is not truly moka and is not worthy of praise or prestige. Moka is in this regard distinguishable from trade, in which the parties have to be satisfied with the qualitative/quantitative equivalences set up in the transaction but do not have to use the occasion to show generosity, although they can also do so if they wish as a means of strengthening friendship. Important men have historically gained their prominence through moka, in conjunction with other capacities, and thus through their ability to make increments on gifts they have received, hence the system can be described as marked by both generosity and competition. Increment, equally, is what makes friendship; and friendship, in turn, is what is needed to acquire a sufficient number of items from partners to achieve an incremental gift to a particular partner. Goods obtained for a moka can be described as traded, since either an item was given in immediate return or the promise of an equivalent return was made, for example a (certain sort of) pig for a shell (of a certain quality).

Since the 1970s shell valuables have been dropped from the moka and replaced with money (see A. J. Strathern 1979; Strathern and Stewart 1999a; cf. also Finney 1974). Nevertheless, the history of how shells entered the moka nexus and the meanings associated with them are of the greatest importance for defining the moka itself, since although pigs and shells were both used in it, in the narrow sense it is especially associated with pearl shells.

Shells came into the Hagen area from several geographical directions (see A. J. Strathern 1971:102–106). Older informants in the 1960s would give conventional attributions of sources in accordance with their own group's geographical position. One old man (Lap) among the Minembi Yelipi people (interview of September 28, 1965), in the course of enumerating moka gifts he had made, said:

> [Pearl] shells all came to us [the Yelipi] via the [Minembi] Nambakae and the Kope [two groups to the south] and there was a ceremonial ground made at the place Krapna [among the neighboring Minembi Engambo clanspeople] long before the white men arrived. We used to help each other to raise the items needed. All the customs of moka were performed by the grandfathers of us old men, but some customs were changed over time. [These were changes in the decorations of pearl shells, significant because they record the process whereby innovatory practices spread from south to north over time.] Previously [before getting enough pearl shells] we would give sets of eight nassa mats or cowrie ropes for equivalent returns. Nassa shells came from Kopon [to the north], cowries from the Wahgi [east], and pearl shells from Hagen [south].

Lap added a more mythologized version regarding the pearl shells:

> People used to say that the *Kewa Wamb* [mythical beings associated with the sky] dropped valuables at the *Mukl Kömb* ["Legs of the Earth, the Horizon"] and the *Mbowamb* [human beings] fashioned them and sent them on trade routes. We at first [also] thought that they [shells] were found in *mur* [mines, caves] in different places. They used to say that the man Kanggop from Tambul [far to the southwest] put many pearl shells round his neck [in a style known in the Tambul and nearby Ialibu areas] and came to Hagen with these. . . . The people would line up pig stakes for him and he would give a *kopong mambokla* [bamboo tube of decorating oil, from the south also; see below] for a pig's backbone, a nassa mat for the stomach, and a pearl shell each for the front and back legs.

More prosaically, another informant, Numndi, added: "That is just a story. In fact they would give a whole pig for a single pearl shell in the past."

Lap's elaborations show some of the romance and mystique associated with wealth items from the south and elsewhere. The name Kanggop means "assignment, agreement to meet," so that the figure portrayed is like an exemplary partner in trade. He is represented as wealthy and generous, as well as exotic. Shell valuables themselves were given an origin beyond human production and thus represented powers of creation in the cosmos as whole. In fact, they were pictured as coming from Sky Beings, the originators of all things (Strathern and

Stewart 2000). Numndi's addendum underlined the more prosaic fact that shells were expensive: a whole pig (of variable size) would be needed to get one whole shell.

Partners in practice had to be persuaded to give. The man seeking an object was the one who would expect to go on a visit and ask for it. Some forty miles to the south of Lap's place, in a different language/dialect area known as Temboka, an interview with Ambra, another aged but knowledgeable informant, who was both a big-man and a ritual expert, yielded further insights on the sources of pearl shells, the beginnings of the moka, and how to persuade a partner to yield a prized valuable (interview of July 28, 1965).

Ambra told of a man of the Muni group, to the south of his own group the Ulka, called Pundi. The Muni people did not make moka with shells but wore them as decorations round their necks (see illustration in Strathern and Stewart 1999a:173, also 168 and 169), and this man, Muni Pundi, gave a pearl shell to a man of the Kulka tribe called Wara, who gave it to a Poyaka man called Mbokwa, who gave it to Merua, Ambra's father. From there it passed northward to Central Hagen groups.

Another man of a group to the south of the Ulka, the Koka, who lived in the Kambia area north of the Muni, gave an interview on August 5, 1965, which included some further remarks on pearl shells and moka.

> Before the white men came only a few men had pearl shells. Partners used to give us cooked pigs' heads but now we have plenty of pearl shells and don't eat the pigs' heads. . . . If I give a man a big pig and he gives me only a small pearl shell or ones that are white [rather than yellow] in color, then we complain. This is called *mineimbil ik*. I send the word by women and children as my messengers. Then I go to see him myself. I frown and he is ashamed and gives better gifts to me, so I am happy. Pearl shells came to us from Ialibu [to the south, place of the Muni] but not in moka. The moka was begun by Merua, the father of Ulka Ambra. That is, he put the red resin backings around the shells [for use in moka exchange. Ambra is credited with first putting the larger resin backings on the shells and turning them into more grandiose exchange objects]. (Interview with Koka Kintmöl)

The same informant then continued with a conventional list of rates of exchange for items traded from the Ialibu people south of his own area. A baler shell was equivalent to a pig or a pearl shell or a stone ax; a cowrie necklace to a piglet; a nassa headband also to a piglet; a steel ax obtained before the arrival of Europeans was worth a big pig, a knife a small pig.

Ambra himself detailed a whole range of spells connected with spirit cults and moka. One he described as being for removing the special cover that was used to wrap pearl shells. The images here have to do with the magic a man makes to persuade a trading partner to unwrap a shell in this way as a prelude to giving it to him. The following version gives an idea of the language involved:

I am in an open place.
Where will I find pearl shells?
I think I will find them if I work hard.
My heart rises up and I desire the shells.
I am sorry in my heart.
A dog looks at a man and he gives it food.
I am asleep. I am sorry for myself.
The Ndan tree has prickles,
The Atinga tree has prickles
[And I will prick my partner in the same way]
I will be tight on his skin like a liana,
I will mark him like a *kindklamb* prickle
He will be sorry for me, sorry for me.
The covering for the pearl shell,
The hoop-pine tree bark, it will be removed
    from it.
It will have marks from the Mumbuma reed,
Its woven handle will shine.
My mother's brother,
My wife's father,
My affine,
The shell will be in the open.
He will be sorry for me as I turn my
    back and go out through his house door,
My affine.

Several points may be remarked on from these materials. First, the Koka informant corroborated that Ambra's father, Merua, was an early participant in shell moka, indeed he credits him with inventing the larger backing for pearl shells that came to distinguish the Melpa style of shell decoration from that of Ialibu and Tambul. Ambra himself confirmed this and also said that Merua had been the first to put a bamboo strip on a chest pendant (the *omak* or *koa mak*) as a mark of having given a moka. Merua belonged to one of the large and politically strong groups in the central Nebilyer Valley, which had accreted smaller groups around it as an ally cluster. He was well placed to become a successful in-novator, and his putative action in enlarging the resin backings of the pearl shells may be correlated both with aesthetic and political criteria. Here we may find at least a partial answer to the question posed by Jeffrey Clark (1991:337, n. 5), who notes that "the literature offers no explanation for this aesthetic elaboration." Our point here is, first, that while for some purposes it is valid to separate aes-thetics from politics in order to ask "why" questions, in terms of a theory of his-torical practice it is more effective to consider how aesthetics and politics go together. Second, moka-making is described as special to the Temboka area, that is, again to Hagen and not Ialibu or Tambul custom. Third, there were conven-tional exchange rates in trading for goods, but the equivalences clearly left much room for negotiation. Fourth, Ambra's spell captures well the uncertainty and tension associated with going to ask for a pearl shell and the need to make the partner "sorry" for one (i.e., sympathetic to one's feelings). The rhetorical mo-dality played on is the human agency and sympathy of the partner, imaged as constrained by the singer's magic song. The words express both the coercive idea of the spell and the contradictory fact that the shell's owner must be freely sorry for this partner, sorry "for his back" as he leaves empty-handed or sorry for him as a man is sorry for a hungry dog that begs for food. Both hyperagency and hyperdependency are represented here. The Koka man's discussion emphasized making a partner not "sorry" but embarrassed so as to exact an honorably equi-table return for things given. Both informants' statements make it clear that the desire was to obtain adequate returns or adequate gifts: moka and trade were both equally infused with the idea of the qualitative adequacy of giving. Gen-erosity takes off from this point of adequacy, which has therefore to be agreed on, and trade and moka exchange grade into each other.

To understand the dynamics of partnerships as revealed in magical spells it is important to realize that the traders were often members of different political groups or indeed language groups, and the mechanisms whereby shells were ac-tually moved along trade routes were social in character. Those in need of wealth for social transactions were the ones who traveled to cultivate trading ties with persons nearer to the points of origin of the wealth items. They therefore were always placed in a situation of potential risk to themselves, counterbalanced by their desire for the items and for the prestige of obtaining them from others. All of the spells for magically "pulling in" shells have a strong geographical reference and in fact constitute the images of trading networks within certain social fields that crossed political boundaries. The spells are thus like mental maps of the local geopolitics, seen as forms of landscape that are in fact forms of human activity in the process of creating networks. It is also interesting to note that the Ulka big-man, Merua, was also cited as the first leader to bring the Male Spirit cult to his group in the past, a point that links the history of the moka and of these cults to-gether in a single vision of sacred trading trackways.

How did ordinary people participate in the development of the moka? One informant in 1965, Kwan of the Minembi Yelipi clan, who was then in his thirties, modestly said that he did not take part in moka because he was "unimportant" (wuö korpa, a "rubbish-man" without wealth). He did, however, see how his own father prepared pearl shells for display. He would put resin or juice from a hoop-pine tree on it and also dried pandanus leaves as a backing to strengthen it at its edges. Kwan himself had to work hard to obtain a single cowrie shell in wage labor. People would divide a string of such cowries into two, each part hanging from the head to the navel, and say that a single part was worth a pearl shell. Half of a nassa shell mat, divided by a "navel" design in its middle, was also worth one pearl shell. The implication was that pearl shells were a store of value, and the smaller shells, obtained in working for Europeans on the early coffee plantations in the 1950s, were stepping-stones to obtaining them. Such wage labor, then, re-placed the older nexus of trade friendships. (It later turned out that Kwan was being ironic when he said he did not make moka; he had in fact made it often.)

Another Yelipi man, Numndi (quoted above), said that pearl shells all came in via the other Minembi groups to the south, and because shells were scarce, people helped one another to raise the numbers needed for an occasion. Lap's brothers, he said, were old-fashioned in not putting resin backings on the shells but only pine-tree juice, and they covered up the shells with ferns and *mongndamb* (a large moth cocoon) and put them into a netbag, smeared with red ochre, so the shell could be seen gleaming inside its container. Numndi's generation then decided to put resin all the way round the shell, as was described in relation to Ambra and Merua from the Nebilyer Valley. Such details indicate that fashions gradually permeated the Hagen area, altering the aesthetics of shell preparation away from the patterns that held in the Southern Highlands, where the shells came from in trade, and increasing the size of the shell and its backing as its use in the moka became more pronounced.

These accounts may be compared with two others already published from the northern Melpa area.

ONGKA AND RU: TWO MODELS

The Melpa big-man Ongka Kaepa discusses various aspects of making moka exchanges, including his role as a middleman, in his autobiographical account from 1979. The time frame here is around the late 1940s or early 1950s.

I gave moka to everyone. . . . Everyone said "Let's go and see Ongka Kaepa" if they wanted to raise some wealth for an occasion. My own long tally is hanging on the wall of my house now, it's as long as the wall itself but I'm embarrassed to wear it now that the white men are here. I had partners in distant places. . . . The Hagen men brought me cassowary headdresses and packs of salt, of the round or long kind. The Jimmi Valley people brought plumes of the white bird of paradise, eagle feathers, parrot feathers, woven decorations for bark belts, cassowaries, packs of sago. The eastern valley men brought plumes of the red bird of paradise, white marsupial furs, parrot wings. Even Enga men came to see me, with big marsupials and necklaces of cowrie shells. They brought all these things and I acted as a middleman, switching things round between them, giving things from the Jimmi people to the Hagen men and vice versa, and so on, so that people said, "He is in the middle of us all and he is generous." From all sides they came to me, and I also used what they brought for my own moka making and bridewealth payments. (A. J. Strathern [trans.] 1979:68–69; see also Strathern and Stewart 1999b).

Likewise, Ru Kundil, another Melpa big-man, discusses moka exchange in his autobiographical account from 1993 (see also Strathern and Stewart n.d.a.). He started making moka exchanges when he was a boy and made many throughout his life. In his narrative of how moka partners interacted or should have interacted, he often refers to the sympathy that a trading partner feels for his partner when a debt is in need of "being reciprocated." "I am really sorry for you. You have not recovered your debt and yet you have been strong and are giving to me. I understand. I will make returns to you quickly for this" (A. J. Strathern [trans.] 1993:26). This is reminiscent of the anticipated sympathy expressed in Ambra's spell (see above). The partners are concerned about the feelings of each other and the perpetuation of the relationship.

Ru also, unlike Ongka, emphasizes that a man who observes the unwritten rules of respect for his partners is a "good man." For example, he reports himself as saying to one partner: "Ndip, you are a good man, you have given me a big moka here. I fear I may not be able to make a proper return for it, your pigs are all so big. You have given me all these big pigs. Well, anyway, don't worry. I can give to you next time if I find a pig or two" (A. J. Strathern [trans.] 1993:27).

These two excerpts correspond to two different models of behavior that apply to both trade and moka. Ongka's model here is a middleman/broker image. He sees himself as switching goods around and thereby attracting people to himself. His emphasis is on the items, their diverse provenance, and what he does with them: the big-man as trader. (In practice, however, big-manship was by no means based solely on such a capacity.) In Ru's model the big-man is represented as the magnanimous giver, the one who delights others by giving well and quickly, the prompt repayer of debts, the pro-social team player. The point here is not that one model is more accurate than the other or even that the two men adhered more to one than the other. Rather, their statements represent different facets of a complex ideology, as we also saw above in the excerpts from Ambra and Kintmöl.

GENDER SYMBOLISM OF TRADE OBJECTS

Gender symbolism in trade and friendship relations can vary enormously between trading partners from different areas. An example of this can be seen in the symbolism of a kind of tree oil exchanged in trade. Among the Highlands peoples, including the Melpa and others to their south, trading takes place for this oil from the *Campnosperma brevipetiolata* tree, called *Kara'o* by the Foi people, a mountain Papuan group among whom it originates. As James Weiner describes it, trade in *Kara'o* oil existed between the Foi and the Highlanders (Wola- and Kewa-speakers), who gave pigs and pearl shells in return (Weiner 1988:63–77). The oil was tapped from the *Kara'o* tree and collected in long bamboo tubes that were carried by several men into the Highlands for this trade. The pigs and pearl shells that were obtained for the oil entered into the ceremonial exchanges of the Foi among themselves.

Kara'o oil is used by the Foi and the Highlanders for decorative purposes, and frequently dyes are used to color the oil black or red. The Foi mix charcoal with the oil to make the traditional black battle covering and mix in dye from the seed pods of the *Bixa orellana* tree to produce a reddish-colored oil used for dancing. The collection and trading of the oil is intimately associated with male status, and it is the item that is primarily needed in order to acquire all other objects of value.

Trade in *Kara'o* oil continues to date, with adult men making at least one trading trip each year. Weiner notes that it has increased with pacification, presumably as a result of the easier flow of goods through networks and the consequent expansion of the networks themselves. Transactions take place between established trading partners. In the past very large and highly prized pearl shells would have been traded for the oil, but today the oil is obtained with money, thus again probably increasing its circulation. In addition to these transactions of goods, Foi men provide sago flour to their long-standing Highlands partners, who in reciprocal manner invite their Foi partners to their pig feasts where pork is given to them (Weiner 1988:65), thereby reinforcing the bond between the traders through the friendly act of sharing food.

The symbolism of *Kara'o* oil is discontinuous along its trade route, having one meaning among the Foi and a very different one among the Melpa. For the Foi as for the Wola people the *Kara'o* origin myths equate the oil with menstrual blood, the tapping of the oil from the tree being likened in myth and spells to the opening of a vagina that stimulates a menstrual flow (Sillitoe 1979a; Weiner 1988:66–68). Weiner describes the exchange of *Kara'o* oil from the Foi for pearl shells from the Weyamo (Wola): "Foi men supply the Weyamo with 'female' substance or wealth, *Kara'o*, and receive 'male' pearl shells and pigs in return, just as Foi men provide each other with wives exchanged for the same wealth items" (Weiner 1988:68). This symbolism is altered for the Melpa, who traded in the past as well as today for the oil, which they call *mambokla*. The Melpa decorate themselves with the reddened oil for dances such as the Female Spirit cult (*Amb Kor*) performance. It would be a complete anathema for Melpa men to apply any substance to their bodies that might be equated with the potentially harmful powers of menstrual blood (although blood in itself is a mark of vitality and without the fact of the menstrual flow of blood reproduction could not occur, as the Melpa recognize [Stewart and Strathern, 1999a]). Rather, the oil is seen to be a kind of kopong (grease), a substance that can be associated with masculinity and equated with semen. This does not mean, however, that there are no positive associations of a female kind associated with grease and with wealth objects. The pearl shell for the Melpa, although a "male" wealth item, was itself also closely associated with the female powers of fertility. This is also the case for the Wiru (Clark 1991). For example, during the closing segment of the Female Spirit Amb Kor celebration the male dancers hold pearl shells in their outstretched arms as representations of the Female Spirit (Strathern and Stewart 1997a). Also, Melpa pearl shells were often coated with red ochre, a "female" color (A. J. Strathern 1979:535). The gendering of colors also varies cross-culturally, since for the Wiru red carries male connotations (Clark 1991:318). The conflation of the color red with the grease-like properties in the mambokla oil may be interpreted as a fusion or mingling of the potency of semen and blood in the context or reproduction, at least among the Melpa.

A COMPARATIVE LOOK: MENDI AND MARING

The Melpa materials show an elaborate set of ideas that underpinned particular transactions in pearl shells before they were replaced with money. The pearl shell culture was an historical invention, as we have seen, since the moka practices based on it developed in situ in the Temboka (Nebilyer Valley) area. But many comparable practices and ideas were found elsewhere. We discuss data from the Maring to the north and the Mendi to the south of Hagen.

Exchange is as highly developed among the Mendi people as among the Melpa, and their category of *twem* expresses an arena of action similar to the Melpa moka or mel etemen. Rena Lederman (1986) has discussed twem partnerships in great detail, and we can ask to what extent these partnerships resemble those of the Melpa and are underpinned by ideas of friendship.

Lederman discusses twem under the headings of etiquette, initiating and maintaining relationships, incremental gifts, and generosity. She also points out that twem activity represents the achievement of social personhood through conducting exchange in a "good way." (This idea is reminiscent of Ru's self-account among the Melpa.) The primary sense of twem is a spouse's relative or affine, but not all affines make twem and not all twem partners are in practice affines. There is an expectation that such partnerships endure over time, with varying intensity and frequency of transactions. If they are affines, an incremental gift made as a repayment on an original gift is considered to be a mark of appreciation. Increment is called *nopae*. Twem transactions are initiated by requesting (whereas intraclan relations are produced by unsolicited giving), although giving is often constrained by obligation and relationship. Promises are not always kept, and it is not polite to ask where items have come from. Repayments are structured in terms of the ideology of interdependence and equality between the partners. Failure to repay at all is considered shameful, but if partnerships are unsatisfactory they can be dissolved or allowed to lapse. The partners may promise to "look for" valuables along "roads" (i.e., networks) they have in order to help each other.

Lederman also refers to an "ethic" of twem that encourages people to give away valuables not yet marked for another. It encourages them also to give nopae gifts that seem to express the equivalence of wealth to the human person as a whole. She argues that "thus, the quality of social relationships generally can be expressed in terms of gift exchange" (Lederman 1986:149). Since nopae also constitutes generosity, it is apparent that the generosity in exchange has to do with the recognition/achievement of social personhood as such. Interestingly, Lederman points out that sorcery is seen as the inverse of the successful pursuit of personhood in this way. A "rubbish man" who cannot exchange well may poison a partner. Sorcery may be resorted to out of resentment, but the good person will try to recreate relationships through nopae gifts (Lederman 1986:150).

Lederman's account makes very clear both the structural framework and the negotiated practice of twem. What is not apparent from her treatment is whether it is based on an ideology of friendship such as we have indicated for the Melpa. It is clear that it has to do with personhood and that sorcery is the inverse of good personhood and exchange. The underpinning of such notions by embodied ideas of "health," "grease," and the like does not emerge. This may either be because it is absent or because it is not the focus of Lederman's analysis, which is cast in terms of analytical concerns centering on big-manship and gender relations.

Earlier discussions of Melpa sociality in general and the moka have also missed the point that both moka and trade are based on a set of sentiments insofar as both depend on an ideology of friendship. Christopher Healey, in his extensive study of Maring trade and exchange, brings out another dimension— the creation of trust between trading and exchange partners. This is done at least partly through generosity, that is, giving more than is required to meet debts so as to promote the relationship. Trade is highly developed among the Maring, largely because their area is rich in the plumes and furs that are used in self-decoration not only among themselves but in the Hagen and Wahgi areas to their south (Healey 1990). Trading partners need to visit one another in search of these and other valued objects and as a result need to stay in each other's houses as guests.

The extension of hospitality is an expression of trust and goodwill that binds trade partners together. A man must feel assured that his host is a friend and not an enemy who will poison the food given to him or harm him in some other way. Acts of sorcery that might otherwise be conducted against a stranger are not likely to be expressed when the persons involved have a trusting (friendly) relationship. Networks of trade are established within networks of trust in which a person is not going to do harm to someone who is indebted to him. Even before trading and gift giving can be begun, one has to know that the trade partner will not harm one's body, that he will not betray the trust that exists at the core of the relationship. Unrelated friends are termed *yemp nunt yu* ("he-gives I-can-eat man") (Healey 1984:52). This reveals something basic about friends—they are people from whom one receives goods, food, and shelter and to whom one entrusts the safekeeping of the body.

The Maring term for trade is *munggoi rigima* (valuables exchange). This system of interactions is intertwined with prestation, *munggoi awon* (valuables give), in which many of the objects obtained through trade are used. These transactions are conducted under the elaborate set of moral pressures that regulate them in Maring society. In addition to these forms of interactions between men, Maring women also trade marsupial furs with men, and among themselves they trade furs, string bags, and vegetables for sums of money.

Through munggoi rigima transactions, wide-ranging personal networks are constructed that bring people together in amicable social interactions that involve elements of growth in personal agency, as well as what we might simply call "fun" or entertainment. In addition, we must not overlook the sense of venture that must have accompanied these traders as they moved along trading pathways.

The element of friendship in trading relations appears very clearly, then, from the Maring as it does from the Melpa case. (This is perhaps not surprising given that the two peoples speak languages of the same family and Maring territory lies just to the north of the Melpa.) The Maring emphasize trade more than the Melpa do for the simple reason that their area is an important source for marsupial skins and bird of paradise plumes used as decorations in dances by the Melpa and other Central Highlands groups. Ceremonial exchange, in contrast, is more elaborately developed among the Melpa, but in its origins shows its connections with trading for scarce and highly valued items of wealth, as we saw in the discussion of how pearl shells originally entered the Hagen area. Ceremonial exchange is also highly developed among the Mendi and the nearby Wola (Sillitoe 1979b), and pearl shells are an important wealth item presented to affines, but neither Lederman nor Paul Sillitoe seems to have been able to discover the complex gender symbolism of shells that Clark discusses for the Wiru (Clark 1991; cf. Sillitoe 1979b:143). Melpa moka exchanges consisted of an amalgamation of individual transactions by men that took place in the context of, and as constitutive of, intergroup relations of friendship and alliance, to a greater extent, it seems, than among the Mendi (and Wola), where twem exchanges remained tied to the interpersonal context of links between affines. In such a context we might expect to find that shells had the same kind of "reproductive" symbolism attached to them that we find in the Melpa (and Wiru) cases, but the available evidence does not allow us to conclude that this is so.

It is evident that "friendship idioms" provide an intriguing and underexplored arena of discussion in Highlands ethnography. Their configuration with other institutional practices and ideologies should prove an interesting topic for comparative analyses in the future. This chapter provides an initial look at this problem, primarily from the viewpoint of the analysis of materials from the Melpa, Mendi, and Maring peoples. In Melpa, as we have seen, monge etemen indicates a stress on the aspect of friendship, while its equivalent, mel etemen, rather carries a stress on the material objects themselves. This duality of phrasing (reflected in the narratives of Ru and Ongka) represents neatly the constant interplay between material and social concerns found in both trade and gift exchange.

As we have said above, the historical forms of currency in the Hagen area have altered over time in dramatic ways. In the next chapter this point is considered in more detail. From the present chapter we conclude that an enduring element throughout a number of historical phases has been the conceptualization of both trade and moka in terms of friendship. Thus we can see how friendship ideas have formed a bridge enabling people to travel between local groups and to extend the networks of sociality, both separately from and along with ties of kinship and marriage. These ideas have thus been important in shaping the background to the development of big-manship because people achieved prestige through making outside trading contacts. Equally, the ideas employed in the expansion of trading networks were deeply tied in with magical practices, themselves extensions of human practical agency.

THREE

▶▶▶▶▶

Pigs, Shells, and Locality

During one of his to-camera soliloquies in the film *Ongka's Big Moka* (Granada TV 1974), the leader Ongka explains to the uninitiated that "pigs are our strong thing," the basic form of wealth in Mount Hagen society, needed to pay for bodies, brides, insults, injuries. Ongka's explanatory schema in this speech was that pigs are original; they were reared and used as wealth long before the white people came to his area. He does not mention pearl shells, but he notes that the white people brought their own money with them, and we know that their currency replaced the pearl shells that were a hallmark of the prestige economy in Hagen in the years following the incursion of the white outsiders and up to the 1960s, when money was first introduced into moka exchanges. Implicitly Ongka is bracketing shells and money together and suggesting this as a reason why shells, rather than pigs, were replaced in exchanges. Why should this be so?

Two answers can be given, both of an historical kind. One is that pearl shells were associated with the incomers because they were brought into Mount Hagen in the 1930s in large numbers to pay for food, labor, and the use of land. They had entered Hagen from the south before the arrival of the Europeans, each shell tending to have its own name and history of passage between exchange partners. In this regard, pearl shells had been seen as exotic but indigenous, coming from the fringes of the known world and carrying with them a magical aura of beauty, power, and mystery. Subsequent constructions of their provenance and meaning depended on an alteration in the geographical perceptions of the Hageners. When they first traveled to the northern and southern coasts and learned that shells came from the sea and that white people in a sense also belonged there, they made an historical reinterpretation, backed by their experience of shells being freighted in by airplane, that these wealth items truly were a part of the white man's world as then understood. They were *kewa mel*, "foreign things," where the word *kewa* also applied to those people living beyond the Hagen lan-

▸▸ *Tiki coffee plantation, belonging to John Collins, in the Baiyer River valley. This was one of the plantations developed in the 1950s and 1960s where Kawelka people worked for wages (Dei Council, 1970s).*

guage area to its south and to a class of cannibalistic demons akin to sky-beings (*Tei wamb nui wamb*). Europeans, too, were known as kewa and were held initially to be cannibalistic spirits. Whatever wealth they used was connected closely to them and their perceived power. Hence pearl shells came to represent, in a sense, both the acme of indigenous values and the power of exotic, introduced values.

The second answer, which follows from the first, is that shells were not produced locally, as pigs were. There was no way to make them increase other than by magic or exchanges, and the magic itself was directed toward attracting shells to a men's house door like parakeets attracted to the fruits and blossoms of a resin-bearing tree whose sap was used as a mounting for the shells themselves (*nde kilt, nde elua*) (see below for further discussion of the symbolism of this reddish resin and mounting of the shells). The shells are imaged as mobile, flashing with color, and able to choose a particular communal men's house and ceremonial ground rather than another to make themselves available. This image of agency and mobility essentially represents their character as objects of pure exchange, counterbalanced by a second image, also invoked in magic, of single large pearl shells, wrapped carefully in barkcloth binding and stored in the back recesses of men's houses, that would themselves "pull" other shells to them (cf.

Weiner 1988:70–71 and 1993). The large shell is in this case like the big-man who lives in the house, and it stands as his symbolic equivalent: the big-man who has a firm base but is also highly mobile is in fact like both kinds of shells, the ones that move and the ones that stay in the house. The overall point here is that shells were highly likely to be compared with introduced forms of currency since they already represented in essence both forms of personhood and exchange values in the same way as European money does, albeit in contexts of restricted rather than unlimited exchange.

If, then, shells and especially pearl shells in Hagen embodied inter alia funds of free-floating power, and therefore were closely tied with big-manship, it is evident that there is a difference between shells and pigs, for pigs are produced on home territories, if not on one's own territory then on neighboring ones, and are the mixed products of the labor of the sexes (being more strongly associated with female senses of personhood and their productive/reproductive powers) and of the fertility of the land and its crops, tied to specific localities and ancestral connections. Their capacity directly to represent the idea of the local group (even if individual pigs have been "financed in" from elsewhere) is what gives them their special continuing place in the arena of exchange practices. Obviously, as many writers have pointed out (e.g., Rappaport 1968; Modjeska 1982), their role as sacrifices to ancestral or local spirits reinforces this nexus of meanings in relation to locality. It is interesting to note further the division of use between pearl shells and pork in the major fertility cult, the Amb Kor or Female Spirit cult. Cult performers were especially expected to carry pearl shells in their hands, with outstretched arms, as emblems of the Spirit (Strathern and Stewart 1997a; Strathern and Stewart 1998a; see also below). These shells were not given away to recipients, they were markers of wealth and fertility and thus of the Spirit, but were in this instance retained by their users (or simply returned to those from whom they had been borrowed). Pork, however, steamed in long earth ovens in the sacred enclosures of the cult, was distributed widely to recipients, both on a group basis and individually. Shells were here a *marker* of fertility, pigs its *product,* made available for consumption. The fact that these two categories belonged to the same "sphere of exchange" in a formal sense, because they could be brought into correlative exchanges against each other, does not alter this symbolic difference between them, one which is therefore repeated in the contemporary interplay of money and pigs. Pigs, as Ongka has told us, remain a basic form of wealth because of their connection with locality and therefore with local representative identities. They are thus an indispensable component of compensation payments for deaths and injuries between individuals and groups. Money has become perhaps the dominant element in these events, but in no case so far (up to

1999) has it taken over from pigs. Money and pigs go together as did shells and pigs previously. By association with pigs and through its handling in these contexts, money also, we may argue, acquires a representational capacity, but it cannot stand alone in such a context.

Shells and Economic Change

If we look back again at some historical contexts in Hagen we can give this argument further specificity. Until early contact in the 1930s with Australian prospectors, pearl shells were very rare in Hagen and possession of them was a marker of outstanding big-manship. When the Australians came they altered this situation dramatically, in two ways. They made shells available wherever they explored or settled, turning upside down or randomizing pathways by which these forms of wealth had previously traveled; and they also gave shells out directly in return for vegetable foodstuffs, labor, and pigs, thus creating an entirely new, and colonial, nexus of exchange and dependency. Shells, therefore, were commoditized in this new context and later made integral to a capitalist mode of production in which they were handed out as wages to workers on plantations established a few years after first effective pacification in the 1950s. Earlier they were used by the Leahy brothers to pay carriers and workers at the Kuta gold mine. This commoditization of shells was accompanied by their reabsorption into the local exchange economy as wealth objects. The equivalent nowadays is the sale of coffee for money, which is then plowed back into bridewealth and compensation payments. They thus looked two ways, as money does now. Such a process of what we may call *precursion,* in which an indigenous valuable is itself reappropriated into a new nexus of relationships and thereby paves the way for a special sequel in the reception of money, gives us the clue to explaining certain aspects of the reception of money itself into previously nonmonetized contexts.

The commoditization of pearl shells was accompanied by a similar process affecting other forms of shell valuables that circulated in the Hagen area. These included, for example, cowries and nassa shells, both traded into Hagen from surrounding, less densely populated areas, to the north and south. Cowries had circulated in precolonial times in exchange for vegetable foods and tobacco. Nassa shells were rare and were sewn onto barkcloth backings to form headbands or nose decorations. The Australians brought quantities of both with them and distributed them in payment for labor in mines and later plantations through to the 1950s. Hageners then stitched the cowries onto long ropes and the nassa shells onto enlarged versions of headbands that became "mats" and were used in bridewealth prestations. These shells were thus ceremonialized and dignified, turned from "loose change" and body ornaments into large objects for display and prestation. The cowrie ropes were worn as elaborate baldrics by females for dances, as the illustrations in Georg Vicedom and Herbert Tischner (1943–48, vol. 2) show. In other words, with the increase in their supply in the colonial period, these shells were recreated as a store of value in ropes and mats and immobilized from circulation and used for other purposes. They were put on a par with the pearl shells and balers that were traded in from the south and also imported by the Australians. A plethora of wealth items of more than one category was thereby brought into being and placed into the nexus of bride-wealth and moka. This creative-transformative process played itself out among the Kawelka and Tipuka in two movements. First, in the 1950s, the Kawelka, who had both traded and worked for the nassa shells, gave large quantities of these and the cowrie ropes in a moka gift that had developed out of postpacification compensation/reparation payments. The supply of these shells was by that time diminishing and in the 1960s plantation owners were switching to the use of Australian dollars as payment for labor. Meanwhile, pearl shells had accumulated in the northern Melpa area where the Kawelka and Tipuka lived, passed on in moka from groups close to their new source of supply around Hagen township. Shells were also brought back as pay by workers who migrated elsewhere in the Highlands, for example, to Goroka. The accumulated pearl shells were then given in moka by the Tipuka to the Kawelka in 1965 (A. J. Strathern 1971:152–167). When the Kawelka came to make returns to the Tipuka in 1974 no shells were given, and money was given instead. We cannot say that debt-equivalences were calculated and the values of cowries and nassa first commuted into pearl shells and these then into money because no such calculations were made. The shells were just said to be "thrown away" (*rok mondorong*). At each movement the aim was simply to "give a lot." In any case, it is clear that the switch from pearl shells to money had been preceded by the earlier switch, and shells in general had been added to the basic form of pig and pork gifts over time. The immediate impetus for all these changes was an alteration in the supply of shell wealth items, while the supply of pigs remained relatively constant.

Shells and Identities

Before moving on to some aspects of the reception of money in Hagen we consider further the role of shells in relation to agency and personhood (Strathern and Stewart 1999a). Shells were powerful markers of gendered personhood and held aesthetic and religious connotations, as we have already seen. The pearl shell as a wealth item and symbol of prestige moved through time and space as women in the society also must move from one group to another when they become brides. Although the pearl shell in many respects is definitional of male personhood, it also defines aspects of female personhood in addition to symbolizing the powers of fertility. In the Amb Kor festival in which the Female Spirit is honored through a ritual sequence aimed at acquiring the power of fertility, the pearl shell is held up in the outstretched arms of the male performers during the dance at the end of the celebration. These shells may be seen as symbolizing the Female Spirit herself. The roles that women play as sisters and wives in society are encompassed in the powers of the Female Spirit, who ensures that gardens will grow well, women will produce healthy and numerous children, and social order will continue harmoniously. At a later time, the use of the pearl shells in the performance was replaced by hand-held mirrors into which the male dancers gazed while dancing. This substitution might be seen as a direct one: the pearl shell had represented the Female Spirit, and likewise the image seen by the men looking at themselves at the culmination of the performance when they were filled with the power of the Female Spirit served as an embodied representation of her.

Pearl shells in earlier exchange transactions were carried in large netbags associated with females, symbolizing the womb and often used as containers to carry newborn humans and piglets. The pearl shell in a netbag is then like a child in the womb. In one of the myths from the Mount Hagen area described by Vicedom and Tischner we see a description of this:

> The pearl shell acquires a marked religious and cultic significance through its use in the Female Spirit cult and in the closing scenes of a moka exchange ceremony. . . . According to a myth these valuables were at one time stolen by bad people of the Underworld. A brave woman, along with a few men, risked herself in going down to the Underworld and brought the valuables back. This act is represented at the end of the moka festival. In order to display this return of the shells in a truly dramatic manner, they were first hidden from view in large carefully prepared grass-filled netbags, with their shiny sides exposed. At the ceremony men with distinctive decorations carried the shells into the dancing place with many shouts and yells, and were received there with great jubilation. Later the shells were handed to the recipients of the *moka*. (Vicedom and Tischner 1943–48 vol. 1:120, translated from the German)

The myth to which Vicedom refers here is a bit more complex than his exegesis might suggest. The "brave woman" who went down to the Underworld was in fact the new wife of a polygynous man, and it was a pale-skinned cannibal woman who stole, not the man's pearl shells but his two sons Eklimb and Kuklup. The new wife was called Kopona Nde. She made her way into the Underworld through a rock face and an underground lake. She burned the cannibal woman inside her house and rescued the sons, as well as other men kept captive there, and "took all her possessions, valuables, cassowaries and pigs and went home." After this the two sons made the moka shell festival (with the shells brought back in this way). This myth gives a leading role to a woman, whose exploit is commemorated by hanging the shells in a netbag when they are brought into the dancing ground. The predominantly female associations of the netbag are thus conjoined with the male association of pearl shells as wealth into a composite symbol. Carrying objects or persons in netbags signifies their translocation from one place or one state of being to another. The pearl shells are first hidden, then brought into view in a revelatory sequence that is like the event of birth itself. In substituting pearl shells for the two sons in this summary of this myth Vicedom was perhaps unconsciously recognizing the equivalence or substitutability of wealth and people that is a feature of the Hagen culture.

Pearl shells stood for the human body in other ways also, as in the conversion nexus of people ——> pigs ——> shells. When a compensation payment has to be made for a killing, the receiving party may point toward his mouth with his fingers, saying, "Soon we will eat" (akop nondopa nuimin). Here the shells are seen as a substitute for pork (also given), which itself is a substitute for the human body. Human flesh would not be eaten, but pork would substitute for it, and in a further step, pearl shells substituted for pork. Now cash can be used in this way although the symbolism of life itself has shifted in conjunction with a recodification of the human body. This is a result of tentative moves to make land a transactable commodity against human life. Evidence for this proposition comes from the fact that land became a focus of compensation payments in one case between two Melpa groups in 1995 (as seen in the BBC film *A Death to Pay For*, Strathern and Stewart 1998b). Land, which can be seen as the ultimate locus of the embodiment of the person, has become an item that people seek potentially to make an object of transactions, like its products (pigs, gardens, and the like). There is a further correlation here, since the aim of transacting land has emerged precisely at an historical point when it is becoming scarce and some people are unable to obtain it through primor-dial practices of inheritance by which their identity with their own land was reproduced.

Although the pearl shell was a marker of male prestige and was kept mostly in the male sphere, women often decorated themselves by wearing the shells of their husbands, thereby sharing in the prestige of these shells and in the expressions of agency impressed in them. Shells in fact stood for both male and female identities at the same time.

Pearl Shell Decoration and Symbolism

In precontact times, when pearl shells came into the Melpa area they were cleaned of their lime overcoating, shaped, and covered along their outer lip with the resin from the *kilt* tree and sprinkled with red ochre powder. The concavity on the backside of the shell was also packed with the Kilt tree resin/red ochre mixture. These shells were processed further through the application of a mixture of the beanlike fruit and leaves of a grassland vine and pig grease onto the convex surface of the shell (Vicedom and Tischner 1943-48 vol. 1:117). This mixture would be readily absorbed by the porous bonelike calciferous shell matrix, producing a glossy, lustrous surface. These decorating steps were conducted by males, but the tightly woven handles that were attached to the two points of the crescent shell were manufactured by women. Later, when a flood of pearl shells arrived in the area along with the coming of the whites in the 1930s, pearl shells were received in their unprocessed form and the local people had to develop their own techniques for making the shells ready for exchange. This involved washing away the lime overcoating of the shell and shaping the shell into an attractive size and form. In an innovative move the shells were mounted onto a board of Kilt tree resin that extended outward approximately four to six inches from the edge of the shell; this diameter was determined by the actual size of the shell (see previous chapter). This board of resin was an elaboration of the rim covering of resin previously applied to the pearl shells when they were less abundant. After mounting, the shells would, as in the past, be covered with red ochre powder. Vicedom was told that if this red ochre had not been applied it was thought that the owner of the shell would die (Vicedom and Tischner 1943–48, vol. 1:119), thus emphasizing the life-giving powers symbolized by the red ochre. With the greater number of shells now in circulation it became impractical for the women to produce their tightly woven decorative handles, thus another innovation came into force: the men produced simple handles from strips of readily available and inexpensive sack cloth.

We suggest that red ochre, which was used in the decoration of the shell, is symbolic of maternal blood and the calciferous pearl shell symbolic of paternal bone. In the developmental scheme of the Melpa, bone filled with kopong (grease) is surrounded and nurtured in the womb by maternal blood from which a child is produced.

Money, Cash Cropping, and Land

In a wider comparative context, the delineation of such a pathway of transformations explains why money was received enthusiastically into local transactional spheres in Hagen and why such a powerful dialectic has been set up between local and wider economic and political processes since that time. Money is quite often represented in certain ways as both magical and evil in contexts where its introduction has been marked by obvious exploitation or hardship and by the erosion of indigenous social values (e.g., Shipton 1989; Taussig 1980). In Hagen, for a long period of time, at least 1965–1985, it tended to be seen as both magical and good. Though its magical or even sacred character has since then become more marked, its resonances have also become more ambivalent, as capitalistic relations reach further and further into the practices of everyday life. It is to this history that we now turn.

The history is closely tied to cash cropping, especially coffee. We can distinguish the following phases of economic history in Hagen since contact: first, the period of early exchange of valuables for services, 1930s to mid-1940s; second, wage labor on coastal and local plantations, 1940s–1950s; third, smallholder cash cropping in coffee and vegetables, 1960s–present; and fourth, larger-scale business activities, professional employment, and the like, 1970s–present. Cash cropping gave the first independent access to cash for all categories of people because smallholding plots could be and were planted by everyone and both men and women claimed access to their products although on differential terms (A. J. Strathern 1979a). But it also produced a new anxiety, as well as a new objective situation, with regard to land as a resource, because land for coffee was semipermanently removed from the cultivation cycle and thus made unavailable for subsistence use, a factor that increased in significance because coffee required the more fertile land in the first place. Coffee plantings were uneven because individuals had differential access to such land, and succeeding generations since the 1960s have found it harder to find land on which to make new plantings. Coffee prices have fluctuated considerably over the years, and there is heavy dependence on this single crop. Consumption of introduced foods has risen markedly over the years since the 1970s. Finally, large sums of money are regularly needed to pay for deaths sustained in killings, whether in warfare or not, between political groups. The demand for money is thus very high, and its supply rests on a base that individuals find increasingly hard to extend. It is evident therefore that tensions over inequality, perceived or genuine, in land resources nowadays translate easily into quarrels and accusations between members of local groups. By 1994, the Tok Pisin term *jelas* ("jealous") had entered into local discourse as a way of describing the ordinary tenor of *intraclan* relationships. This attribution of rivalry and competitiveness over *production* within the clan signals a reversal of context from the past, when such rivalries held sway in *interclan* contexts and had to do with *exchange* capacities. And the rivalry or bad feelings overtly have to do with money, not with pigs.

Another factor has influenced this situation. Since the mid-1970s it has been a practice to gather lump sums of money to purchase pigs that are used in compensation payments for killings. Pigs bought in this way are notionally similar to those financed in through networks in the moka system in the past, but obtaining them necessitates an immediate outlay of cash. These pigs also become an expression of the cash amounts needed to secure them for an event, and their significance can be seen in monetary terms as a result of the capacity of the land to produce coffee and hence money. This practice increases the pressure on individuals to produce coffee and hence cash for honor-driven activities that ultimately secure the safety of their landholdings. If this were all, we might be able to argue that ultimately interpersonal resentments were transcended by collective activities, but the actual situation is by no means so simple.

The intergenerational context has here to be borne in mind. The attitudes of young males in their twenties or late teens are quite different now from those of men in their thirties or over. These younger men see shrinking amounts of land available for their economic activities; they are accustomed to visiting town and spending money there; they play darts and drink alcohol as well as gambling with cards; and they are less interested in pig rearing and gardening work than the generation above them. Resentment felt within the clan is increasingly along generational lines, younger men feeling cut out of opportunities because of the holdings of their seniors. It also operates strongly between lineage cousins, and especially in cases where one cousin has prior claims to land that has been used by the other for growing coffee without a formal payment between them.

Such rivalries are further exacerbated by patterns of political patronage that have sprung up during the 1980s. Politicians use large amounts of money allocated to them for direct distribution in their electorates to build and maintain support among factions. These patronage networks amplify existing jealousies and tensions between persons in clan groups. Elections are fought bitterly by candidates and lead to recriminations and violence following extensive practices of bribery. Subsequent killings make the demands for cash even higher (A. J. Strathern 1993c).

It is unsurprising, therefore, that money has begun to acquire aspects other than that of the simple "good thing," a direct replacement for shells, which it was seen as in the 1960s. Shells were then dismissed as "rubbish," the worthless skin surrounding a creature inside that white people ate, and money was accepted as strong because it was white people's true wealth and currency (cf. Merlan and

Rumsey 1991:27). Now money is seen as itself producing problems between people. One of the early indications of this problem occurred in the context of changing bridewealth rates.

The adoption of money as an integral element in both bridewealth and moka transactions has had profound implications for the trajectory of exchanges in Hagen. As might be expected, an earlier sharp increase in the numbers of pearl shells used in bridewealth was followed by a similar rapid rise in the size of money payments after shells became unfashionable, pari passu with an increase in the supply of money from wage labor and cash cropping and the continuing fact of prestige associated with high bridewealth payments. The monetary component of bridewealth fluctuates while the component of live pigs has tended to remain stable among the Melpa: again, as we would expect from the fact that the pig supply is relatively stable. Among Melpa the amounts of cash that are distributed to women have also increased along with the importance of female labor in cash cropping. Bridewealth is central to social reproduction and to the balancing of transactions between people and a focus of intergenerational cooperation and tension. Complaints about the size of payments, especially their monetary component, also indicate the development of inequalities between local groups in their access to cash. It is money, not pigs, that becomes the focus of discontent here simply because control over its acquisition is less secure than control over pig production.

Money as "Sacred"

What is interesting to observe, however, is that while money acquires a "bad" aspect it also has acquired a "good" aspect in two contexts. One is its use in contributions to local Christian churches. Offerings and tithes that are regularly demanded and made in both old mainstream (Catholic/Lutheran) and newer (Seven Day Adventists, Evangelical Alliance) churches become sacred in the act of being offered to God in this way, and as happened much earlier on the Papuan coast (Gregory 1982) there is competition to build more impressive church buildings than one's neighbors have.

The second context is even more telling because it involves indigenous religious notions. In cases when persons are very sick it has become a practice to collect sums of money as contributions from their group-mates and other kin and take these to show them to the sick person as a part of the process of seeking to heal the sickness. The contextual meanings are that, first, the collection of money indicates the solicitous care that kinsfolk feel for the sick person; second, the money will be used to obtain either special foods and medicines or to procure pigs for sacrifices to spirits that may be implicated in the sickness; and third, money itself has acquired certain quasi-sacred characteristics that derive from its supreme value in the new economic world and its historical association with pearl shells.

Money in fact easily took on the fertility imagery that had previously been found both in shells and in stones, as that of the river stones that are collected by men who are going to perform the Amb Kor, Female Spirit cult. In this cult the stones serve as a home in which the Female Spirit can reside when she comes to share her fertility powers with the group.

When money was first introduced into the area it was in the form of the Australian shilling. These metal coins were referred to as *ku* (stones), by a classificatory approximation linking them to the earth. The shilling coins were often ones with a hole in the middle and thus for the Melpa were reminiscent of magic stones used for both rain-making and fertility. During the 1970s, when money was used in compensation payments, the bills would be artistically laid out in a fanning, centripetal shape with an empty circular opening at the middle. These bills were spread out in this fashion on top of brightly colored fabrics with flower prints on them. These are the body wraps and head coverings that had been worn by women.

During the 1960s a particular cult emerged, called the Red Box cult, in which the powers of currency were conflated with the types of power resident in stones used in the Amb Kor celebration. The cult may have been introduced into Hagen from Madang, where it was started in 1966, by a cult leader called Yakob Masu (Bieniek and Trompf 2000, with references to earlier literature). The Red Box cult members placed stones in metal boxes and waited for the stones to be converted by a kind of automatic alchemy into money (A. J. Strathern 1979–80; Stewart and Strathern 2000a). In the original image, the Female Spirit could manifest herself as a stone; in the new image, stones themselves could become wealth.

The powers of money and its close links with the Hageners' perceptions of their own history are also shown in commentaries that have sprung up since the 1980s on the designs that are found on Papua New Guinea's currency notes. The most obvious characteristic of these designs is that they are all versions of indigenous valuables from different provinces of Papua New Guinea, for example the stone ax on the K2 note, the pearl shell (kina) on the K5 note, the pig on the K20 note. Perhaps surprisingly, less symbolic note has been taken of these representations than of the design of the K50 note, which was introduced much more recently and corresponds in Hagen to a significant unit of wealth (notionally a "bicycle," *wil-wil kat,* or "one leg," *timb tenda*). Here what is picked on is the fact that the note has on it the head of Sir Michael Somare, Papua New Guinea's first prime minister and current elder statesman. The note is called *Somare peng,* "Somare's head." Attention to this fact is related to the realization or consciousness that money is a national symbol and also stands for governmental power, which is thereby potentially given the same quasi-sacred power that we find in its use in sickness rituals at the local level. It is also predictable that since leadership is seen as personal, the associations with "the nation" were not made until Somare's head appeared on the K50 note. And it is for this reason that a further semantic twist was given later, from 1991 onward, in a belief that was articulated by Ru that Somare's head would be taken off the valuable notes and replaced with the pope's head. Since the pope is a major religious figure, it is obvious that money's sacralization is intensified in such an image, but the symbolism is also connected with prophecies of the end of time, as will be discussed later.

Johnny Parry and Maurice Bloch have developed an analytical scheme that helps us to make sense of the dichotomized picture of money as both good and bad that has emerged so far here. Money is involved in the "relationship between a cycle of short-term exchange which is the legitimate domain of individual— often acquisitive—activity, and a cycle of long-term exchanges concerned with the reproduction of the social and cosmic order" (Parry and Bloch 1989:2). The problem is that money is used in both of these domains. It facilitates individual acquisition, but it can also be used as a vehicle for intergenerational social reproduction. Conversions of it from one sphere to the other are marked by ideological practices and also by the potential for conflict. The relational-individual stands at the center of such tensions between collective and personal aims and desires. We turn, therefore, in the next chapter to questions of personhood again.

FOUR
▶ ▶ ▶ ▶ ▶

The Relational-Individual

Terms such as *person, self*, and *individual* have been deployed in anthropological writings to approximate concepts and experiences in people's lives. Some writers have proposed definite and rigid meanings for these terms; others have used the terms interchangeably. But most writers have found some difficulty in attempting to come to terms with appropriate description for terms and meanings that cannot be adequately defined in English. Some have used ideal-type distinctions to contrast Western notions with those of "others." Some have theorized that ideas of individuality are found everywhere. A review of the earlier debates on this topic reveals that straightforward distinctions are hard to maintain. But what is clear when we examine the materials from Hagen is that by listening to what the local people say about themselves in words such as *noman* ("mind") we can better analyze the indigenous vision of "self," "person," and "individual." In addition, forms of ethnographic materials like speeches and life-history narratives are invaluable to the anthropologist who wants to listen honestly to what members of the society are saying about itself so as clearly to be able to place ethnography into the most appropriate theoretical frame.

A review of concepts as used by anthropologists generally in this complex field of debate is particularly appropriate because of a shift of focus in analysis away from ideas of the "individual" into notions of personhood putatively particular to Melanesian contexts and summed up under the idea of the "dividual," as noted earlier in the book. Further, since male leaders in Highlands New Guinea societies were often portrayed as strong individuals, the counterstress on the dividual appeared to negate such characterizations. Our own position, as we have already indicated, is that we need to look at all aspects of personhood and not rule out any of them a priori on grounds of typological contrasts. By reviewing some of the literature on this problem we will show that the problem is indeed complex and writers are not agreed on its solution.

We have previously reviewed the dilemmas that arise from variations in usages in particular semantic fields (Strathern and Stewart 1998c). Here we will elaborate on this issue owing to the level of ambiguity surrounding it and in so doing will move beyond the Pacific region before moving back into it. Efforts to synthesize and improve the concepts of person, self, and individual have been attempted for well over a decade now. Grace Harris (1989) forthrightly begins by pointing out that person, self, and individual are often conflated as terms and that this hampers both cross-cultural and cross-disciplinary work. She therefore regards these terms as analytical tools, for which clear and universal definitions are required. We may note that not only are these terms sometimes conflated, but the meanings given to them can differ and that these differences often emerge from attempts to match them as translation terms to indigenous concepts that are the focus of analysis. For a given case we can try to match indigenous ideas with glosses of our own; or we can represent them periphrastically; or we can cut across them with analytical terms that may prove relevant. Harris is interested in the translation of terms, but she also wishes to use her definitions as cross-cultural sorting devices. Her triad is stated clearly: *individual* refers to living entities among many such entities in the universe; *self* refers to human beings who are centers of beings or experience; and *person* refers to human beings who are members of society and have agency in it. She labels these three dimensions biologistic, psychologistic, and sociologistic and suggests that these concepts can be present in a local system without being the same as (coextensive with) Western formulations of these same dimensions. What this approach, which allows for many variabilities of specific context, does involve, then, is the supposition that a triadic division of dimensions into biology, psychology, and sociology holds universally. If this were intended simply as an outside observer's device for description, the translation problem would not arise; but if it is also intended as a cross-cultural universal picture of the actors' own classifications, the difficulty with it is that these classifications may crosscut the scheme or be quite divergent from it.

Despite this initial problem, Harris's paper provides some useful pointers. For her, *individual* is a neutral term, equatable with "human beings." Individuals in this sense are differentiated as entities but undifferentiated socially. "Not all individuals acquire the standing of full persons," through the acquisition of language and other ways of creating the "normal" individual who is recognized as a person. She points out that individual seen in this light is not the same as the "Western" individual (p. 601). Indeed, she at least partly dissolves the idea of separateness associated with this term when she goes to the cross-cultural record and notes that boundaries differ, by way of notions of shape shifting, gender differences, and connections with the nonhuman world. The "asserted biophysical processes" associated with individuals vary greatly, she argues. In general, the individual in her scheme becomes a somewhat residual as well as a highly variable ontological category.

Self is also variable. Harris contrasts the putative Western concept of the bounded, reflective self with other ideas (noting also Clifford Geertz's argument that we cannot know private but only public selves). The examples of variability she gives here play on the dimensions of passive/active, continuity/discontinuity of identity, and accessibility/inaccessibility to knowledge. Nevertheless, she argues that the idea of a persisting self is necessary to notions of accountability and to concepts of the person.

Harris reserves the attribute of agency for the person. A person authors action. In this sense, another dimension is added: a person need not be a living human being. (Meyer Fortes, for example, in a passage widely cited, pointed out that among the Tallensi a crocodile may be a person, Fortes 1987.) The concept of *person* may therefore also appeal to very variable ontologies. What is common to the domain of personhood is the picture of a moral context of social action. Morality implies choice, and choice again implies accountability. The person is a roster of interconnected active capacities as seen over time and as having a development over time, a career. Personhood implies also judgmental capacities, that is, abilities to choose between evaluations of actions. On the whole, then, Harris strongly links personhood to the moral domain, which we will see is close to the approach of Fortes.

Harris uses her distinctions deftly in constructing a criticism of Richard Shweder and Edmund Bourne's well-known distinction between the egocentric-contractual view of individual-social relationships in modern Western societies and the sociocentric organic view of these in Orissa, North India (Shweder and Bourne 1984:193). Harris argues that Shweder and Bourne conflate person, self, and individual, and she suggests that in fact the closed social networks among the Oriya subordinate the self to the person, while open networks in the American context studied permit or lead to the reverse, the subordination of person to self.

Harris therefore effectively shows the heuristic value of her distinctions and maintains her tripartite division by allowing for great variability within each domain. Questions of translatability and matching remain, but she usefully suggests that we need to see how the three concepts of individual, self, and person configure and relate to one another in particular cases. Individual, however, is not for her so strongly marked a term as self and person. In Nancy Rosenberger's scheme, however, self is made to encompass both individual and person.

One of the terms proposed in Western sociology is the individual/society relationship, seen as dichotomous. This dichotomization has been challenged in Rosenberger's preamble to her analysis of "the self" in Japan (Rosenberger 1992:2–3). Rosenberger argues that this concept has idealized a certain concept of the "Western individual" as rational, versus "others" who are swayed by emotion or context (this is reminiscent of Harris's representation of Shweder and Bourne 1984). Rosenberger notes that this putative "Western" concept has itself been destabilized, and she argues instead for a view of "self" that "attains meaning in embodied relations to other people, things and ideas and implies that 'people' 'are creative, as they produce as well as reproduce culture (p. 3, with refs.).'" She therefore adduces embodiment and creativity as further markers of the self that she makes analytically central.

She goes on to discuss the sense of the self in Japan as being an interactive process with the social by examining how the self and the social constitute each other. She posits that the Japanese self emerges as neither entirely collective nor completely individualistic but that the self is molded through the processes of social relationships (p. 3). She finds it unnecessary to place her analysis of the Japanese concept of self into the dichotomous framework of individual and society that conceptualizes the individual as acting in accordance with abstract principles, independent of social influences. Rather, she sees the self formed by complex processes and as heterogeneous, making sense only in relation to other socially constructed meanings (p. 3).

From her descriptions and her articulation of her theoretical position, it is clear that Rosenberger conflates what Harris would distinguish as person and self into a single term, *self,* and attributes to it also embodiment and creativity which others might locate in the individual. Her choice to privilege *self* as a central term relates to her stress on consciousness implied in the title of her edited collection, *Japanese Sense of Self.*

A. L. Epstein in *Gunantuna: Aspects of the Person, Self and Individual among the Tolai* has traced some of the definitions and uses of the three terms in his title, giving utility to each and acknowledging the virtue of making distinctions as Harris does (Epstein n.d. 4). He rejects, however, universalism or essentialism of definitions, saying it is a mistake to suppose our terms have some "proper" meaning. They are instead tools needed to address particular contexts or issues. One context is that of the differentiation between humans and others. This, however, is in itself moot because the boundaries of differentiation vary (as Harris herself notes), or are context-dependent. This observation would apply to the category of "individual" = "human being." The term *person* also presents problems. If we reserve it for an idea that is general, with constant moral value, in some cultural contexts it will not appear, and instead we will have only "social individuals." *Individual* further presents problems if we restrict it to the "egocentric contractual" model of Shweder and Bourne. Citing Brian Morris (1994:193), Epstein notes that this may leave no scope for individuality or the autonomous individual outside of the Western tradition. Epstein himself is reluctant to allow this because the Tolai people, with whom he worked, "with their entrepreneurial ethos and emphasis on individual achievement," think of themselves as making their own destinies. Epstein implies that ideas of both personhood and individuality are found among the Tolai and that individuality is here a part of the achievement of personhood. His "individual" goes beyond Harris's "human entity." He also devotes some attention to the self and defines it in psychologistic terms (thus falling into alignment with Harris) and citing Michele Stephen's study of Mekeo ideas in Papua New Guinea relating to "the hidden self," the self "inside" as opposed to "outside" (Stephen 1995). This is a distinction shared by many Melanesian peoples (for example, the Melpa of Mount Hagen) and one that can be investigated further through the study of dreams.

In sum, Epstein argues that it is preferable to apply the perspective of a continuum as opposed to the absolute notion of "Western" society versus most other societies in these analyses. We suggest that through this perspective a clearer understanding of personhood and of the specific ontological pressures involved is obtained. By the term *ontological pressures* we mean to combine two ideas. The first is that cultural categories imply ontologies of being (cf. Douglas 1996). Although there may be variable representations of such ontologies, they nevertheless form a framework for people's thinking that is relatively unquestioned. Second, these frameworks are employed by people in their interactions in such a way that they enter into social action and perception itself, thereby exerting pressure on forms of behavior. A strong idea of "individuality," for example, may constrain people to behave in a certain way. Thus ontological pressures do exist. Also, by exploring how the person is open to experience, and we might say opened by experience, an exploration of what constitutes a person can be greatly enhanced. In this regard, we can enrich the idea of the person by including within it aspects of the self. Epstein, for his part, would agree that these terms can enrich one another and reserves a place for "individual" that goes beyond Harris's usage.

The picture that Epstein paints for the Tolai is one of much complexity, and he points out how overgeneralizations and misconceptions about meanings make it difficult if not impossible to make cross-cultural comparisons or in some instances even to understand how the indigenous ontological pressures are working to move human beings into and along the processual pathways toward personhood.

Epstein's retention of the term *individuality* for aspects of achievement among the Tolai resonates with the global treatment by Anthony Cohen (1994), who argues, like Harris, for the probable cross-cultural universality of concepts of self and individual, but, unlike Harris, does not feel that we can clearly distinguish between a triad of terms. Cohen's treatment of the issues is both comprehensive in its reference to the literature and clearly articulated in terms of his own position. He refers, for example, to "the indefensible contention that the individual is a peculiarly Western concern" (p. 14) and relates this fallacy to a conflation between individuality and individualism (of which the Western "possessive individualism" is again only one kind). Cohen places some of the blame here on Louis Dumont and some on Émile Durkheim, arguing that the privileging of "society" as a concept led to an anthropology in which people qua individuals were almost incidental (p. 16) and that this is counterintuitive because we would dislike such an elision in relation to "ourselves." He is not arguing that "the individual" is the only reality. He does not wish to reinvent the wheel of methodological individualism or to allow individuality to obscure commonality (p. 17). But he does note that the sharing of symbols does not preclude different interpretations of them (thereby constructing an analytically important space for "the individual").

Cohen tends to see "person" as the precipitate of Durkheimian sociology with its theme of the transformation of "individuals" into "persons" shaped by society. Although he uses the term *person* in a sense equivalent to Harris's "agent in society," he is clearly more interested in the individual and the self and stresses both consciousness and authoring in relation to the self. His self and his individual are not amoral units, however. They are socially constituted and defined, but they are also creative, as in Rosenberger's usage.

His distinction between individuality and individualism enables him to treat the former as universal but the latter as resulting from capitalist thinking. In this usage, "individualism is a dogmatic posture which privileges the individual over society" (p. 168), whereas individuality refers to "a property of selfhood, the perception of an individual's distinctiveness" (ibid.). With this there goes the idea that the self is not passive, but active, creative. "Constituted by society and made competent by culture, individuals make their worlds through their acts of perception and interpretation" (p. 115).

Cohen thus recognizes a triad of terms but declines to separate them sharply by means of definition. In his own treatment, person is backgrounded, while individual and self are foregrounded and enrich each other in an interlocking manner.

His view of "individualism" here develops out of his concern to mount a critique of Thatcherite ideology in Britain, with its strong form of bourgeois possessive individualism. It is worth noting here that this term is not without its conflicting usages in anthropology. Carol Greenhouse uses it to characterize "Hopewell," a community in the state of Georgia in the United States of America where the values associated with the Southern Baptist version of Christianity prevail (Greenhouse 1992). Greenhouse illustrates what she means by individualism by linking it to an extreme adherence to norms of group harmony and a corresponding avoidance of conflict behavior. "The avoidance ethic is one expression of individualism" (1992:238). People would keep silent and transform complaints into prayer in terms that emphasized the irretrievable separateness of individual human experience." Furthermore, "it was the tenacity of individuality that rendered any overt attempts at conflict resolution futile—since people . . . cannot change other people" (1992:238–239).

This use of the term individualism clearly differs from its Thatcherite or capitalist usage. It is also striking that Cohen himself is able to cite Greenhouse's earlier work (Greenhouse 1986) in which she argues that "Jesus eliminates individualism" (Cohen 1994:142), whereas Cohen argues that the Hopewell parade of shared symbols such as "selflessness" could be "a posture put to the service of the highly individualized self" (p. 144). Definitional problems here seem labyrinthine, but Cohen's "take" on Hopewell does still seem to be different from that in Greenhouse's 1992 paper.

In Brian Morris's book *Anthropology of the Self: The Individual in Cultural Perspective* the first sentence of the introduction states: "The present study is a critical introduction to cultural conceptions of the person." Thus he begins by conflating self, individual, and person. He then outlines the three concepts applied to the term *person,* which are connected but that he believes should not be conflated: human being, cultural category, and individual self (pp. 10–11). He states that the first is a universally recognized concept and one that is determined in part by the process of intellectual construction resulting from social praxis. In this view, a person is conceptualized as embodied, conscious, and as a social being with language and moral agency. In this treatment, therefore, *person* is the salient term and has swallowed the other two. The second, cultural category, is a concept of the person that is specific to the culturally articulated representations of a community. Morris explains that this definition encompasses experience and that these cultural representations are embedded in the practical constitution of everyday social and material life. He elaborates by pointing out that cultural conceptions of the person may extend to include ancestral spirits, animals, and the environment (pp. 11–12).

The third conception of the person, individual self, Morris states, is a universal category delimited by social context, and the self is an abstraction that has been created by each human person (p. 12). This concept of the person, he argues, refers to a process rather than an entity. Morris rejects the use of the Western conception of the person to evaluate and define the person in other cultures (pp. 15–18). Morris's study also presents a descriptive analysis of conceptions of the person in six different cultural contexts, classical Greek, Buddhism, Hinduism, China, Africa, and Oceania (p. 18). He outlines how the Hindu conception of self (*atman*) is molded by the priority given to self-realization as a spiritual quest. He discusses the distinction between the self and the mind (or ordinary consciousness) considered in Hinduism to belong to the material order of reality. He concludes that "the suggestion that the Hindu view of the person is 'sociocentric-organic' in contrast to the 'ego-centric contractual' self of Western culture (Shweder and Bourne 1984) is highly 'Eurocentric,' in that it ignores completely the religious dimension of Hindu thought" (95). Morris here underscores from a different viewpoint the similar judgments made by Harris and Epstein. He provides a discussion of African conceptions of the person, those of the Tallensi, Ashanti, and Lugbara of Uganda. For the Tallensi, he relies on the work of Meyer Fortes, noting Fortes's dual concern with social structure and psychology, derived from his own training. The Tallensi have a complex set of ideas about "destiny," a configuration of ancestors who choose to oversee a person's life cycle. "Given a good destiny a person's life will prosper and if a man he may achieve full personhood" (p. 126). Ideas of this kind serve post hoc to explain misfortune, and they also "recognize the individuality of human life—and the Tallensi have a shrewd understanding of individual differences in character and disposition" (ibid.). The human individual is seen as crucially involved in the process of achieving personhood and the person is the result of a "dialectic interplay of individual and social structure" (p. 127, quoting Fortes 1987:265). Personhood grows through life but is completed only by ancestorhood.

Morris identifies Tallensi terms that signify human beings (*nisaal*), soul as a part of the person (*sii*), person (*nit*), and self (*meng*) closely associated with soul, noting that they make "the crucial distinctions between the individual, self, and person" (p. 129). The Tallensi recognize the individual but give little scope for "individualism," stressing rather ascribed status (p. 130).

In summarizing his findings from the Tallensi and other cases, Morris rightly stresses the complexities and variabilities of African ideas, the interpenetration of ideas of soul, breath, spirit, and body, and the recognition of the individual without the stress on individualism supposedly found in the West. The achievement of personhood among the Tallensi is seen as conditioned both by "destiny" (from the Tale viewpoint) and by individual actions (from the observer's viewpoint). Any notion that the Tallensi lack an idea of the individual is precluded, but Tale perceptions of variabilities of fortune are explained by the Tallensi themselves in terms of the agencies of ancestors as well as of living individuals. In addition, Morris stresses the recognition of the body as the locus of the person in these cultures: embodiment is therefore a criterion of personhood. On the whole, the effect here is to retain centrality for "personhood."

The three studies Morris cites for Oceania are also, at the outset of his discussion (p. 151), said to have sociocentric conceptions of the person. But this does not rule out individuality, for example among the Gahuku-Gama described by the ethnographer Kenneth Read, since they have a stress on self-assertion and "people have a strong sense of their own individuality" (p. 180). Bodily expressions are important. "Skin" is an expression for "personality," and *menu,* situated in the neck, is also seen as a concentrated site of the "self" or personality, seen as a marker of the individual that ceases to exist at death. Morris follows the terms of Read's argument that the Gahuku-Gama have no idea of the person in a Western sense separate from his or her social roles, but he repeats that a sociocentric concept of the individual may still give full recognition of individual idiosyncracies. "'Person" is here elided (though only in a Western sense), while individual and self are foregrounded.

Our excursion here into the comparative literature, ending with a return to Melanesia/the Pacific by way of Gahuka-Gama materials, has been designed to show two things: first, there are complex, overlapping variations in the ways that terms such as *person, individual,* and *self* are used in the anthropological literature. These observations are particularly relevant in a Melanesianist/Pacific context in which emphasis in the literature switched from a 1960s emphasis on "the individual" in relation to Highlands New Guinea big-men, their leadership strategies, and their ability to move swiftly into capitalist-oriented forms of business activities (see above, this chapter, and chapter 1), into an apparent 1990s consensus that "the Melanesian person" is a "dividual" rather than an "individual," that is, is defined by relationality rather than individuality (this seemingly arising from Marilyn Strathern's "as if" distinction between Melanesian and Western forms of sociality and her statement that "Melanesian persons are as dividually as they are individually conceived" 1988:13). Subsequent to this claim, it seems that "dividuality" gained currency at the expense of "individuality." The cross-cultural debates reported on above suggest strongly that there needs to be a rebalancing of the two concepts. In pursuit of this aim, we propose here the concept of "the relational-individual," a form of personhood in which elements of relationality and elements of individuality coexist. The particular dimensions of these elements, the tension or harmony between them, as well as their practical realization, can be expected to vary within certain ranges; but we expect to find relational individuals all around the world, and as much in Melanesia and the Pacific as elsewhere. This point about relationality can then be separated out from other debates about "partibility" and "permeability." Specific ideologies of embodiment give a definite cast to notions about, for example, gender and personhood in the Pacific, which have been described in terms of "partibility" and contrasted with ideas said to hold in the West. But ideas of partibility also exist in the West itself, as when we write that "a person puts his or her heart and soul" into a task or relationship. The special idioms in which such notions are expressed may be diagnostic of cultural differences, but the fact of partibility in the broader sense is found widely across cultures. What does seem to be quite characteristic of Pacific materials is the idea of permeability, broached for South India by Cecilia Busby (1997). Busby suggests that Melanesian "partibility" is quite distinct from South Indian "permeability" (e.g., 1997:275). On closer inspection, however, it appears that permeability is also a powerful notion in the Pacific. How else to explain the great concern throughout New Guinea and elsewhere with sorcery as a force that breaches body boundaries?

We can, however, adapt the idea of "partibility" without enclaving it in Melanesia but using it to refer to an aspect of the agency of our indigenous field collaborators and narrators of their lives. As self-conscious persons in Cohen's terms, their aim in these narratives is to give the world some idea of themselves, to show themselves in this sense as "persons of parts," and to "impart" this to the anthropologist and through the anthropologist to others, both within and more particularly beyond their own society. When we realize this, it is evident that it is particularly important not to squeeze such narratives into categories such as "the individual" versus "the social" but to base our understanding of their stories on their own cultural concepts. One way to achieve this is to employ indigenous terms when possible. Hageners often speak about their noman, which is the most significant term in this domain. The noman of a subject is seen by Hageners to be in a continuous process of change over the span of life's course and to encompass ideas of process, relationality, creativity, and identity. The successes and failures of a Hagener's life are gauged through an examination of one's noman (Strathern and Stewart 1998c).

Noman can be glossed variously in English as mind, intention, will, agency, social conscience, desire, or personality. These ranges of meanings need to be considered processually, in relation to the life cycle and the social interactions of the person. Noman distinguishes human beings from most other beings in the world. Dogs and pigs are the only other animals said to have a noman. The noman is not something a child is born with. It is a growth that comes into being when a child begins to understand and use language, and language use is the most powerful indicator of the state of the noman.

The noman develops through the process of interacting with other persons, the environment, and the ancestral/spiritual world. This process of differentiating the noman over time is done by relationality. This exemplifies what we have termed the relational-individual. Throughout a lifetime a person will experience many different noman, or states of mind. The goal for most people is to obtain a strong and unified state of the noman. The relational interactions that produce a strong noman are the ones that follow the dictated moral code of the society. At the same time, a strong sense of the individual person is conveyed by the idea of a strong noman, and the term can be used to refer to people's insistence that a certain line of action which they favor should be followed although such lines of action may or may not be normative.

Noman is a guiding, self-referential concept for all Melpa speakers regardless of sex or age, and people spontaneously refer to events in their noman. Life-history materials that have been gathered from Hageners demonstrate this point very well, as we have shown in previous publications (Strathern and Stewart 1998b, 1999b; Stewart and Strathern 2000). In addition, the concept of the noman and its support for the model of the relational-individual are clearly represented in the verbal forms used by Hageners, for example, in the contrast between the use of the term to signal "individual will or desire" and its use to indicate "social conscience." Thus *noman pindi* means "to make a noman to be placed there," that is, "to desire," while *noman petem* means "the noman lies there," that is, the person is mindful in a moral sense of others (*petem* and *pindi* belong to the same verbal root, the latter containing an ergative infix).

These complex different ways in which noman is used indicate to us that it spans the various aspects of the Hagen ethnotheory of the person and in particular the two poles of relationality and individuality that sometimes harmonize and sometimes conflict with each other in people's actions. The situation here can be further compared with what Jeannette Mageo has written for Samoa (Mageo 1995, 1998). Mageo distinguishes between egocentric and sociocentric discourses regarding the self, which she defines as the experience of being a person (Mageo 1995:262–263). She points out that cultures usually recognize both forms of discourse, foregrounding one but backgrounding the other so that cultural premises "retain a background that subtly confounds" their dominant appearance. She further distinguishes between moral, compartmental, and strategic forms of discourse (ibid.). In moral discourse people evaluate each other; compartmental discourse belongs to particular genres of social occasions; strategic discourse occurs when people try to manage "the messy flow of ongoing events and relationships" (ibid.). She goes on to exemplify all of these forms for American Samoa, concluding that "the three discursive practices here are not part of a unified cultural model of the self" (p. 291). (See also her discussion of the social realm as one of multiple "performance" 1998:38, with references.)

For Hagen we would like to comment further that there is a balanced blend of the egocentric and the sociocentric shown in uses of the term *noman,* and its various apparently contradictory senses also correspond to the discursive genres outlined by Mageo. The strategic level of discourse may also be involved with the moral and may "scramble" the latter, as when a speaker wishes to cast action in a certain light so that the same action may be criticized by one person as proceeding from "desire" and upheld by another as exhibiting "social conscience." Emotional terms themselves may convey both: *popokl* anger can be either "righteous anger'" or a "willful tantrum" depending on its contextual evaluations. Further, we argue that the sum of these discourses, for a given person, does add up to a theory of self, though not necessarily of a unified self. Our relational-individual concept captures this point. It regards the person as the unique site of the dialectic between relationality and individuality (the sociocentric and the egocentric), and the experience of being that person through the different contexts and genres of discourses is what leads to the search for consistency and "strength," the making of the person as a process through time. All these ideas are encapsulated in the range of complex referents of the Hagen term *noman.*

A further arena in which concepts of personhood and of action can be examined is that of myths and narratives. An early collection of these is available for Mount Hagen (Vicedom and Tischner 1943–48 vol. 3). Some of the stories included in the collection are ones Vicedom calls "stories of cunning" and "stories of social relations." These tell the tales of particular human characters and their adventures, escapes, or vicissitudes, though including magical elements such as transformations of people into creatures. Many of these narratives could be used to exemplify the lineaments of the relational-individual as we have outlined this concept. Here we do not enter into an extensive analysis but refer to three narratives, nos. 64, 74, and 84 in the collection (pp. 82–83, 101–103, and 119–120 in A. J. Strathern 1977b).

No. 64 is a narrative of Miti and Kukil, two antiheroes who go around tricking people. Such narratives are made to make people laugh, appreciating the cunning shown by these two characters in deluding others, whereas their behavior itself would be thought reprehensible if enacted in real life and within the community. In the first part of the story the two terrorize an old couple, set them at loggerheads, pretend to take sides in a fight between them, simulate a wound with pandanus fruit juice, then demand and get compensation from the two: a paradigm for the sometimes extortionate practices of demanding compensation in real life, showing us that deceitful extortion is not a new idea in the society.

In no. 74 a man lives with his sister, who is lazy. She killed an errant pig with a stone, and the pig's owners came to fight her kin, furious at its loss. Her brother defended her, hid his valuables, and changed her into a cassowary as a disguise. He fled and took cucumbers to eat from a garden, where a young woman discovered him and took him home. He was adopted into the group and one day cut off one of his fingers while up a tree and looking in the direction of his old home. He went with a companion back there, found the cassowary and tore off its wings so that it turned back into his sister, and recovered his valuables. They returned and he married the woman who first found him while his sister married his companion (a sister exchange).

This story reinforces relational norms, while portraying individual resourcefulness and bravery. It also begins with a deficiency in the sister's character and her mistake in killing a pig, producing an inordinate response from its owner. The brother shows initiative by escaping and is accepted by hosts. He recovers his sister-cassowary and redomesticates her by tearing off her wings. An exchange marriage is arranged. The shows of surprising individuality are appropriately consummated in the creation of relational bonds.

In no. 84 one sister chooses an ugly husband and the other a handsome one. The one with the handsome man taunts the other, who is affronted and suggests that they swap husbands (an inappropriate exchange). When this offer is refused, the insulted sister hangs herself in revenge and comes back as a ghost to kill the other. The living sister suspects this and tries to escape by sleeping with her husband in his men's house, but she is refused and the ghost kills her, stringing her up by a cord. The husband wails and lops off a finger, and his dead wife's ghost comes back as a particular kind of bird and shows herself to him in this guise.

This is a tale of errors, with tragic results. It reveals the patterns of shaming that also exist in real life between people, the competitiveness we also saw in the women's dispute in chapter 1, and the patterns of negative reciprocity that can result. The sisters are very much individuals in their choices, including "wrong" ones such as taunting and revengeful ones (suicide and murder). They are also locked into a dance of deadly relationality: the implication is that sisters should not taunt each other and that husbands should listen to their wives in need even if it means letting them into the men's house, normally tabooed. Everything may be a judgment call, and so individual decision making may be needed to retain one's relationships.

Until recently, stories of this kind were told regularly to children, primarily by their mothers, and women still predominantly offer to tell such tales to the anthropologists, although middle-aged people of both sexes know a range of them. Our point here is twofold: first, narratives of this sort make an impression on people early in life, which they carry with them into adulthood; and second, the portraits of action in them are dramatized versions of conflicts of role and agency that occur in people's own lives. The stories thus reflect this everyday reality while also highlighting and condensing some of the problems people deal with in quotidian contexts. In general, the genres classified as folktales in Highlands storytelling are heavily laden with admonitory comment and implications, rather than being simply for entertainment. In entertaining, they also set horizons on behavior. People do not necessarily commit suicide or murder in their own lives, but these narratives warn that severe consequences hinge on choices people make, and that it is up to them, with their *noman,* to make choices that are "straight" (*kwun*) rather than "crooked" (*kröya-möröiya*). We need to recognize, therefore, the connection between such folktales and the moral choices that press on people in their actual lives.

PART TWO

TRANSITION

Everything, of course, is always in transition, or at least changes continually happen. When we speak of transitions in this part of the book, we do so in two ways. First, we signal the change from colonial to postcolonial life since the 1960s. The Australian administration in the Highlands deliberately set out to enable the people to prepare for self-government not many years after the first new institutions such as local government councils were introduced. Both they and the people, therefore, were conscious of a directed transition, summed up by Hageners in terms of "law" and "custom." Second, this indigenous formulation, with its implication of an uneasy coexistence of law and custom, points to the sense of contradiction between elements, such as the introduction of bureaucratic and parliamentary government in the face of the personalistic, exchange-based modes of sociality and leadership of the past. These two senses of transition are obviously connected. They stand in ironic juxtaposition to the implications of terms such as "development" or "modernization." Modernity in Papua New Guinea today is not modernization, but a hybrid mix of contradictory processes and values resulting from earlier transitions.

FIVE

Transaction and Rhetoric

Analyses of exchange practices in the Highlands have tended to concentrate on the material items used in exchanges and on the nonverbal meanings encapsulated in the actions of exchange, for example the basic idea that wealth can be used to pay or substitute for the human body or can stand for the human person. But it is important also to attend to the verbal exchanges that take place on these occasions, for these reveal to us the explicit, creative, even manipulative consciousness of the speakers, who construct meanings around the material exchanges themselves. No exchange occasion goes by in Hagen without an elaborate barrage of speeches and counterspeeches, and these form the crucible in which meanings are forged. Such speeches are amalgams of historical interpretation, diplomatic formulation, and political claims, and as such they are the sensitive mechanisms whereby a changing historical horizon is explored and tested. They are one of the sites of the improvisation we alluded to at the end of chapter 1 and of attempts to establish legitimacy and respect for viewpoints that may be in competition with each other. It is of great importance to realize that we are dealing here with the category of the egalitarian society. Although this is not the main focus of the present study, it is a concept that is significant in its own right. The concept does not of course mean that everyone in such a society is equal (see Jolly 1987). On the contrary, it means that everyone is in one way or another slightly unequal but that there is an ethos of self-assertion based on a dogma of basic equality. (It has been a difficult question to determine whether New Guinea Highlands societies are to be characterized as showing gender hierarchy or basic gender equality. An assertion of inequality may conceal aspects of practical equality, and practical inequalities may belie assertions of equality. Here we argue simply that both men and women can take fiercely independent stances in situations of conflict that amount to a denial of overall hierarchy in social relations.)

In the context of the egalitarian society, speech-making takes on some special characteristics. It is a major context in which persuasion is exercised. It is governed by forms of etiquette that avoid appearances of coercion between persons and groups. These involve not saying certain things as much as saying certain things. And agreements have to be based on appeals to common sense, common interests, and historical necessities, matters that appear to lead inexorably to a certain solution. At the same time, they may contain coercive undercurrents, as when a remark contains a latent threat, but in deference to both diplomacy and the egalitarian ethos the threat is not expressed openly.

Hageners have developed particular forms of speech that handle the above requirements. The two main forms are "arrow talk" and "folded talk." The first constitutes part of the title of this book, one of whose concerns is the ritualization of conflict behavior in political contexts. "Arrow talk" sounds belligerent as a term, but in fact it refers to speeches that are usually made when some peaceful settlement has occurred between groups. "Folded talk" means talk that has some concealed element in it. It is the conjuncture of these two categories that interests us here.

In an earlier publication (A. J. Strathern 1975) it was pointed out that the two categories of speech event or types of speech noted above tend to co-occur in Melpa or Hagen usage. Arrow talk (*el ik*) refers to the stylized portion of oratory that skilled speakers deliver on occasions of political prestations and compensation payments. Folded talk (or bent talk in the translation given by Merlan and Rumsey 1991 for *ung eke* in the Ku Waru language) (*ik ek*) can occur in any context but is also prominently found in political speeches, especially in the arrow talk portions of these. Here we explore this overlap further, particularly in the context of changes in semiotic production brought about by postcolonial contexts of the 1990s in which, as we noted at the end of chapter 1, the problems of settling conflicts have increased.

Following on the earlier analysis, we suggest here that arrow talk and folded talk are intrinsically linked by a common structure of concealment/revelation and reversibility of reference. In the term *arrow talk,* arrow can stand metonymically for war. The translation of the term would thus be "war talk." Yet in practice, arrow talk is delivered on occasions of ostensibly celebrating the achievement of peace through the exchange of valuables. The concealed meaning of "war talk" is thus that it is "peace talk." At the same time, the images and stances adopted in it may convey messages of potential hostility or opposition as well as friendship or peace. The meaning is thus reversible: it has inside and outside aspects that may change places. The term *arrow talk* is thus itself an example of folded talk. Further, the image of the arrow that goes straight into the body of an enemy and pierces it so as to kill can be used in two further ways: one to express meanings that are conveyed powerfully ("hit home," as we might say), and the other to convey a sexual image, the male act of copulation with the female (usually referred to in terms of an image of the spear rather than the arrow, but the two images are related). These meanings of the term reveal another dimension that is available for polytropic usage, by drawing an analogy between the spheres of sexuality and politics (war and exchange). Analogies of this kind have been prevalent in Hagen speech-making at least since the 1960s, so we can safely say that this is a well-established pattern and not just a product of recent changes in the conventions of making metaphors. At times, the analogies appear to be decorative intensifiers as when a speakers of the Ndika Kelambe clan, in a dispute with the Kawelka Membo clan over land boundaries at the place Kuk, spoke of the pressures he was feeling: "When the wind blows, it blows up the front apron of a young woman and lifts it so they see her vagina; when the wind blows the pigeon forgets to hide in the rock and flies out and the hunter catches it. The wind is blowing on us Ndika now [and we have to come out and be observed and make our case]."

Often, however, the analogy reveals a close correspondence between event and image. At a moka made in 1969 as part of a compensation sequence between a coalition of clans from the Tipuka-Kawelka alliance and one of the Minembi clans, a Tipuka Kitepi speaker (Wai, who lives at Mbukl in old Kawelka territory) said: "They say if a girl is not good-looking, then one should send a good sow along with her in marriage and hang some good pearl shells on her," meaning that he was apologizing for the gift, which was being given in a hurry and was inadequate and saying that they had tried to make it look better with a few good items. Women are "the roads" of exchange and hence the comparison between a bride and a moka gift reveals them to be contiguous in cultural logic.

An observer at the same occasion who had an interest in the flow of goods but was not directly involved used another image to express his position: "Men go into the courting house and sit close to an unmarried girl [in order to woo her by performing the 'turning head' ritual with her]. If she breaks wind, we can't spit in her face, we have to swallow our own spittle and leave," meaning that he was annoyed because there was no talk made of giving gifts to his group, but he was not in a powerful political position and therefore had to suppress his annoyance: swallowing one's own spittle because of frustrated desire can, however, act like witchcraft to harm those resented, so the metaphor was double-edged, a recognition of powerlessness but also a hint at subversive powers.

Another Tipuka speaker, directly addressing the Minembi, urged them not to be too friendly with other groups into which they had married over to the south but to make their moka gifts only to the Tipuka and Kawelka to their north. He continued: "It was good that I [i.e., his clan in the past] killed Pakla [the man for whose death the compensation was being made]. If I had not killed him, what would you have 'eaten'? Parsley greens or the breast milk of an unmarried woman?" [that is, greens without pork and a breast with no milk in it. He was arguing that killings are necessary to produce compensation payments, therefore from this point of view being an enemy is just a necessary prelude to being a friend. Eating, including the notion of sucking breast milk, is compared to receiving ("consuming") gifts.

In general, speakers of el ik (arrow talk) also maintain a constant oscillation between self-deprecation, in which they treat those they are addressing as superiors, and self-praise, in which they remind listeners of their status. In self-deprecatory vein (from the same event in 1969):

> Pakla of the place Kindöpit,
> He was like a *mamnge* marsupial, you know,
> He was like a bat, you know,
> He was like a banana-leaf bustle, you know.

He was hard to find, swift, rustling but not seen—all these expressions praise the memory of the big-man of the other side for whom a payment was being made and thereby indicate the speaker is humbling himself. "I am like a frog that urinates" (My gift is small, like the urine of a frog). In self-praising, the same speaker said:

> At Kotndong they said
> There is a tree trunk standing up
> There is a red lake, they said,
> Down by the Mökö river
> There is a cannibal man from the sky.
> Who was it that they saw him eat and spoke of this?

The speaker, a big-man of the Tipuka Oklembo clan, Kele, compares himself to all these dangerous, impressive things associated with magical power including the sky beings, sometimes seen as cannibals, who are regarded as the ultimate originators of groups in Hagen.

Another speaker combined the modes:

> I see another habit of yours.
> You Minembi clansmen get big breadfuit

leaves but you only have little rats
Inside them to eat. That is how
You must eat this moka now.

These oscillations reflect the constant seesaw of egalitarian relations between groups. Arrow talk is honorific but interspersed with home truths. This prevailing ethos of intergroup relations is also carried through to contemporary contexts: self-assertion alternates with meiosis, and both are intertwined in sequences that similarly intertwine relationality and individuality.

In the contemporary context, the creative potential of arrow talk has been extended by including election politics in its scope and by bringing Christian imagery to bear on issues of creation and control of communication. We will first sketch out the relevant features of context into which this creative symbolic work fits and then we will illustrate it.

Contemporary Problems and the Limitations of Speech

Sharpening since independence in Papua New Guinea in 1975 although set in motion well before that date, several factors have coalesced to stretch the speechmaking powers of orators who wish to mediate disputes by talk as well as or instead of by fighting. These factors all represent the erosion of trust between groups that had been given a fragile existence through colonial pacification and the introduction of police and courts. In early colonial years ceremonial exchanges engineered by big-men leaders brought about widening arenas of peace, but within these arenas new causes of conflict emerged. The widened scale of social relations brought people into contact who sometimes engaged in violent conflict as a result. Guns, gangs, and alcohol consumption further diversified and intensified the contexts and bases of such conflict. Guns in particular increased killings beyond the levels that could be dealt with easily by compensation. Christian churches preached unity but themselves caused divisions through sectarian attachments. The creation of constituencies and election contests between rivals have exacerbated all other contexts by providing a recurrent arena of competition in which the stakes are high and divisive (see Saffu 1996; Ketan 1996; A. J. Strathern 1992, 1993a, 1993b).

Thus it is not surprising that forms of rhetoric for peacemaking are stretched. Compensations have occurred in the late 1980s and 1990s at which arrow talk was not made at all for fear that it would be misunderstood or because the recipients wished to get away in trucks so as not to be assassinated. Trouble Committees have been set up with limited powers to stipulate levels of compensation. Skilled negotiators still need to be able to employ tropes as devices of persuasion, however, and folded talk reenters in this context.

Contextual Uses of Arrow Talk and Folded Talk and Their Expansions

The skillful deployment of ik ek (concealed talk) in mediating conflict is a talent not easily acquired but one that is developed as a rhetorical form through a combination of mimetic osmosis and individual creativity. The strategic ingenuity of ik ek lies in the ambiguity of its meanings, which can fall either on the side of diplomacy or of threat depending on the situation and the reply delivered from the opposing side. The familiar imagery that is used in ik ek when placed in the heated context of political transactions takes on a subtle and poignant force. The suggestions here closely parallel those of Francesca Merlan and Alan Rumsey for the Kailge people (Merlan and Rumsey 1991:102ff.). Ik ek is primarily used in political interactions between different groups, thus heightening the potential for ambiguous verbal interchanges. As with the ancient Greek oracles of Delphi, much of the power behind ik ek lies in its inherent indeterminacy. A few carefully chosen words may suffice in obtaining a particular end because of the implicit unspoken text that the listener mentally constructs from the contextual cues. There are also parallels with dreaming. In Melpa dreaming, as in René Magritte's *Ceci n'est pas une pipe* painting, the vision of a bird does not represent a bird but the spirit of a big-man who is soon to die (A. J. Strathern 1989:313). Likewise, in the film *A Death to Pay For* (produced in 1995 for the BBC, Strathern and Stewart 1998b), the two leaders Ru and Ongka report that when they heard the cry of a *kot* bird (a form or an emissary of an ancestor) the night before a compensation settlement was to be agreed upon, the bird's cry was an omen that the settlement talks would not go well and a delay in acting on the matter needed to occur. In these contexts, statements and appearances all require interpretation and partake in a common structure of concealment versus revelation, but the specific interpretations always have to be supplied in context. This interpretation of events is also equivalent to the interpretation of verbal statements, so we can regard omens as nonverbal equivalents or expansions of verbal actions. Leaders while making el ik move to a metonymical from a metaphorical mode of expression in this way, for example by displaying a dirty and then a clean piece of clothing as a sign that a problem must be brought out into the open and made clean (see the historical example given of this in chapter 4). Imagery of this kind often has added Christian elements today, as we explore further. The trope involved (unclean: clean: killing: compensation) can easily be given a Christian cast. Here also value is placed on bringing matters out into the open, reducing ambiguity. In this

▸▸▸ *The leader Ongka-Kaepa, dressed in colonial style with tie, shorts, long socks, and councilor's badge, harangues his people on an occasion of a money-moka payment (1970s).*

arena, ik ek can acquire a pejorative connotation since what is concealed may be an attitude of hostility. On one occasion, a leader (who was also a modern parliamentary politician) challenged the speakers at a moot held to discuss a death caused by a road accident to say whether they were discussing compensation or making ik ek as a sign that they wished to make a revenge killing. Folded speech between certain categories of people, for example co-wives, is always interpreted as a mark of hostility. Co-wives are proverbially jealous and are described as *wölik* from *wöl ik,* speech that is wound around like plant rope round a spindle. Big-men who are rivals are described by the same term and also expected to make hostile folded speech to each other. (Nowadays the Tok Pisin term *resis* is used to cover all forms of hostile competition, including that between the genders as well as within gender contexts.) By contrast, el ik belongs only to formal contexts where peacemaking is the overt aim. Folded speech is intrinsically ambiguous. Arrow talk may or may not be so, but in its primary sense it has a clear purpose, however this may be subverted in practice. Leaders from the 1960s onward have continued to use arrow talk, throughout different colonial and postcolonial contexts.

Next we look at two spheres of metaphorization that use the potentialities of metaphor to create contexts of rapprochement between groups in contemporary life. While the first sphere retains ambiguity, the second aims to expel it.

THE SEXUAL METAPHORIZATIONS OF POLITICS

As we have seen, the term *arrow talk* contains the kernel of a sexual image. The image is also dyadic and falls into the domain of pairing, as Merlan and Rumsey (1991:113–116) have noted. They also note that in Ku Waru (closely related to Melpa) "taking a bride" means soliciting the help of an ally in warfare. We suggest that this form of expression contains a play on equality/inequality that is ambiguous. The male bride-taker is portrayed as active, but the female must agree and her kin must be paid (and in practice exchanges are made reciprocally). The female's agency may be stressed by portraying her refusal or agreement. Agency is thus reversible, as is power. The trope, therefore, is a good one for representing the uneasy character of "alternating disequilibrium" that is a concomitant of the egalitarian exchange-based society.

Melpa metaphorical images in general are rooted in bodily experiences and are transformed by being applied in new contexts, in which one set of meanings is mapped onto another through their experiential connections. A taped interview with a Kawelka leader, Ru-Kundil, from 1991, shows this process at work for the domain mapping sexuality/politics, as an extract will indicate:

The Kuta and Raembka tribal coalitions used to be enemies and fight, and they subsequently were rivals over the elections of MPs to Parliament. At first Raembka held the MP position but later the Kuta people obtained it. Anticipating the next election of 1992, the Raembka people sang:

Kwiya kep-e mana ndoklmba
Welyi Kuta amb-e tipi mon ndoklnga
Na nggörli pent o e
[Pa pi wa yo e
E pa ya
Pang e wa yo e]
Ponom ile mbi nilmba
Wete mon nilinga
Wör ile moklp a
Na yand pamb o e
[Pa pi wa yo e
E pa ya
Pang e wa yo e]

I (Raembka) come down the banks of the Kwiya river, and
The Welyi (= Kuta) woman turns her back on me

> I am ashamed
> I said I would go where she goes, but
> She said no
> I'll stay at the edge, then,
> And retreat back home.

The words in brackets are a refrain with no semantic import. Courting imagery is used here to express a veiled message of political rivalry. The intention is not peaceful, as it might appear. "Retreating back home" is in fact a prelude to fighting. We see that the original image of the song is deflected or "turned" so that it acquires a new, transferred meaning. The self-deprecating meiosis of the singer is thus to be interpreted as its opposite, a veiled threat, and the presentation is ironic. In formal terms we can recognize the semantic transposition of reference involved as "metaphor," but what is most important is to understand the logic of the transposition itself, to know the force of the recodification of experience in terms of the parallel/contrast between courting and fighting in Melpa sociopolitical life as two potential modalities of sociation between ambiguously related groups. The operation of the song is thus like the operation of tropes as they occur in political speeches and belongs to the same context.

A parallel to this image-pairing among the Melpa is found among the Mae Enga. Mervyn Meggitt, in an article on dream interpretation among the Mae Enga, cites the dream of a man, Anggauwane, who reported that in his dream he encountered a good-looking young woman of a neighboring clan whom he proceeded to befriend sexually and have intercourse with, staring down her male relatives who came to cut off his head with their axes. Anggauwane interpreted this dream of a sexual conquest for the clansmen to whom he narrated it as meaning that their clan (Kara) would be victorious over the neighboring clan (Meraini) in a land dispute that had lasted for a decade or more. The Kara clan did in fact prevail in the court dispute, and Anggauwane declared that his dream had made him confident they would (Meggitt 1962:228–229).

Two elements appear in the story that Meggitt does not emphasize. One is that although the dreamer represents himself as active, the female is also seen as active. The other is that the dream takes place outside of the localities of either clan. These two features, we suggest, represent the open-ended character of experience and the duality of agency implied in the sexual metaphor. They represent the woman as an ambiguous trope, who transports the man to a new place and seduces him. The dream could thus also represent the conversion of hostility into alliance as happens when a sexual encounter is further transformed into an alliance. Sexuality and desire represent a potential, then, for both hostility and friendship, depending on how they are taken and developed over time. The trope sexuality/politics is able to reflect this ambiguity fully in today's ambiguous political relationships. The trope also expresses the interplay between individual actions and collective outcomes, and in this context two further points can be made. One is that as a result of sexual liaisons in the past men have been able to get information about the plans of their military enemies and thus to win battles. Sexuality is here put to the service of the politics of killing. The other is the more general point that the ability to attract women represents the power of collective reproduction for the clan and the numbers of persons within a clan are directly correlated with the clan's military and economic strength. In this case, sexuality and politics are part of a single overall complex of intergroup competition. The trope (sexuality/politics) thus acquires a powerful depth of meaning.

In the next section we look at a form of metaphorization that attempts to transcend ambiguity, the appeal to the Christian God seen as a first ancestor.

THE CHRISTIAN METAPHORIZATION OF POLITICS

The impact of Christianity with its promise of guidance and revealed knowledge to church adherents has added yet another layer onto the political complex. In a scene from *A Death to Pay For* Ongka explains how he took the head of a sacrificed pig as an appeasement to a group of youths to persuade them not to drink. Off camera in a further interview Ongka related that the jawbone of the pig was to be nailed up on the church as a Christian mark of the sacrifice and a promise to God that the youths would not drink again. In another scene in *A Death to Pay For* the men involved in discussing the compensation payment after a killing gather in the Juma Lodge meeting room near to Mount Hagen township, take places around a long oblong table, and before beginning any negotiations bow their heads and pray to God to provide them with insights into how to resolve the matter fairly. By implication, they appeal to God to reveal the proper approach to solving their problem. A metaphorization of politics has occurred. In the past, prayers were made to the ancestors to ask them to go forward during warfare to facilitate a successful outcome in the battles. Now, prayers aim for the opposite result—for a peaceful resolution to disputes. God is the mediator in conflicts. Through the Christian ideology of the Bible, the killing between the two groups depicted in the film is seen as an internal killing of one brother by another, as in the case of Cain and Abel. In many ways, prayer has replaced arrow talk. Under God the political context is shrunk down to the familial context, presenting a shrinking trope like that of the shrinking trope of politics into sexuality. In 1995, during a film interview, Ru's wife, Mande, explained clearly how God is seen to be in charge of the ancestors. She said that previously the ancestors could make one sick directly, but nowadays the ancestors must go to God first before making anyone sick and seek God's permission to act. This places God the mediator back further in time than the ancestors and also hierarchizes politics. God is the first ancestor, and other ancestors are below him because they are later in time. Pork sacrifices are made to ancestors but validated by God. The trope ancestor = God resolves all ambiguities into a single overarching statement that transcends any recourse to ik ek and turns it into "straight talk," *ik kwun*. Power is also represented in terms of ancestry, and God as the first ancestor of groups appears as the reason why such groups should live in peace. This idea was expressed graphically by a speaker (Pakl), who made arrow talk at the conclusion of the compensation ceremony portrayed in *A Death to Pay For*. Pakl, referring to the fact that the killing had occurred in a drunken brawl, said that "God first put us together and only beer has separated us." God was portrayed as the first ancestor, who produced the ancient alliance between the two groups (Mokei and Kawelka) involved in the compensation. The trope ancestor/God turns collective difference back into collective unity. God as an individual figure thus collapses all collectivity into himself; he is the ultimate collective individual, we may say. Tropes such as sexuality/politics and ancestor/God both represent an individualization of the collective (e.g., an interclan relationship is signified by a sexual encounter) and a collectivization of the individual (since the individuals become markers of the collective). As shrinking tropes, they are thus also expanding ones.

More generally, these two tropes are examples of attempts that individual speakers and leaders have been making to reinvent for themselves the models of social process among them and thus to reduce the inchoate, in the terms of James Fernandez, to the meaningful (Fernandez 1986). (Dream narratives can be seen as examples of the same form of experiential production.) Attempts to link complexly and confusingly constituted domains such as those emergent in contemporary politics to themes that are familiar from other practices can be seen precisely as conative efforts at meaning construction or semiosis that are then shared and used as counters in public rhetoric. Tony Cohen has referred to such a process in quite a different context, that of fishing in the Shetlands community of Whalsay in Scotland. In his book *Self Consciousness* (1994:141), Cohen notes that expensive high-tech fishing machinery would be described in terms relating to earlier forms of fishing boats. We may compare this with the pulling of God into the sphere of the ancestors in one of the two Melpa tropes we have outlined here. Making God into an ancestor makes him into a tool to think with in social relations. Analogously, comparing politics to sexuality enables speakers to bring out aspects of the negotiability, uncertainty, and reversibility of power that is inherent in politics in a way that the formal introduced language of bureaucratic and parliamentary structure could not do. Such tropes represent, then, the open-ended edge of individual creativity working in contexts of fluidity and uncertainty, in the constraints of an egalitarian context.

The tropes also represent offers of transactions or commentaries on transactions refused. They are counters in the rhetoric of diplomacy. Referring to a refusal of political alliance by way of imagery derived from sexuality and courting is a method of softening the impact of the statement by converting it into the imagery of interpersonal cross-sex behavior rather than intergroup same-sex behavior. Rhetoric works, then, by converting certain dimensions of reference into others, creating a new domain of meaning based on the contrasts as well as the similarities invoked. The political song sung in these terms by Raembka men could be heard by Kuta people as though it were a kind of failed courting song. They could express their anxieties that the other political faction might threaten them with warfare, while ostensibly saying that the situation was like a girl turning her back on a suitor, an individual act that would not ordinarily cause a fight.

The trope ancestor/God that was used by the speaker Pakl (an elder in the Catholic church) was an offer of a transaction, suggesting that instead of seeing themselves as different, the two sides involved in the prestation should see themselves as one. Christianity offers an expanded possibility of the idea of unity generally, but in this case Pakl's innovation lay in his alignment of an ancient myth of origin with both a recent political alliance in contemporary terms and the attribution of ultimate causal agency to God. Pakl's suggestion was a true example of arrow talk in the sense that he intended by it to create a new political arena, and he announced this as a fait accompli from the past: God first joined us together. The message of the compensation payment itself was thus modified and enriched by Pakl's claim. Rhetoric therefore is involved in transactions and adds its own set of meanings to material gifts. Where rhetoric breaks down,then, we can expect that diplomacy and transaction also fail. Hence, again, the effort made by speakers to incorporate the contemporary significance of the Christian religion into their speeches in order to bolster their material transactions. The issue behind their efforts is *lo pemba mona mon*? Will "law" prevail? That is, will the new ways of handling conflict and settling disputes prevail? It is a question that must have been recurrent in Hagen history since early colonial times and was directly posed by a Tipuka politician on one occasion in the 1970s. We shall see its manifestations in events of the colonial period from the 1960s onward in the next part of this book.

SIX

Early Administration: Kiaps and Councils

Mount Hagen town in 1964 was very different from its appearance in 1998. Many of the government offices at this time were constructed from wooden posts, woven cane, and swordgrass thatch and were built by the conscripted labor of prisoners. There were no vehicles other than those used by government personnel and plantation owners. Roads were narrow and flanked by miles of canna lilies, introduced by the Australians. All areas within fifty miles or so of Mount Hagen were pacified, and it was safe for outsiders to patrol by foot or vehicle in any clan territory. The prevailing mood was one of optimism and anticipation. Both administrators and local people talked much about economic and political development as the key to the future. The first national elections for a House of Assembly (forerunner of Parliament) were held in 1964. People turned up dutifully for the occasion of the elections, presided over by colonial officers, gave their votes to any candidate they had heard of or listened to, and returned to their homesteads and gardens wondering what all the new rhetoric signified. In one, Dei Council, a Local Government Council survey had been done by Patrol Officer Max Allwood in 1962, and the council had been newly instituted in 1963.

In spite of being subjected to colonial control since 1945 (with "first contact" in the early 1930s; see Connolly and Anderson 1987), the Hageners in Dei Council appeared to be exuberant, self-confident, and intensely curious-minded people.

Looking back at this time, it is impossible not to be struck both by the degree of security at the time and by the tenuous character of the forces that had brought this about. Several reasons can be adduced for this historical conjuncture. The most obvious and powerful reasons lie in the local response to European penetration: first, the intruders were initially classified not as humans but as powerful spirits (*kor wamb*) (see A. J. Strathern in Levine and Ploeg 1996 for a discussion of this point); and second, they brought with them desired kinds of shell valuables for which the Hageners were eager to trade, and thus were called the "valuables people" (*mel wamb*) and accorded a kind of humanity on the basis of these exchanges (see chapter 3). Their ability to fly in planes and their possession of wealth gave them great prestige. In addition, firearms gave them superiority in hostile encounters. As a result of these factors, a very small number of settlers and government officers had been able to set themselves up in a dominant position among a very large number of local people. The valuables they brought were quickly funneled into bridewealth, compensation, and competitive exchange payments. (At the same time, they were able at small cost to themselves to purchase huge amounts of food and labor with these shell valuables, which were cheap at their source of supply on the coast and immensely prized in the interior.) Hageners proceeded to elaborate the complex of big-manship and competitive ceremonial exchange, and during 1964 a major chain of prestations passed through the Möka Valley area between Dei and Mbukl (A. J. Strathern 1971).

Hageners were undoubtedly in some sense preadapted to the early social transformations made possible by the arrival of the Australians. Big-manship and exchange effloresced from the 1930s onward but had not been invented overnight. Rather, what happened was to make the contests for leadership more open than they may have been before. There was no hereditary chiefship, but earlier big-men had certainly monopolized access to shell valuables (cf. also Vicedom and Tischner 1943–48; Strauss and Tischner 1962; Feil 1987; A. J. Strathern 1987 on controversies surrounding these issues). When the outsiders brought shells and traded with all comers for them, this monopoly was broken. Hageners were also curious about the outside world, and this was a major reason for their willingness to travel on labor-migration schemes to the coast, where they expected at first to be able to secure shells for themselves. With the idea of government and the notion of access to public funds that came with it through the structures of local government councils, they were also rapidly persuaded of the advantages of political involvement and activity. The Finance Committee of the council became a new center of power, as well as a new forum for bringing together leaders of disparate groups within the council area as a whole. From the council there emanated the doctrine of development which gradually began to contradict the process instituted earlier of expanding the sphere of ceremonial exchanges. From this moment, at once economic, historical, and political, stemmed the tensions of the ensuing years, which by the 1980s had created a situation of "neotribalization" in which major military confrontations between groups were commonplace and fear of them a part of everyday discourse.

Before the introduction of the council, which the Australians saw as a necessary part of political evolution for the people, big-manship had reached a high point of efflorescence and had been greatly responsible for the spread of pacifi-cation. Big-men sought new marriages and exchange alliances with formerly hostile groups, freedom of movement made it more possible for youths to court girls of various groups, and there was a general feeling that life was uniformly better than it had been. The steep rise in the size of bridewealth payments was made possible by the ability of people to call on wider and larger networks of kin to support them in this endeavor. This result of big-men's activities was not widely acknowledged by administration officers. In 1964, it was notable that Kiaps referred to local big-men as "fight-leaders," sometimes romanticizing these characters as the "true leaders" by contrast with "bigheads" and "spivs" whom they saw as currently emerging among those who had returned from wage labor on the coast (a process the administration itself instituted). The precise role of leaders as peacemakers and extenders of political frontiers does not seem to have been well appreciated at this time.

Kiaps held the elections for councilor positions every two years, and a mix-ture of older and younger men tended to be elected. A councilor could be either a stoogelike nonentity or a preeminent big-man. Only younger councilors, with some ability to use pidgin English (Tok Pisin), could function well in the Fi-nance Committee or in council debates at large. Several early politicians made their way into higher levels of politics via the council system. Already in the 1960s, some began campaigning against the exchange system, arguing that it kept people away from cash cropping, business, and development, that is, progress. The conflicts they instigated made the indigenous pacification system falter and turned people's attention to activities which in the longer run induced the begin-nings of a social class structure in their society. Kiaps encouraged these younger "progressives" while at the same time nostalgically praising the old "fight leaders" who reputedly had true control over their clansmen. In both regards it can be seen retrospectively that they missed the point: the progressives would over time become patrons in an unstable system of quasi-capitalist social relations, while the supposed fight leaders had in practice come to be eminent through participa-tion not so much in fighting as in the expanded arena of exchanges made pos-sible by the presence of the Kiaps themselves.

The flamboyantly impressive prestations that linked partners and groups vividly together in the Möka Valley in 1964–65 stood out as affirmations of iden-tity against a patchwork of changes that were much more evident on a daily basis: people engaged in unpaid communal road work every Monday, sometimes combining together in large posses to drag huge *Nothofagus* (mountain beech) logs down from high forest areas to repair bridges on the narrow dirt roads that snaked through the valley areas and up into the mountains. Most men had participated either in supposedly communal plantings of coffee trees or in establishing family plots of this cash crop, and the trees had begun to bear coffee beans. A few small trade stores had been built, dotting the roadsides, either with the sponsorship of NAMASU, an economic arm of the Lutheran mission, or with private savings. Money (Australian pounds at the time) had entered the bride-price system and was about to enter the ceremonial exchanges (moka). Throughout Dei Council the Lutheran church was predominant, and its prestige was increased by the presence of a mission hospital at Kotna (just west of the Dei Council chambers) staffed by Americans at the time. From time to time the missionaries held baptisms, at which a selection of older people would appear in white robes for induction into the church, thereafter abandoning their residence in scattered homesteads and joining together in nucleated rows of small family houses near to their local church, abjuring participation in moka exchanges and other practices of the pagan past. Big-men usually delegated to unimportant or senile members of the community the task of pleasing the missionaries by volunteering to join the church and observe its novel taboos. Christians thus joined forces with secular progressives in attacking the moka system and paradoxically contributed to the eventual breakdown of the neotraditional methods of social control exercised through this system. Christian cosmological and ethical notions had also subtly penetrated into and modified people's conceptions of the world and of themselves in it.

The role of councilor began to combine many functions that were subsequently dismantled. People built special houses for their councilors. The councilor had Komiti men from the various subgroups in the group he represented, and with these he constituted a mini-hierarchy: small disputes were supposed to be dealt with by the Komiti, who would bring larger or intractable matters to the councilor. If the councilor could not settle a case, it would go to the Kiap. Yet Kiaps did not recognize this arrangement. Unlike their predecessors, the Luluai and Tultul, councilors had no legal standing as dispute settlers in the colonial regime, only an informal standing as mediators. Kiaps frowned on councilors settling cases and even talked of putting them in jail for exceeding their powers. Yet they themselves could never have handled all the disputes that arose. By refusing to sanction the councilors' judicial role, they effectively weakened the local system of control, conducing toward later patterns of confusion or rebellion. Village courts, introduced much later, after independence in 1975, have only partly filled this gap.

The point here is an analytical one, revealing a mismatch in perceptions between the people and the Kiaps. Kiaps saw themselves as generalist field officers with very wide powers of command administratively and also as combining

‣‣‣ *Using a megaphone, a Kawelka orator promotes the claims of a particular candidate in an election contest (1970s).*

magisterial and police powers. They saw councilors as largely there to carry out their own directives at the local level, not as independent leaders in their own right. Nevertheless, they were supposed to introduce these same councilors to "democratic" forms of debate and decision making within the framework of council meetings, with their motions, speeches, votes, and minutes. With the advent of councils, aspects of the Kiaps' own roles at the community level became ambiguous. From the viewpoint of the councilors, some of whom were also big-men, the situation was different. They saw their role as giving them the chance to become like the Kiaps in their own sphere. Leadership in Hagen was generalized, and Kiaps were also seen as powerful general figures, whose powers councilors wished to emulate. Yet Kiaps denied them this in practice. The colonial context ensured further that they regarded local leaders as inferior, in need of education, and were therefore reluctant to grant them more power than was minimally necessary. These attitudes spilled over easily into everyday conduct toward the people.

Narratives that circulated in the mid-1960s reflected the considerable desire of the people for European forms of property, a desire that crystallized only a few years later in the elaborate money cult known as "wind-work" (*köpkö kongon*) that swept through the Hagen area (chapter 3). They represented the hidden underside of people's attempts to enter the economic world of the incomers, attempts that formed the topic of much speech-making by leaders in the 1960s and through to the mid-1970s, when concerns over law and order problems began to predominate in public discourse. A speech made by P., a "progressive" leader of the time, who had been a prominent local government councilor and subsequently became a member of the national House of Assembly, indicates this concern with money and development. The speech was made on February 4, 1974, at a marketplace next to the council chambers in Dei. P. stated:

> Money is a strong thing. It is not to be thrown about on useless purchases like long trousers and on buying the services of prostitutes. If a man wastes his money like this and neglects his true wife, the wife will die of hunger and the crops and gardens will be spoilt. As for the prostitute, she too will grow old without finding anything worthwhile in her life. Keep your money and use it to buy food and to pay your taxes. One man has already been jailed for refusing to pay his council taxes.
>
> Hey, you! The man down there who is spitting out betel nut juice with one side of your mouth and with the other flirting with a girl, you're not listening to me! But, believe me, you won't marry that girl, you'll go home and sleep with your own wife.

The occasion was a meeting at which prominent local councilors tried to persuade the people to acquiesce to an increase in the poll tax paid to the council. There were complaints that the rate of (Australian dollars) $12 per head for men and $2 for women was too much because the price of coffee beans had declined and so the tax should be cut to $6 for men and $1 for women. They were also discussing how people should set about voting in the upcoming election for the members of the House of Assembly, but little campaigning took place because "only God knows who will win."

The original speaker again berated the young men for running pointlessly after girls they would not marry. Another councilor now complained:

> Before the people pay tax we decide along with them what the tax rate should be, but you people are lazy and you don't come to the meetings, you think of your pig exchanges and your wives instead. Yet when we put the rates up you get upset and say no, but what will you do? You'll be put in jail. Or will you pluck out the eyes of the white government officer who comes to collect your money? Where will you go? Will you go into a pig's arse or into a cave or

where will you go to hide? Hold your meetings and decide properly about this, so that later we don't have to spend more council money on gasoline to go around hearing tax courts. You people just think of copulating and fighting, rather than of business and buying cars and working at good projects.

Surely you have all heard what has been said, that we need money for our own self-government, but even now you're throwing your money around and wasting it. Australia is ready to give us self-government, but we will be short of money. . . . Vote carefully at the elections. When we want to steam-cook taro in the earth ovens we take strong wood like casuarina and the *olka* tree and the stones in the oven glow with heat, and consequently the taro cooks well. If we use soft woods for the fire to heat the stones the taro will be raw. . . . In Australia the government is strong because of money, through income tax which is divided to the army, navy, and police and other departments to buy iron, bombs, guns, all the strong things. Others are saying that the price of coffee has gone down and so tax rates should go down too. But we should have more than one business, so that if the price of one thing goes down the price of another will rise and make up for it. We grow coffee only, that is our mistake. Here! [he gestured to a rival speaker] come and sit down on this finger of mine! How can we make self-government and be strong if we don't pay taxes? We shall be like those people of Irian Jaya [west of Papua New Guinea]. We will get into trouble over self-government if we don't have enough business. . . . On the coast they have learnt all this, but we haven't.

The tone of the discussion here was hortatory, and the issues of taxes, consumption patterns, and political change were tied closely together. The assumption was that the people would need more cash to run their own government, and that would mean diversifying businesses and saving up money. Anxiety regarding the future is reflected in these comments, together with a feeling that the bulk of the people were feckless and ignorant of what the future would hold for them. The anxiety of the leaders was in fact well founded, and their perception that after self-government and independence matters would become more complex and difficult to handle was highly realistic. Their speeches located the ultimate solution to problems with government and the possession of strong things like bombs. In this way a rhetoric of force was interwoven with a rhetoric of economic change, in a manner that was to become increasingly emphasized as time went by.

Inspection of the number of speeches from the years up to 1974 indicates that the typical concerns mooted just at the time of self-government for Papua New Guinea had all been articulated by leaders appointed in the council system. They also confirm that leaders saw themselves as prodding their constituents into a reluctant realization of political and economic changes for which they were unprepared. On March 1, 1968, a deputation from the United Nations visited Dei Council as a part of an inspection tour on progress toward self-determination in what was then the UN Trust Territory of New Guinea. As soon as the entourage had left, the same prominent leader (P.) whose speech in 1974 has been quoted seized the opportunity to make an extended address on change:

> To begin with, the white men appointed "boss-boys" and *luluai,* and we thought that these were appointed to make moka exchanges or pay bridewealth for wives. We were not forceful enough to ask the government officers what was to come later. We had no ideas! Now that we have councilors we are more strong.
>
> Do you remember Pena of the Römndi group when he was a luluai? He gave us pigs and pearl shells in moka gifts, and when we didn't repay him he came to seize goods and shot at us with arrows. That was the old way. He did not think about "law," he just thought of what was owing to him, even though he was a luluai. We didn't ask the government properly in those days, we could have got the right knowledge faster and already received self-government. The people who live on the coast do not have such good ground as we do [but they know more, he implies]. Here the ways of the past are still with us. We stare at whatever kind of car or plane of the white people comes to us, and we think that these people come because they do not have good ground in their places, but this is not true. They have good ground, but they come here to help us. . . .
>
> The government was first established in Moresby, while Germany controlled us still, but Australia was strong and took us over. Now we have councilors and our House of Parliament is also strong. We do not need to be afraid of any country coming to take us over. Our Parliament is strong and they won't get us. My father was a traditional leader, he killed men in war and made moka exchanges, then they gave me a councilor's position and began listening to my talk. I am not being cross with you, I'm just telling the truth. We can keep our own customs, wear our bark belts and long aprons, the government will not think that we must give these up, we can keep our ways and adopt the ways of the government too. Do not think that self-government will be delayed until all the old ways have been abandoned.
>
> A sapling grows and later it turns into something else. So it is with political offices. Luluai turned into councilors, and these into Members of Parliament. But we are too busy with our moka exchanges rather than at real work.

Do you know about how the politicians to our east and west have succeeded at development projects? You older big-men, I am telling you about this. We cut big posts to make the supports for bridges, we can't pull these just as they are. We put rollers underneath them and then drag them. In the same way we must find ways of beginning work in Dei Council, and in our neighboring area Mul Council. If we are not strong this work [i.e., development] will not happen. The United Nations comes round to see what people need and how they are progressing or if there is trouble, and they come to help us with new medicines or teachers. But we can get money by our own efforts from our land. I have seen where money is made, in the bank [in Canberra]. . . .

In the Western Highlands we cry for money, but it doesn't come free. Companies obtain a lot of money. If we are strong as they are we can get money too. We are going to reduce the size of bridewealth payments, down to £20 in cash, with or without a cassowary. We are always disputing over women, but the new law will put an end to this. A part of us is ready for change, but a part is not, like the growing beak of the sickle-billed [*Epimachus meyeri*] bird of paradise. We have forbidden bridewealth to be paid for divorcees within our own council area, but now people send them to other areas beyond Dei. . . . All the time we have court cases over women and we want to stop these. Only those who refuse to do community road maintenance work and thieves are brought to court otherwise nowadays. If we can stop all this we shall be free of crime in future. Small cases can be handled by the councilors, they are not to be brought to the District Office.

[He goes on to discuss his doubts about the administration's plan to join Dei and Mul councils into a single electorate, a plan that later ended in disaster, see, e.g., A. J. Strathern 1974, and chapter 7 in this book.]

As to money, we shall get it through business, this is the true *nde neng* [he refers to the tree leaf sacred to his own tribe]. You think money is only in the white men's places. No, there is as much money in the bank at Hagen as would fill up the Mbekl rock south in the Nebilyer Valley.

[He continues to discuss the upcoming election in which he stood against a candidate from the neighboring Mul council, who actually won on that occasion.] I have paid my fee to stand for election. Princess Stephanie birds of paradise at first have no tail, and we call them *köi mek pe.* Then they grow short tails and we call them *köi alingönd,* and finally the long tail grows. So with me. I was a councilor, then vice-president of the council, then president, and now I'm standing for Parliament. [He praises their own council, Dei, and denigrates two councilors who have switched their allegiance to Mul, then turns his attention again to haranguing the people.] As to you people, you are always trying to persuade the councilors to settle disputes instead of thinking properly about business. You think only of having sex with other men's wives, of eating pork, of making moka. You have sex with your brothers' wives and omit to bring good food to sell in the market. The councilors are thinking of jailing all of you. You stand up and talk and make eyes at women. Do you know we've set the tax at £5? [= $10; the currency had changed to Australian dollars by this time] In Goroka [a town in the Eastern Highlands] recently they jailed two hundred men for not paying taxes. I heard this on the radio. . . . Some of you big-men are councilors, but you don't hold meetings about business, only about women and moka, and some of you have only bush areas in your land without any business projects.

At a meeting of the kind this politician was urging should be held by councilors, Ongka, a leader of the Kawelka people who was at that time also their councilor, did his best to exhort his constituents (the meeting was on August 11, 1969). He began by raising the issue of a land dispute with two other tribes (chiefly the Ndika Kelambe clan) that was restricting the Kawelkas' use of their recently reoccupied territory at Kuk (see the speech reported in chapter 5 from this time). He pointed out that those of them left in their old mountain territory would have to make money from it. Some people in a backward area had not known about the new tax rate of £5 ($10) for men and $1 for women, and twenty had been jailed. Everyone would have to work and cooperate. Young people would be taxed too. He continued: "When we make moka or obtain wives we like to get pearl shells, but now they are telling us to give these up, even though the white men themselves filled our place up with these shells before. So now we need money. . . . And just wait till P. [the politician] gets self-government. If any of you have sex with women against the rules or you steal pigs then, you'll get your throats cut!"

These speeches reveal clearly many of the crosscutting issues of the time: on the one hand a pride and confidence in the council system, on the other a fear of not having the resources and knowledge to sustain self-government, since it was already understood that at this time the white (or "red," *kundi*) men would go. Some councilors were opposed to independence and preferred the idea that Papua New Guinea should become a state within the Australian federal system of government, fearing that they could neither afford nor manage independence.

SEVEN

"Law," "Custom," and Violence

In the speech by P. from 1968 a clear distinction is made between the old and the new ways of handling disputes: the old-time luluai (indigenous government official) from the periphery of Dei Council started to shoot arrows when repayment of his debts was refused. He did not think of "law," only of his own desire to enforce his claims. Pacification in the Dei area had been effectively begun after 1945, when the civilian administration once more took over from ANGAU (the Australian New Guinea Army Unit), and coffee trees were planted from the 1950s on, both by settlers who bought or leased plantation lands and, sporadically and with administration surveillance, by local smallholders. The pace of development, however, and above all consciousness regarding it, increased greatly from the time that the Local Government Council was instituted in 1962. Councilors were seen explicitly by the Australian administration as the spearheads for change in their local wards. But in the midst of the establishment of the council, issues concerning social control were ignored, thereby contributing to the later resurgence of intergroup fighting.

The quotations in chapter 6 make it clear that leaders saw their roles as primarily legislative and educational. They would make rules that would turn people away from the old things, such as disputes over women, and encourage or force them into increasing their incomes so that they could pay higher taxes. Economic development was seen as necessary for political progress. An important link was made: as one government interpreter remarked during a council meeting at Dei in 1969, the people must work to get money, but the politicians must "open up the road of business" for them. The idea of political patronage is clearly expressed here and has subsequently become deeply entwined with processes of change at large in the society.

At this time leaders did not present themselves rhetorically as the settlers of disputes. Records of disputes indicate that a wide range of prominent men

▸▸▸ *Kuri, a preeminent old leader of the Tipuka Kitepi clan, casts his vote into an election box (1960s).*

would become involved in their resolution: councilors held no monopoly, indeed, as we have seen, they actually had less power than the luluai and *tultul* who previously were appointed directly by the government patrol officers. Political leaders were both trying to restrict the kinds and numbers of cases that would be brought to the District Office to be adjudicated and to argue that councilors could settle small "rubbish" cases at their own homes. In their rhetoric leaders also denigrated the moka and bridewealth systems as though they were insignificant but also time-consuming and troublesome, the source of disputes. What they did not thereby acknowledge was that, no matter what disputes might emerge out of moka occasions, prestations of this kind were the *only* effective means of controlling political relations between people and of consolidating the gains of pacification.

Whatever optimistic picture the new politicians were imagining, its dimensions were dented by a major dispute that convulsed both Dei and Mul councils from 1967 onward. The events involved showed very clearly how *new* political enmities could be created through the very process of supposedly "progressive" change adopted by every public speaker in the 1960s.

Under pressure from the United Nations, the Australian administration had to show what steps it was taking to educate the people for independence, and the agents of this education were exactly the same colonial public servants who

▸▸▸ *An Australian government officer (Kiap), Roger Gleeson, explains the structure of government that is to come with independence to a set of listeners, mostly women. At the apex of the two sticks, he says, are the people themselves (1968).*

had only recently established their external control over the people. Therefore, a certain sense of logical contradiction or paradox was present from the 1960s onward. Australian Kiaps sometimes behaved toward the local people in the overbearing ways that had facilitated their initial success in subjugating them, yet at the same time they were required to instruct the people about how to free themselves from this kind of control. To make the imagined narrative of their actions seem more internally consistent, they were obliged to adopt the United Nations' imperative and make it a part of their own "founding myth," overlaying the older narrative of colonial discovery and expansion. The bridge between the old and the new founding myths was found in forms of political and economic ideology pertaining to the "new order" which the whites saw themselves as bringing. Local leaders were instructed through the council system to promulgate among their ward constituents the mechanisms seen as necessary to replicate this new order beyond the colonial context. Hence the emphasis in their speeches on taxes as the sine qua non of progress: very much an "administrative" way of looking at things both communalistic and bureaucratic. New political structures were seen as the means to the new ends of development rather than as sources of power and patronage in their own right. But the brief observation of the council interpreter

Warike that politicians would "open the road of business" for their electors in fact contains the seeds of both the "bureaucratic" and the "patronage" messages regarding the future. The competitive, segmentary context in which council elections were fought became the model for the new wider-scale political processes of election to Parliament (or the House of Assembly, as it was then known). In this context, one piece of colonial policy had severe consequences. This policy was that Local Government Councils should be merged over time so as to create wider spheres of social awareness and cooperation and to work toward concepts of national unity. The two councils picked for this amalgamation in the Hagen area overall were Dei Council and Mul, their neighbors to the south and southwest. Amalgamation of the councils was supposed to go with their merger as a single electorate in the second national elections that were to take place in 1968. In retrospect, the speed with which this policy idea was imposed is startling. Councils had begun only in the early 1960s, and Mul and Dei had not yet been joined at the council level when they were put together by fiat of the Electoral Boundaries Commission for the 1968 elections. Such a decision represents the dominance of the bureaucratic model of development with a concomitant downplaying of the patronage model that ordinary people had. In the event, leaders themselves became the targets of the contradictions set up by the new structure.

Before the council merger could take place, in September 1967 the driver of a passenger vehicle from the Mul council area was attacked in Dei after his vehicle had knocked down an old man. Relatives of the old man seized the driver and struck him with wooden planks, and he died from head injuries (the old man was in fact not seriously hurt). From all the settlement places in Dei as a whole cries went up, announcing this death and calling everyone to collect at the council buildings to discuss what to do. The extraordinary feature of this response is that instantaneously a new level of political structure was created that grafted together concerns derived from the indigenous polity and frameworks created by the drive for "political development." It was assumed by everyone—and this could *only* be because of the administration's plans, for such a reaction never before occurred—that all of Dei Council would be held responsible and would have to meet compensation demands from the relatives of the dead driver in Mul and that if these demands were denied, anyone from Dei might be a target for revenge. Dei Council became the first unit in the neotribalization of politics in Hagen. The Australian officer acting as council adviser participated in this process by coordinating the efforts of the councilors to collect wealth for the compensation payment and by witnessing the actual handover of wealth when it took place, in front of the council chambers. Another feature that tied together ele-

▸▸▸ *Kuri's son, Parua-Kuri, who became a long-standing Member of Parliament in the Dei Council electorate (1960s).*

ments from different levels of structure was the position of the Dei Council president as an affine of those who had led the attack against the driver. He embodied in his own person both old and new aspects of "responsibility" in the case. Furthermore, he was shortly due to stand in the election, which would pit him against two prominent leaders from the Römndi tribe in Mul.

While all the Dei groups participated in compensating the Mul people, a major established division within Dei itself now issued in further complications. The dead driver came from a small interstitial group of people right on the borders between Dei and Mul, near to the government station Muglamp, which served "Hagen north," an area encompassing Dei but also parts of Mul. This small group, the Nengka Kuklanggil, had ties both with the main segments of their own tribe in Mul and northward with segments of a large (more than five thousand people) Dei tribe, the Minembi. The Minembi as a whole were traditional enemies of the council president's clan in Dei, the Tipuka. An outlying segment of their tribe, closely allied to the Tipuka and therefore at odds with the bulk of the Minembi, was responsible for the attack on the driver and was also tied to the Dei president by a relationship of affinity. Rumors circulated in 1968 that the president's own clan was secretly suspected by the Mul people of being responsible for the attack. The effect of such rumors was to open up again the question of revenge and to detract from the effectiveness of the compensation payment that had been made. In addition, the admixture of elements deriving from political rivalry is clear. The Minembi were jealous of the political eminence of the Tipuka (an enmity that has continued to be important through to the 1990s) and even of the fact that the Dei Council chambers had been built in the vicinity of Tipuka rather than Minembi territory (i.e., at Dei itself rather than at Muglamp). The first president of the council had been a Minembi leader from a clan that neighbors the Nengka Kuklanggil, and he had been ousted in a competitive vote in 1966. His clansmen were implicated in the rumors about the current president, and these in turn were generated from the new context of rivalry in politics, since the Minembi also resented the Tipukas' hegemony in this sphere and vainly sought candidates whom they could convincingly put up against the president. The net effect, as can be seen with hindsight, was to favor the Mul candidates in the 1968 election because Mul at the time had no major divisions internally of the sort that pervaded Dei politics, and both Mul candidates came from a single tribe, the Römndi, who also had a network of ties with Dei people. The younger and more vigorous of the two Mul candidates thus won in the election, declaring that by his efforts he now would unite Mul and Dei together (A. J. Strathern 1974:250–252). This did not happen. In the next setting of electoral boundaries, they were in fact split into two separate electorates for the elections of 1972.

Speeches made by candidates and their agents on campaign trips through Dei and Mul generally did not delve into these underlying causes of dissension. The Dei president, P., himself was reluctant to visit Mul, and his chief Mul opponent, Mek, was the only one from the opposite side to campaign in Dei. The other Dei candidates actually traveled around together, making formal speeches and leaving the rest to the people. Patronage was not in evidence. They all conventionally declared that they did not mind who was elected. Mek was already stressing the unity of the two areas and how people could move freely within them, and generally the outcome was said to depend on God and the free votes of individuals. Mek politely advised his people to think carefully. "We have been to Dei Council and slept there too, now we will go again, they will not abandon us, they will give us some votes too. You must think and put a strong man into the House of Assembly. If voters don't want us, we won't be cross or put anyone in jail or ask why, this would be a 'rubbish' way to behave. There is no boundary between our councils, we are gathering here to find a good man for both areas, and you people must get this straight in your minds."

Mek also promulgated the theme of economic development and community change, presenting parliamentarians as advocates for their people.

The women used to work on the roads to get gravel and their shoulders and backs were sore. We candidates took pity on you people and so we paid our fees to stand for election. Many people think we are going just for our own ends, but this is not so. . . . We made bridges with posts and our hands were swollen with pain. . . . The white men struck us for not working on the roads too: we thought of this and stood for election. Our children have to walk long distances to school and take their own sweet potatoes to eat, it is hard for them. We want high schools nearby, so all the children can go. We want hospitals nearby. We work hard and plant coffee and the white men buy coffee beans from us and pay us only £10 or £12 per bag, they cut us short with the price. There is a lot of money in the House of Assembly, we shall go to find it, we will ask why the white men cut our coffee prices.

Mek's words here mingle the standard bureaucratic picture of change with the beginnings of a criticism of the economic role of Europeans in the cash economy. He also used images derived from his own culture, comparing Parliament with the Hagen mountain and saying that in it one must follow the talk to its source like the head of a river; he told voters to wrap up all the talk as though in a netbag and empty the bag later by voting; and he said that they would later see what all this was about in the same way as one sees directly how the blade of a stone ax is bound to its hafting with bark. Finally, he said that an election is like a marriage: candidates have come to woo voters and the giving of votes is like the giving of a bride in marriage (an image that shows the crossover between "courting" and politics which is characteristic of Hagen political language, as we discussed in chapter 5). He compared the election to the swaying head of the casuarina tree blown by the wind (a motif applied in songs to the wishes of a woman) and to the winding oxbow patterns traced by the Wahgi River to the east of Dei, both expressions that convey freedom of choice and uncertainty of outcome.

Other speakers agreed with Mek and added their own images. One said: "We cook pigs and when we want to steam the fatty pieces we take ginger and salt and spit them on the meat to make it tasty. Without the salt, it is not really tasty" (i.e., the talk of the candidates will not be worthwhile unless they make good points). And talking of relations between the two councils he made a political moral: "We candidates are like the jealous, competitive wives of a polygynist. The children see that their mothers are jealous of one another and they burn down the houses of the other women. Yet in fact many of them sleep together in the same house and they burn together. We of Dei have sixteen thousand people and you of Mul fourteen thousand, but we are together. . . . We do not want to continue acting like children when we go to Hagen town." The people believed Hagen town was ahead in terms of development. Another Dei candidate urged the electors not to listen to blandishments but only to straight talk. "The talk must not go astray like a crooked waterfall or like the curving tail of an eel," seen as slippery and elusive. Mek himself made a further set of comparisons: "A marsupial leaves its feces on stones, and butterflies collect on this to eat from it. This is how you see us and perhaps you think we are mad, but no, we have a task to perform. In times of rain the rivers carry sticks and stones and dirt with them from their heads and we are like that, we are carrying all of you along with us. . . . The job of the Member will be hard. The head of a *korloma* fish is strong, but a hard stone heated in fire can penetrate it" and the Member will have to speak with words like hot stones to get what his electorate needs.

A major feature of this election was that European and indigenous candidates were competing with each other, which probably brought out the issue of relations between these categories generally, always couched in terms of economics, suspicions of exploitation, and trickery. In this campaign a fiery young politician from the Chimbu area, Iambakey Okuk, came and directly challenged his white competitors for the wider regional seat, declaring they were all liars intent on making profits for themselves and putting himself forward as a "black man" to set all this to rights. Other concerns were articulated regarding the Japanese cars (Toyotas) entering the market at this time (cf. Salisbury 1962:209 on "novel capital investments"): "We spend a lot on cars, as much as £2,000, and repairs are expensive too. The Japanese make these cars and we like them and buy them. Do the white men pay only a little for these cars? They charge us a lot for them and for their repairs" (Pung, of Römndi tribe, a candidate). And regarding problems with women: "Women are disobedient, they are always getting involved in courts which are difficult for us men to settle, so let the women be their own councilors and *Komiti* [councillors' assistants] and settle these court cases themselves" (Maep, of Römndi tribe, a senior leader).

Nikint, of the Kawelka Kundmbo clan, commented on the race issue: "People said that if we elect only the white men they will hide the talk among themselves, but if we send our own people they won't understand things. So we should send both of them together and the black men can check on what the white men say and stop them from hiding things." In 1998 Nikint was still concerned about the issue of deceptive behavior by whites and was inclined to blame social problems on the influence of films coming from the outside world.

Similar remarks were made by Kundil, of Minembi Kimbo clan, but with some disappointment, too: "We thought the white men would hide talk from us, and so we elected one of our own people, Kaibelt from the Minj area, but he didn't come to see us either."

Kundil further articulated early concerns about development and plantations:

> We have to do government work [on the roads] with one hand and work for the white men on plantations with the other, now we want to know if they give us one shilling but take two shillings for themselves. The Member of Parliament should go down to the capital city, Port Moresby, and find out about this. And about roads. . . . Two generations have passed since Kiap Taylor [an early government official and explorer who came in the 1930s] came, but we're still hard at work on the roads. Do the white men make roads like that or do they make them quickly? We want to find out.

Talk of bribery ("grease talk") was also in the air. Welyi, a Kawelka Kurupmbo man, reported: "All the white men have been coming here and greasing the people. Our own men have been greasing them too, offering to go on campaign for them if they give money and a car. Two councilors got $12 from John Colman [an Australian businessman candidate] and others got $22 to patrol into the Jimi Valley for him. The white men are believing this and eagerly giving money. They bring plenty of cars. It's a pity they're doing this. Grease talk should belong to us local people only."

Most notable in the campaign was the absence of the Dei president P. Declaring himself to be sick and sending emissaries on his behalf to Mul along with the other three Dei candidates, he confined himself to a few appearances inside Dei itself and especially occasions near to the council chambers. He adopted a lofty, forceful tone in his speeches, stressing his own knowledge of politics and the future, as in a speech made on February 2, 1968:

> We have talked to you and some of you have heard, but others have not. There is talk inside the government which you don't know about yet [he alludes to self-government]. Now that the government is here we have built our council chambers and whatever talk comes up to do with road building or other projects we are in line to do it. The source of this talk is hidden from us, it lies underneath the surface. You think that the member will get a big salary, but this is not so, we want to do the important work of raising up Papua New Guinea [*Papua Niu Gini koma ruimin,* "we will carry PNG on our shoulders," as a parent does a child.] You do not really believe us, you think we are joking. We will talk to you now and later you will see what we do. The Kiaps will come and tell you too.

From time to time he berated his listeners:

Some of you men who are walking about here are not listening, instead you are cutting your mothers' vaginas [i.e., thinking about sex not politics]. . . . We are not talking about being "bigheads" and having sex, we are talking about something different here. . . . You people are keeping quiet because your mouths are full of pork, but are you listening to what we are saying? We have not paid our election fees for no reason. You tell us that you do not have enough money, that only in Australia is there sufficient money, and for this reason we are standing. We are sorry for you younger men, you men of "law.". . . If you young men oil your skin, put on long trousers, shirts, and glasses, you are not thinking of your work, you are thinking only of drinking beer in the hotel. You won't start any work to improve your area. You are thinking of prostitutes and of decorating yourselves. Now, however, listen to me carefully and remember, because the older people will forget. . . . We must choose a strong man who is like a crowbar to break the strong cement in the House of Assembly that has been made by the government. We don't know what is inside the cement, but a strong man must go there and let us know. We want this place with its many people to develop, to prosper under the law. We are not thinking of ourselves, we are thinking of you. . . . The members will find us ways to get good food to eat at night as the white men do. . . . You must elect a man who has no shame and can defeat a white man in debate; the kind of man who succeeds in having sex with a woman when others fail. . . . This man will go to the House of Assembly and he will not hide the talk, he will get iron for bridges, trucks, bulldozers to cut mountain roads and a large school for this area. We candidates are all strong men who have spent £25 on our election fees. . . . We are men who eat stone [i.e., are tough].

Candidates in fact used a range of sometimes contradictory images to explain what the role of the member would be. While the prevailing accent was on "strength," a characteristic of existing big-men, they were anxious to deflect any idea that they were in the competition for their own advantage (as big-men sometimes are held to be in their affairs) and to profess altruism. They wished to "raise" Mul and Dei, to prevent them from being the "servants" (*kintmant*, assistants to big-men) of the Central Hagen Council area. One candidate compared himself to such a kintmant: "Just as an unimportant man [*wengen*, lit. bachelor] fetches sugarcane for a big-man, so will we take your talk to the capital Port Moresby and fetch back things for you. We shall be like men with facial decorations like raindrops (i.e., like women), with ashes on their skins, ragged front aprons" [*ndamong mong waep iti, king kik rui, mbal ping rui*]. Yet the same speaker added: "The man who goes to the House of Assembly will give talk to all the unruly people, he will be like a white man (*masta*)" and thus unlike a servant.

Speakers also alluded humorously to the suspicion that they might be exercising "undue influence" over others in the campaign. As P. said: "Our daughters are not grown up yet, so we can't send them to you in marriage and get ourselves elected in that way. Nor will we give you a large pig. That would be 'grease.' No, you yourselves must think and look and vote for the man you want." These references read ironically when compared to the meteoric rise in bribery in elections of the 1990s (A. J. Strathern 1993c).

Generally, speakers avoided saying much about the murder that had brought enmity between the two councils. The leading Mul candidate, Mek, did so, however, on at least one occasion in Dei when he said: "There has been this murder between Dei and Mul and they are broken apart. But I don't want this, I am only young but I am strong enough to join you together, if you vote in Dei for one of your own men as your first choice you can give either myself or Pung [the other Mul candidate] the second preference vote, and we can work for you too. I want to raise up all of you people in both Dei and Mul."

In the event, Mek's suggestion was a shrewd one, for he did indeed win the election by securing most votes in his own area plus second preference votes in Dei (A. J. Strathern 1970). But he did not succeed in "joining Dei and Mul together." Instead, following a pair of "omens" that happened, there was an attack on the Dei president, P., while he was attending the opening—of all things—of a new police post at Muglamp station, near to the home area of the Nengka Kuklanggil, who had earlier received compensation from the Dei people after the killing of their clansman while driving in Dei. The attacker was a Kuklanggil man, R., and P. narrowly escaped death from the blow, which struck him in the neck.

He was treated in the hospital at Port Moresby and was back in Dei on October 8, 1970, when he returned, almost as a hero or martyr, greeted by a concourse of men in mourning clay, his mother's relatives clasping his knees and grieving over the injury, which had left one side of his face partially paralyzed. In retrospect, this leader's long success in the political arena probably owed a great deal to the event of his wounding and the affront to the whole of Dei it implied. His injury literally embodied a far more powerful discourse on his behalf than could be encompassed in speech-making. The new politics of violence, or the violence of politics, found its impetus from this major event and its various forms of aftermath. As with all such "conjunctures," in the term that since the foundational work of Marshall Sahlins we have become accustomed to use (Sahlins

1985), there was a combination of old and new elements. In the old political system, P. would never have had occasion to enter the vicinity of a hostile group in the way he did, nor would he have been held responsible for what men of a different clan from his own had done. It was in his role as politician and president of a council, now seen as a kind of "super-clan," that he was attacked. Yet the attack bore all the marks of an old-fashioned act of revenge. The attacker was a man of low status, who seemed to harbor a resentment against his low standing; he was closely related to the victim of the car accident; and he was said to be unhappy with his share in the compensation or even to have been left out of it altogether. He played the role that P. himself had attributed to another Mul man in the past, coming to Dei and shooting at his debtors without waiting to negotiate. He followed custom, not law, in this regard.

R.'s choice unleashed similar choices in response. Some Dei councilmen, at first thinking P. dead, at once drove to a plantation inside Dei where a clansman of R. was employed and battered him with the blunt ends of their axes. Although he survived, there was now a reverse demand for compensation, which meant that either side could exhibit anger and escalate its demands. Claims and debates of this kind in later years were to frustrate attempts to bring other situations under control. A new web of history, based on overlapping conflicts, was being spun.

In an effort to handle the broader implications of the case apart from the criminal trials (held on October 11, 1970), which were treated by the people as largely irrelevant to the serious issues at stake, the administration appointed a respected officer, Roger Gleeson, who for long was the Dei Council adviser, to run a joint Mul Dei Committee of twenty men (ten from each council), including the Member of the House of Assembly, (MHA) Mek. One meeting was held late in September 1970, in which it was decided that the two victims on either side should themselves settle the amount of compensation they wanted to receive and that the question of removing the Nengka Kuklanggil from their territory should be seriously considered. At the second meeting held by Gleeson on October 20, 1970, P. declared that he would not demand a sum in compensation from the Nengka Kuklanggil, nor did he think that Kerua, the counterpart victim, would do so because he "really" belonged to Dei and not to his original clansmen (in this way he sought to neutralize the opposing case for enmity). He was bitter toward the Kuklanggil themselves:

> We elected an MHA for both Mul and Dei. Römndi Kei established a single police post for both councils, and there the Nengka Kuklanggil struck me. I don't want them to stay living with the Römndi. The MHA [Mek, also

of Römndi] is in the middle between Dei and Mul and I don't want the Nengka to be with him. This is what I say, let the Joint Committee find a way to settle this. I thought we would run the law well, but there are some troublemakers around. Mr. Gleeson, I told you the Kuklanggil would ax me. They gave my name to a child and sang at a dance calling his name [a concealed form of threat] and now they have truly wounded me. These Nengka, they speak another dialect, I have nothing to do with them. I don't want pay from them.

In reply, the Kuklanggil councillor questioned P.'s intentions: "R. struck P. I and my people didn't know about his plan to do this. K. is also of Dei Council and P. says he will pay compensation directly to him. P. also says he will not accept compensation for himself. Why? What is in his mind (noman)?" Here, the councilor is suggesting that P. may be harboring thoughts of further revenge.

P. repeated that a child had been named and sung about, and how could that have been by chance? That is, the claim not to have known R.'s plan must be false. The Kuklanggil councillor became truculent, competitively offering compensation to K. and demanding that if his group were expelled from their present living place the group of those who attacked K. should also be moved. We can see here the beginnings of a highly skewed discussion, in which a demand is met by intransigence and a counterdemand because the original demand is potentially too severe in its impact. Gleeson then weighed in with a variety of observations, blaming both sides but in particular the Nengka Kuklanggil for being troublemakers and for mistakenly thinking that P. had been party to the killing of the Kuklanggil truck driver since he shared a name with one of the men who actually had been involved but was of a different tribe (the Minembi). The councilor for the Römndi, who had hosted the Kuklanggil as immigrants, now said that his own group would compensate P. and that the Kuklanggil must leave his place. He added: "If the government doesn't move them, there will be trouble, we shall fight for four days and on the fifth the government can break the fight." At the same time, another committee member asked: "Where can the Kuklanggil be put? These days every group is holding tightly to its land" because of cash cropping and population growth. Gleeson suggested that the government could put them anywhere, acting instead of the clans fighting and driving them out, as would have happened before. The council interpreter noted that the people were indeed ready to fight if nothing was done, and so the Kuklanggil should be removed by a decisive act by the government to forestall their doing so. Gleeson then spoke of the practical difficulties in the way of this solution, adding that even if they were moved, desires for revenge might remain and be acted on when members of the opposed groups met in Hagen town or elsewhere. He now suggested instead that they be kept where they were and made to do heavy community service as punishment.

Koi, a Minembi leader from near Muklamb, commented: "No, they must be banished to a bad place. You white men, you raise us up and then knock us back down again. If you don't settle this, trouble will come again. And besides, if people refuse to take pay, they are thinking of killing." Gleeson, in reply, criticized the ancestral ways of taking revenge for death. But P. insisted he would take no compensation; the government could receive it instead if they liked. His attitude clearly polarized the meeting between the Dei and Mul participants. He requested the miscreants be removed and Mul representatives said there was nowhere to put them. With this deadlock, the motion that the Kuklanggil be resettled was voted on and carried by thirteen votes to seven. The meeting broke up in tension.

The case contained further complications because R. declared that a relative of his among the Kimka had actually urged him to strike at P., saying that he had removed P.'s necktie by stealth and so P. would be without "strength" to resist an attack. A motion was made to drive out the Kimka from their territory, but it never came to a vote. The detail regarding the necktie is significant, showing how the situation was continually invested with indigenous values having to do with the embodied power of leaders. It is worthwhile to mention these here because they reveal the way the people thought. Before the attack an eagle belonging to P. had been stolen from his house, and some clothing of his was also stolen at a showground near Hagen town where preparations were being made for the Hagen Show. Both of these events were interpreted by P.'s kin as omens, *temal*, that his enemies of Mul would attack him. The eagle, a proud, strong bird, and the clothing, which contained P.'s own sweat, were both interpreted as signs or parts of himself (whether metaphorical or metonymic, as we would say). P.'s kinsmen called in the Dei Council adviser, an expatriate, who also telephoned the police in Hagen. The adviser seemed genuinely perturbed, but the policeman who came to investigate, also an expatriate, appeared to miss the point altogether. He commented that P. should not really be keeping a bird in this way because it might be illegal to do so and departed. The necktie episode belongs to the same sequence of events, and the same cultural logic, as the first two "omens," with the twist that a specific power is attributed to an introduced piece of clothing which only high status/urbanized persons could or should wear. The tremendously emotional greetings lavished on P. and his body by kin and supporters on his return contributed to a charged atmosphere in which all aspects of his self and his body gained heightened significance. He was welcomed as though he had returned from the dead by a multitude of people who assembled first at the Hagen airport, and he was then led home in a motorcade. He was embraced by the vice-president of the council at Dei and "installed" in the council chambers almost as though he were a sacred king. Clan meetings were held widely among his own tribe and their allies the Kawelka (his mother's people) in which arrangements were made to pay him sums of money and threats were made to fight the Kuklanggil and drive them out unless the government removed them first. Ongka, the preeminent leader among the Kawelka, mused that P. was still angry (*ararimb*) with some of the people, specifically certain of the Minembi, for secretly being glad that he had been attacked (they were jealous of him for a long time because he had eclipsed their own leaders) and hypocritically expressing their sympathy for him. P.'s wound was not healing well, Ongka thought (in fact, as the physician at R.'s trial had testified, there was a likelihood of permanent partial paralysis on the right side of the face where the nerves had been cut). Ongka attributed this lack of healing to P.'s anger, implying that should P.'s condition worsen and he were to die, who knows what conflict this would unleash. Gifts which Dei leaders planned to make to P. were therefore to help assuage his feelings and thus help him to get better.

A further meeting was held on November 2, 1970, attended by the expatriate advisers from Dei and Mul and run by Roger Gleeson, who announced that the way to settle troubles was by talk, not fighting, and fortunately neither P. nor K. was dead. The Kuklanggil arrived decorated with marsupial furs, cassowary and cockatoo feathers, and charcoaled faces. To the spectators this was an ambiguous display. One Kawelka leader said that the Kuklanggil were pretending to be good, well-decorated men, but in fact they were decorating because they were happy they had attacked P. (*P. rok tek nongk onomen, P. nomb mint mor pilik ong*, "they have struck P. and laid him low and eaten him and they come, they are saying 'I am still eating him and have come'). On the Dei side, only a very few men were decorated, but these included P.'s namesake, who actually had been among those that committed the first killing. The Kuklanggil might well have interpreted this as a hostile act of communication toward themselves.

Gleeson began by recounting the decision to remove the Kuklanggil but noting that there was no introduced law that could give them power to do so, although by custom people in the past had been driven out by violence. Gleeson enumerated twelve wrong actions by the Kuklanggil, including thefts, threats, and actual attacks, and pointed out that in the past these actions would have provoked a coalition against them which would have driven them away and so only the presence of the Kiaps themselves was currently stopping this. He told them they had followed the ways of wild dogs, pigs, rubbish men.

The interlocutor for the Kuklanggil, Römndi Köi, an aged leader, spoke next, reciting the historical "lineage" of Kiaps and how they had forcibly stopped warfare in the area since the 1930s. He had worked with them and been given a luluai's badge. The councillor of the Kuklanggil was his own sister's son, he said, but when he received the compensation on their behalf for the first killing and offered it to his nephew, the latter refused to take it. "Therefore I don't want him to stay in his place. I am now baptized in the Lutheran church and if I say I will kill him I will go to Hell but I am saying that he must leave. You MHAs, Kiaps, councilors, vice-presidents, presidents, all of us must think now. These arrogant, troublesome ways must be stopped. Will our country be run well? I am old and I will die. The Kuklanggil have done twelve wrong things. P. says he will not take their compensation. What shall we do?"

The Dei vice-president pointed out that in custom if an immigrant group without independent land rights is worsted in fighting, their hosts will not protect them, they just flee. He concluded that the Römndi had no obligation to the Kuklanggil and the latter must therefore move. Another speaker agreed and added, "We want 'law' to spread everywhere. The government came and gave us 'law.' We want to join Mul and Dei together, but if we don't settle this trouble, our place will be bad (*kona kit moklmba*). Köi was young when the government first came, now he is old, when shall we find and make this 'law'?" A famous old leader from the Central Hagen area, Mokei Nambake Wamb, also attended and added that he was alarmed by the Kuklanggils' actions in ignoring or refusing compensation because this was a sign they would not accept "law," and peacemakers such as himself would even be resented. "How can we achieve self-government when we still hold spears in our hands?"

Wamb also wanted the Kuklanggil removed; but Gleeson now decided that if they really wanted to follow "law" they could not physically drive these people out and yet no law as such could empower the government to remove them either. A Kuklanggil speaker now replied, repeating the line that they had no part in the attack on P., it was all R.'s doing, and adding that as to the ground on which they lived, "two generations of my paternal forebears have been on this ground and so it is my true home [*möi kela*]." He meant they should or could not be removed, but they would be prepared to pay P. At this point, P. himself was enraged and threw off his jacket, demanding again the removal of the Kuklanggil, "otherwise there will be no 'law.' The committee has voted previously, what is this talk about now, if we are not following 'law' here then the 'law' is not true. We made this Joint Committee so that it could make laws." That is, decisions; Gleeson objected that the committee could not make laws, but P. contradicted him.

Another Mokei visitor now remarked that the committee was failing in its work; the two sides were simply opposing each other. Gleeson agreed and said that if they fought, the government would separate them; it was up to them.

Would they follow the government or would they follow their ancestors' ways? He reviled them for reverting to the old customs. Pung, a Mul leader and council president, announced that they would gather "pay" for P., whether he wanted it or not, similar to that given before for the death of Nengka Kiap (i.e., $2,000 Aust., 100 pigs, 20 cassowaries). In fact, he offered to return the compensation paid for Kiap first. Deadlock was reached repeatedly, with Mul speakers offering compensation and P. demanding instead that the Kuklanggil be removed. Mek (the MHA), Gleeson, Wamb, and others were reduced to commenting from the sidelines on how futile this all was, and the meeting ended at 6:00 P.M. with no conclusion. In another two days P. had decided that "the government would not help him" and so he would just have to accept compensation. An assistant district commissioner, Ross Allen, came to the next Dei Council meeting in mid-December 1990 and argued that the idea of removing the Kuklanggil was "misguided talk" (*kranki tok*). P. meanwhile squirmed in his council president's chair and tugged gloomily at his beard while the assistant district commissioner further implied that the Dei people had asked for far too much compensation. The assistant district commissioner also told me separately that he thought the Dei leaders were stirring up bad feelings about the issue.

On December 22, 1970, a compensation ceremony for P. was arranged at a settlement place belonging to the Römndi and contributed to by the Kimka. The latter had brought with them five hundred dollars, three pigs, and one long bamboo tube of decorating oil (used for rubbing the skin at dances). The old leader Köi enumerated the amounts from the different men's house groups (sub-clans) of the Römndi, also totaling about five hundred dollars plus eight pigs. The total was thus about one thousand dollars with a few pigs. The relatively small size of the payment indicates that it was not a true compensation. It was rather an apology from groups that were in general well-disposed to P. Old Römndi Köi was one of the speech-makers, and he had set up two sticks taken from the *neng* tree, sacred to P.'s tribe the Tipuka, between which he strung a piece of vine, *kan koeka*. The latter marked himself and his group the Römndi, whose roots were in Mul but whose vine had grown long and extended into Dei. He then hung two towels on the vine and in between these a bundle of old shilling pieces with center holes so they could be strung together. He called on P. to take whichever object he chose. One of the towels was dirty: this represented desire for revenge. The clean one represented "law," the new order. The shillings represented compensation, in between the old and the new ways. Köi next called for a bundle to be brought forward and opened, containing *purl pint*, a plant formerly used as a support for corpses at funerals. Köi took the dirty towel, pressed it on the purl pint leaves, and tied it up with a bundle of cordyline leaves. He suggested that the bundle be buried, and instead he brought out the compensation money. Government officers, including Ross Allen and the two advisers from Dei and Mul (Dick Olive and John Edwards), were present and made speeches, and the occasion ended harmoniously.

The further outcomes of this case have been described earlier (A. J. Strathern 1974:258–260). Notably, the Kuklanggil neither left their territory nor paid compensation. Friendship between Dei and Mul was effectively curtailed, and enmities within Dei were perpetuated. In 1972 the Electoral Boundaries Commission established Dei and Mul as two separate open electorates, and predictably P. was elected in Dei, continuing to hold his position until the mid-1980s and continuing therefore to be a part of the same complex of events and emotions that led to the creation of his electorate in the first place. From then on, he scarcely had to campaign when elections were held. He came to stand for a new hegemony within Dei, crystallized from the conflict with the Kuklanggil and implicitly with Mul. Subsequently, one of his sons, R., was able to capitalize further on this hegemony and succeed to his father's position, until he was defeated in the 1990s.

Studying this case through the discourse of the participants, it is evident that a serious and unresolved (perhaps unresolvable) debate was taking place about the meaning or meanings of the term *law* and its relationship to custom, meanings that had to do with the legitimacy or otherwise of force (or violence when seen as illegitimate). The terms of this debate have continued to this day, and it is therefore important to see its early manifestations in a case going back to the late 1960s and early 1970s. The massive problems of social control that erupted in the 1980s were rooted in these earlier events, which were themselves shaped precisely by the plans and practices of the colonial administration as well as by the actions of the local people.

The debate in the Mul-Dei Joint Committee (as well as outside it) was three-cornered. First, one viewpoint was maintained, though not consistently, by expatriate government officers, such as Roger Gleeson and Ross Allen; second, another viewpoint was held by P. and his supporters; and the third was that of the Kuklanggil and others who supported them. *All* of these parties, explicitly or implicitly, laid competing claims to the concept of "law," an idea introduced entirely through the discourse of the Kiaps in the first place.

First, the Kiaps themselves stressed that "law" meant settling disputes without force, by talking. The old way was to fight, the new way to talk. But such a model depended on consensus and practicability. Faced with a lack of either, the model broke down. More generally, "law" meant the new way of life in its entirety, implying a change of cultural values, a divergence from "custom" in this sense. Second, for P. and his supporters "law" in this case meant following the

▸▸▸ *Prince Charles of England, on an open Land Rover, salutes spectators at the Sir Hubert Murray stadium in Port Moresby on September 16, 1975, during the Independence celebrations for Papua New Guinea.*

stern and forceful traditions of the early Kiaps themselves. Thus they demanded that the Kuklanggil be driven out to punish them severely and show a tough example to others. P. appealed to the idea of "legitimate force" as the basis of law in general and added that without this the latter would not be strong. This model in turn broke down in face of both government reluctance to use force against the Kuklanggil as a whole (i.e., refusal to recognize collective responsibility) and the intransigence of the Kuklanggil themselves. Third, the Kuklanggil and others, less openly than those involved in the first two viewpoints, offered compensation as a basis for a "lawful," that is, peaceful, settlement. Such compensation of course had its basis in custom, just as much as the model of expulsion did. All therefore laid claims to law, but none could agree quite what this would mean. The administration officers in particular were caught between law as "order" in general and law as "specific laws" enabling actions to be taken. P. and his supporters implied that if such specific laws were not made then law in general would not be strong. They demanded government based on force, the kind of force used earlier in colonial pacification. The administration officers, however, were constrained. Though appealing to law, they in fact were involved in promoting consensus and compensation, partial solutions rooted in custom. These semantic twists and contested politicolegal arguments thus issued in deadlock and confusion, born from the colonial encounter and destined to be carried forward through independence in 1975 into the 1980s and 1990s. The rhetoric of the Kiaps became perplexingly interwoven with the rhetoric of local leaders, and

▸▸▸ *An exchange occasion among the Kawelka at Kuk, early 1980s. The Papua New Guinea flag is being carried in a display on the local ceremonial ground.*

this web of contested meanings began to spread itself across political conflicts between other groups in the wider Hagen area (cf. A. J. Strathern 1974:260–266). The speaker who declared that "you white men lift us up then knock us down again" was complaining of the double-bind situation into which he perceived the people were being driven. Exhorted to follow "law," they were denied, as they saw it, the means to make it effective, just at the time when, because of the new expanded scale of political interaction, their own methods of consensus and compensation were also proving unable to bring about peace. As we have already glimpsed in chapter 5, at a later stage the rhetoric of the Christian religion was appropriated to fill in the gaps left by introduced laws on the one hand and indigenous custom on the other, or, otherwise put, to bridge some of the growing contradictions between the old and the new ways.

These conflicts marked the tensions involved in the painful processes of transition toward political independence. They revealed also some of the basic contradictions implied in these processes, for example the strain between the act of creating larger political units and the incompatibility of these with local allegiances. In the next part of the book we consider these contradictions further.

► ► ► PART THREE ► ► ►

CONTRADICTION

Earlier chapters in this book have made it clear how important the practice of compensation is in Hagen history. From a custom designed to obviate blood revenge between small-scale local groups it has grown to be an issue of major national significance in dealings among such groups, the government, and international companies. News clips in the 1990s were full of reports of such problems, analogous to those sketched from an earlier period at the end of the last chapter. Issues surrounding compensation and changes in ideas concerning it show exactly how contradictions in social practices grow up over time. For example, while the payment of compensation can settle disputes, it can also lead to inflated demands and to a disregard of other possible solutions. Or it can be a cause of severe problems between the state and local groups seen as landowners. In this regard, the old perceived conflict between moka and development is rerun with increased intensity in disputes that involve the large-scale interests of commercial companies. In the next three chapters we examine the parameters of contradictions of this sort in greater detail, concentrating mostly on local intergroup levels of action.

The chapters are arranged in the following order. Chapter 8 looks at the historical achievements of the moka system as an example of uncentralized political evolution organized around the principle of the ritualization of aggression, comparing the Melpa with the neighboring Enga in this regard. Chapter 9 considers how this political evolution then intersected with early forms of colonial influence, producing what we call the problem of "crime and compensation." Finally, chapter 10 brings the picture up to date with the decline in the old moka exchange system and the incorporation of ideas of compensation into the schemata of Christian rhetoric, used in an attempt to overcome the growing contradiction between customary and state-based frameworks for action.

EIGHT

▶▶▶▶▶

Honor, Shame, and Agency

The Melpa speakers of Mount Hagen whose history is central to this book are well-known in the literature for having developed the elaborate form of exchange practices known as moka, which are symbolically modeled on compensation payments for killings, although they are also the site for the production of prestige and influence. These exchange practices can be seen as a ritualization of violence. Although this terminology is accurate and productive in itself, it is possible to shift from a functional to a performative mode in analysis and refer instead to a process of transformation from embodiment to objectification, that is, instead of physical violence being enacted on the body of an enemy, wealth forms, substitutive of or equivalent to the body and the personhood of a victim, are used to stand for the victim and are given back to the victim's kin as a means of regenerating new life to replace the life that has been lost. Wealth objectifies the body and obviates the obligation to maintain honor by executing revenge. So much is well-known. But the Melpa elaboration of this shift to objectification, in a framework of ritualization, not only places them at the far end of a continuum of practices in the New Guinea Highlands but is also relatively uncommon in a wider cross-cultural context. Turning revenge killings into wealth payments and turning these into status competitions seems to be a double shift of agency and the definition of honor that has largely been a road not taken elsewhere, although traces of a movement of this sort can be found widely distributed. Why should this be so?

To approach this question, we start a little further back, with another one, equally well-known in the political anthropology of acephalous polities: can we really make an empirical distinction between feud and war? The answer in this particular context is no, because if we define feud as an activity fueled by the motivation of revenge, it is clear that this motivation enters into sequences of fighting that are also labeled as war. The relevance of this point to the argument is that if an embodied element of revenge enters into the calculus of warfare, it cannot be transcended other than by a symbolic objectification realized in ritual. Hence peace ceremonies following wars should be studied with this proposition in mind and their likely effectiveness evaluated accordingly. War-damage payments can be seen as appeasements to avert retaliation and revenge.

Our tack here is different from that of the standard political anthropology of the 1960s in which feud is distinguished from war simply in terms of scale of hostilities and number of deaths. Feud is then taken, as in the work of Keith Otterbein, to be a mechanism whereby the heavier destructiveness of warfare is avoided, either consciously or unconsciously (Otterbein 1994). Such a functionalist argument is bound to draw critical attention even though it has in fact some empirical applicability. The usual criticisms can be offered: the function of feud is to do what it does; it prevents something from happening, but we do not know if otherwise it would have happened. Does war occur only when feud breaks down, or do they simply belong to different political domains, insulated by social logic? The definitional distinction is purely formal and does not entail a further functional proposition. Nevertheless, acceptance of the functionalist proposition is in order in those instances where we see that people purposefully make a choice not to escalate a conflict into a more widespread combat but to restrict it to activities of revenge between families or small lineages. A narrow as against a broad encompassment of conflict can be interpreted as insulating acts of killings from the larger political context. There is another pattern, however, found in Hagen, in which the kin of a man who has been killed deliberately choose to broaden the conflict situation by assassinating a target from a clan allied to that of the killer, thereby *creating* enmity between the two allied groups. The killing is still seen as an act of revenge, one that operates in two separate spheres: it settles the score of the first killing (in the manner of homicide retaliation), but it also opens an issue between two previously solidary groups and makes it less likely that they will unite in war (or else it goads them into doing so). Here, the purpose clearly *is* escalation. In the ensuing warfare, however, elements of revenge continue to enter, and in the calculus of payments that may later be made for killings the numbers of deaths are relevant. With the arrival of guns in warfare from the mid-1970s onward the basis for such a calculus between enemies was made much harder to operate because the numbers of killings rose: hence the relative intractability of arranging for compensation payments; too many deaths, too little wealth, unsettled scores.

Formal distinctions between feud and warfare can be maintained, then, provided we recognize that the theme of revenge is woven into both and in fact forms a thread that connects them. In processual terms this is an important point. When compensation payments are made, they are couched in terms of the transcendence of revenge, not simply as forms of peacemaking. They either avert a wider conflict or, if it has occurred, halt it. It is at this point that we can recognize an analogy with the functionalist theory of the feud, since arranging for compensation payments is certainly a deliberate act of negotiation. But in addition, it is a transformative and essentially redemptive act, moving social relations from one modal state to another (Samuel 1990).

Keith Otterbein, in his review of Christopher Boehm's *Blood Revenge* (Otterbein 1994:133–146), notes that Boehm's explanation of Montenegrin feuding uses the language of intention, so that feuding is "deliberate social engineering," a manifestation of the human capacity for dispute settlement or the management of conflict. Boehm's argument might be seen as the triumph of functionalist thinking (Boehm 1984:87–88). He himself recognizes the paradox: Montenegrin feuding appears compulsive, uncontrollable, honor-driven, an expression of hyperagency. Yet in fact, since the killings are narrowly confined in their scope and can be terminated by political judgment and debate shored up by ritual means, we can interpret them as a form of dispute resolution that avoids greater destruction. Boehm's interpretation is thus a "peace in the feud" argument. Whether or not we accept its overall logic, it is important to notice two things: first, the broader context invoked is that of the opposition between the Montenegrins and the Ottoman Empire, since Boehm's ethnography relates back to the nineteenth century, when certain Montenegrin tribes had achieved a measure of independence vis-à-vis the encroaching Turks and had established a refuge-area tribal zone within which it was to their advantage to minimize internecine warfare. The functionalist argument therefore makes sense only if it is set into history. Second, the form of ritual peacemaking can be compared quite interestingly with Mount Hagen practices.

Boehm distinguishes between the "first homicide" (usually resulting from an incident involving honor and transgressive agency such as seduction or adultery), the "middle game" in which retaliation and counterretaliation were practiced, depending on the relative strength of the kin groups, and the "end game" in which a "Court of Good Men" would intervene to make a settlement. By 1840, Christian bishops, who had become politically important, gained the power not only to arrange truces but to punish blood vengeance itself with a death penalty (Otterbein 1994:138). Previously, the arrangement of a truce depended on the will of the parties and the tally of killings between them. The group that had killed more was expected to initiate a truce because "its honor was in better shape" (Boehm 1984:122). After three periods of truce, the court of judges (*kmets*) could be convened, consisting of highly respected persons, who would eventually distribute liability on both sides and try to find neither party "the guilty one" (p. 132), so that a set of compromise adjustments could be achieved.

In some instances, when the resumption of social relations was considered to be important, a pacification ritual would be arranged. The killer was supposed to humiliate himself (reversing the honor code) by crawling toward the victim's kin with the gun that shot the victim hanging from his neck. If this act of self-abasement succeeded, a bond of godfatherhood would also be set up between the two sets of kin: the killer brought infants to whom the other side would stand as godparents. This ritual was performed in addition to the actual blood-money settlement. Here too the clan that was "winning" (i.e., had killed the most men) had to beg the losing clan to accept the large blood-money sum that was due in obviation of further vengeance. The losing clan in turn lost honor, in a sense, by not taking vengeance. Finally, and rather surprisingly, it appears that the blood money was not actually handed over "since only the rifle, as the actual instrument of death, actually changed hands" (p. 135). The victim's kin received the rifle, kissed the killer in forgiveness, and (re)established a ritual brotherhood on the basis of this act.

If we compare this ritual with Hagen practices, clear similarities and differences emerge. Similarity lies in the fact that, for a settlement to be made, deliberate status reversals have to be effected or staged. But in Hagen, the temporal ordering of the reversal is different because the outcome is also rather different. The victim's kin approach the killers with an offer of a man-bone payment (*wuö ombil ngok ruk ndoromen*), saying, "You killed our man but you did not eat him, so we give you back here his bone and you can then pay us for his head" (*wuö peng iti*, to make man-head). The man-bone payment is much smaller than the man-head one and can retrospectively be constructed as a solicitory gift in a moka sequence. The symbolic construction of noncannibalism is striking here. The Hageners were not cannibals, and the play here is on embodiment and objectification. Eating the victim is seen as an extension of killing him or an expression for the act of killing him. When a revenge killing has been accomplished, the killers are expected to hold dances and sing songs described as acts of eating (*up noromen*) and to kill a pig (substitutive for the victim himself) and roast its liver to eat saying that they eat the dead man's liver. The act of killing is thus metaphorized as an act of consumption, but this itself feeds into a trope expansion whereby such a form of consumption is described as "not real" and gifts of wealth replace it. The embodied acts of killing and eating are replaced by the acts of exchanging wealth, especially pigs. In terms of honor, the victim's side abjures its pathway of recapturing honor through revenge and sets the scene for its reappropriation through the reception of wealth. The killer's group in turn not only raises a very large sum of wealth but must actually hand it over. The idea of displaying wealth but not giving it, as was done in nineteenth-century Montenegro, would be anathema in Hagen. The killer's group must give up a very large amount of wealth in order to recapture its own honor. The recipients respond as though they were overwhelmed. In fact, they benefit greatly and are enabled to use the wealth to make new marriage alliances and replace the dead they have lost. The Hagen exchange ideology thus stands to pacification in the same way as does godparenthood in the Montenegrin case, but the Montenegrin modality is more tied to the body: infants are brought to the ceremony and godparenthood is ritually established as a fictional tie of blood. Wealth appears to "stand for the person" in Montenegro, but this social logic is not followed through as in Hagen, since a part of the same end is achieved by different means. In Montenegro there was no further ritualization of leadership or status into a "big-man" construct. The embodied rituals of crawling, handing over the virile lethal gun (standing for the person?), and kissing kept Montenegrin procedures at the immediate level of the perceived body and obviated the step of actually handing over wealth, as though this step was envisaged (by collecting it) but not enacted (since it was not given). The imposition of rule by the Eastern Orthodox bishops then blocked any further progression of ritualization in such a direction by substituting hierarchy for exchange—a modality which in 1995 was just beginning to emerge in Hagen with the explicit invocation of God or Jesus by pastors and court officials involved in mediating compensation discussions over killings. (This process is documented in the BBC film *A Death to Pay For,* Strathern and Stewart 1998b.)

This micro-comparison shows some of the potentialities of comparing the symbolic construction of compensation payments in widely disparate areas. It also shows that the questions of honor, personhood, and agency are very relevant to such a comparison and that the "honor complex" associated with areas such as Montenegro, Albania, Kosovo, and the Mediterranean easily finds resonant echoes far away in Papua New Guinea, albeit with significant transformations in the Hagen case (see F. H. Stewart 1998 for a general discussion of the concept of honor).

We wish next to erect a comparison with Hagen closer to "home" by looking at Mervyn Meggitt's materials on warfare among the Mae Enga, the Hageners' western neighbors, who have historically developed a system of exchange even more elaborate in its scope and ramifications than the Hagen moka. The aim of this comparison is to examine the relative symbolic role of physical violence in the two cases, set against an apparently equally great stress on exchange practices as a means of settling disputes and achieving male prestige.

Both the Mae and the Melpa (Hagen) cases fall into Otterbein's statistical category of "feuding with compensation" (fourteen out of twenty-two cases in an original "society sample" of fifty, Otterbein 1994:140). A complication in the exercise arises from the fact that Meggitt has always worked with an explanatory model for the Mae Enga that differs from the one we use for Hagen: whereas we have used exchange as a primal category, Meggitt has used land shortage as an ultimate determinant of social patterns (Meggitt 1977:9). "The basic preoccupation of the Mae is with the possession and defense of clan land. Participation in the Te [exchange system], as in other prestations, is but a means to this end." This overall orientation in Meggitt's writings leads to another result in his account of Mae Enga fighting: the motivation of revenge (which we can see as the inverse of positive exchange and thus logically compatible with it for the purposes of trope-expansion or transformation) is subordinated to that of land pressure. Mae Enga fighting therefore tends to be presented as a form of warfare over material resources rather than as a form of feuding based on a calculus of killings themselves. In Meggitt's analytical scheme, land stands as an ultimate material counter outside of the generative field of symbolic constructions. It is an engine of history in its own right (even though he also is describing land as it is perceived and valued by the Mae Engans).

The way in which Meggitt's argument is constructed can be seen in his working definition of war as "a state or period of armed hostility existing between politically autonomous communities, which at such times regard the actions (violent or otherwise) of their members against their opponents as legitimate expressions of the sovereign policy of the community." Warfare he then takes to be "the actual military operations effected by representatives of these groups" (1977:10). He soon confronts the question of feud and retracts from his use of this term in earlier writings. Considering the well-known segmentary contextualization of modes of conflict which forms a part of indigenous models in acephalous conditions, he wonders whether intraclan fighting should be called feud rather than war but rejects this idea on the basis that the mode of fighting is "substantially the same" and that its motivation is both to "secure a material advantage" (e.g., land) and to redefine the group's position in the segmentary hierarchy (pp. 10–11). This may be so, but the taking of revenge as such may still form an important component in the dynamic processes of such conflicts, and Meggitt's terminological ruling tends to gloss over such a possibility. War is presented as a rational, strategizing male activity, and the clan is depicted as a small-scale sovereign community. This may correspond to one set of Mae indigenous rhetorical models, but it is contrary to another set which stresses both the importance of exchange and the agency of women as players in the *tee* exchange system (Feil 1978, 1982).

The model of warfare as rational, goal-directed action is reminiscent of David Riches's handling of the category of violence within a framework of trans-actionalist theory (Riches 1988). It tends to suggest that, by contrast, the motivation of revenge and its correlate feud are irrational, based on emotions, disruptive but not purposive (an argument that Boehm explicitly subverts by maintaining that feud is *also* a rational form of conflict management). Our categories of rational versus irrational do not, however, seem to be very relevant here. We are dealing in all contexts with cultural ethos, pursued with varying degrees of effectiveness or consistency. Emotions are involved in warfare just as much as in feud, and the Mae Engan men's attachment to their land is just as emotional as it is material.

The split between revenge and land as motivations of conflict is shown in Meggitt's Table 1, dealing with stated causes of war in the period 1900–1950 among some fourteen clans, a total of eighty-four eruptions of fighting between principal contestants (those to whom the cause of war belongs and who are therefore liable for any compensation payments flowing from it). The table purports to show the significance of "land" as a cause of such fighting. In its reckoning, 57.7 percent of the cases resulted from disputes about land, whereas in only 11.2 percent homicide and revenge for it were cited as causes (with another 4.2 percent issuing from quarrels over homicide payments). This division of causes raises problems of a processual kind: if fighting "over land" resulted in killings, did not then a revenge motivation take over? If contemporary perceptions of land shortage in a time of colonization, population growth, land alienation, and cash cropping have come to dominate Mae men's thinking, might this not also retrospectively color their attributions of causes of fighting in the past? Could the whole "fighting for land" syndrome not perhaps be a case of the "invention of tradition"? May there not also be an ethic of revenge-taking over land itself that operates independently of population pressures but is exacerbated by them? Why is the book called *Blood Is Their Argument* if its title should really be "Land Is Their Argument"? Finally, and perhaps most fundamentally, what is the symbolic context in which Mae Enga men construct the category of land as such?

This last question challenges the ontological status of an argument that would place land as a category outside of the realm of symbolic constructions. To pull it back into this realm is by no means a denial of what Bruce Knauft has aptly called "hard world actualizations" (Knauft 1993:14). It is perfectly obvious that population density is relatively heavy among the Mae and that clansmen do attempt to achieve gains and minimize losses of land in intergroup conflicts. But in such a context we would also expect that land acquires a heightened symbolic significance. In turn, however, we cannot hypothesize that such a symbolic significance emerges *only* in a context of pressure. Far west of the Mae, among the Duna people, the "the ground" or "the land" (*rindi*) is a major conceptual and organizing principle that operates in many domains of social life and in some contexts is isomorphic with the concept of "social affiliation"—this in a context of relatively low population density (P. J. Stewart 1998). The Duna equation of life with land finds its parallel among the Mae, as Meggitt himself records in a passage in which he stresses as usual land gains and losses as the major issues in fighting. He is discussing the circumstance of a clan seizing part of a neighbor's territory and then deciding that it should not push the struggle further, either for strategic reasons or because "the invaders were concerned only to retrieve a tract of land which, they assert, was formerly theirs" (Meggitt 1977:114–115).

This is a vital point. Why would invaders fight to reclaim land formerly theirs? Is not honor involved, as well as or independent of land pressure? The meaning of land comes into play here. The moral context is also notable. The invaders may wish to hold back further if the opposing clan is a fraternal one, of the same phratry. Or they may wish to consolidate their gains by making gardens on the land they have taken.

The losers also seem to have their strategies. They need to regroup and to recruit allies. But "this is not to say that the group which yields land in this way accepts the hiatus cheerfully. On the contrary, the men may go into mourning for their lost estates as for a dead brother, holding a 'death house' feast, lopping fingers and slashing ear lobes—all of which serve as stimuli to eventual retaliation. It is small wonder that in these circumstances not only can the negotiations preceding homicide payments easily founder, but also the formal prestations themselves may explode in a pitched battle. Even if pigs are disbursed, the peace that follows is likely to be tenuous and short-lived" (Meggitt 1977:115).

The passage is remarkable. It shows clearly that land itself is morally charged and loss of it is mourned as for the death of a kinsman (a "brother" in this male-centered view—women's positionality in all this is considered only briefly on pages 98–99, and women are represented as essentially powerless in the male realm of fighting). Here the significant point is that land is equated with life and with the agnatic social group in exactly the same encompassing way as it is among the Duna, or for that matter essentially among the Melpa. Loss of a piece of land is seen as symbolically equivalent to the death of a brother, calling out for retribution or retaliation. Hence we can easily understand why a conflict may be initiated simply to recover such a piece of land whether or not it is needed for subsistence. Possession of land is also a source of political standing and honor. Loss of it is a source of shame. Agency must be reestablished by retaking it if possible. Seen in this light, land really is the source of the Mae Enga men's arguments, but since its loss is seen as equivalent to the killing of a brother, it should be symbolically merged with rather than separated from the category of blood revenge. Meggitt's Table 1, with its division between land and revenge, thus sets the scene for a misprision of Mae Enga ideas in the very moment of seeming to report on them.

To pursue the comparison with Hagen a little further, we can argue that while the basic concept that land is somehow sacred because it is tied up with the kin group is the same in the two cases—and is surely buttressed by ideas of ancestrality, the presence of spirits, and their capacities to bless the land with fertility—there also seem to be differences. Land as such is not something that Hagen groups in the past have directly struggled over as a supremely contestable category. One could argue that this was simply because it was not so scarce as among the Mae, but we rather argue that the Hagen form of exchange, which established the possibilities of free-floating funds of power based on transactions in wealth, released the big-man from a reliance on land as a basis of prestige. Today's situation is different: with increasing land pressure and many pathways to prestige dependent on the long-term use of garden land for cash cropping we can argue that there is now a genuine "struggle for land" in Hagen, but this is a situation that has only gradually built up since the 1960s. The explanation for the original difference between the Mae and the Melpa here seems to be the one which Raymond Kelly first put forward in his comparison between the Chimbu and the Mae (Kelly 1968): if flexibility rather than rigidity is adopted as a response to pressure, fighting over land can be obviated. Meggitt may have overgeneralized when he argued that the Mae have a pure segmentary agnatic lineage system. Nevertheless, they have set more rigid parameters of conflict for themselves than have other Highlands populations.

A second difference arises, perhaps surprisingly, in the sphere of exchange and perhaps also in gender relations. Both the Mae and the Melpa (Hageners) place enormous emphasis on interpersonal and intergroup exchanges of wealth in pigs and other valuables that travel at least partly along lines of marital alliance and matrilateral kin ties. But the overall form of the Enga *tee*, in which the Mae have historically been involved, is remarkably rigid: a long chain of exchange ties across many local groups, encountering problematic perturbations in time and space and subject to ruptures, delays, and complications because of its sheer complexity. While Mae (or Tombema, Feil 1978) women did certainly express their agency in exchanges of pigs which they had nurtured in the same way as

Hagen women did (and do), their overall control of events in the tee cycle, like the control exercised by most men, was highly circumscribed by the total form of the exchange circuits. The tee predictably declined faster than the moka has in Hagen; but in Hagen the enchained character of exchanges (A. J. Strathern 1969, 1971) disappeared over time, leading to a broader overall decline. Hagen women have, however, held onto their importance as producers of wealth and entered the arena more as transactors since the 1970s. The local character of exchanges and their immediate placement in terms of the need to make compensations for killing has given a renewed importance to women's productive agency in Hagen, including their capacity to generate wealth by picking and processing coffee beans for sale. This was recognized in their handling of monetary contributions to moka in the 1970s and in the gifts of money made to them as brides and described as "tax" on marriage occasions which have become more pronounced since the 1980s. Our point here is that this aspect of female agency is still vitally important in the 1990s and the more so since the wider superstructure of moka alliances has fallen into disuse.

At the end of his chapter on homicide compensations, Meggitt reiterates his main thesis. These payments are made because land is so short and people are so crowded together that life would be intolerably dangerous were they not made and revenge thus forestalled. He also notes that women would be required to work extra hard to help look after pigs given away and that they received no special notice for doing so. The scene he portrays is un-Melpa-like (Meggitt 1977:142–143). First, among the Melpa women's work is constantly referred to and given as a reason why women must be expensively decorated so that they can participate in dances (a pattern that was disappearing, however, in the 1990s when neither males nor females danced so often). Second, and relatedly, Meggitt does *not* link his reasoning to any further observation that male prestige is generated out of such compensation payments, although they are considered transactions of comparable importance to those that take place in the tee. The cathexis of values in the Mae system thus appears to differ again from that which holds for the Melpa even though Mae big-men certainly do play an important role in negotiating these homicide compensations. With the decline of the tee, the introduction of new political offices, and the resurgence of intergroup violence in the Enga region as a whole, it is doubtful what role is left for the big-men altogether nowadays there (Meggitt and Gordon 1985).

What these data indicate is not just a set of sociological contrasts. We are dealing here with local historically inflected notions of personhood and its embodiment among the Mae and Melpa. Correspondingly, male and female agency are constructed rather differently in the two cases, and this is shown in notions of what forms of violence to the body are considered legitimate or otherwise (granted that "contested legitimacy" is always at work here, Riches 1988). Melpa agency, both male and female, is here constructed in network terms; Mae agency in group terms, even though Mae big-men also operated in large networks in the tee and Mae women were transactors in their own right. These contrasts further mean that the fundamental transformation of revenge into exchange which was encompassed by the Melpa did not truly take place among the Mae. The Melpa have made a transition from embodiment to objectification which is more completely worked through than it is for the Mae. The early assumption of money into Melpa moka and compensation payments tends to support this view.

The Melpa symbolic transition (their own interpretive turn, as one might call it) has been facilitated by an intermediate historical step, as Daryl Feil has pointed out (Feil 1982). The substitutability of shells for pigs which was so pronounced among the Melpa meant that two stages of objectification of the human person or body were encompassed: from people to pigs, and from pigs to shells (and thence to introduced forms of cash).

It is worthwhile to examine this symbolic transition in a little more detail. Among the Melpa the characteristic of humanity is the noman or mind (see chapter 4). Human persons of both sexes have this; though men sometimes chauvinistically claim that men's noman are stronger, they themselves recognize this as rhetoric. The body is represented as "skin," contrasted with noman, but skin records the state of the noman (A. J. Strathern 1994, 1996; Strathern and Stewart 1999c). Shame lies on the skin, either proceeding from the noman or exhibited without a deep feeling in the noman. The "ropes of exchange," debts and credits in exchange, are entangled on people's skins, and only when they are straightened out (implicitly by the choice-making actions of the noman) can an exchange occasion be held. Noman is thus linked to all social capacities, but it is intimately linked with, rather than separate from, the body. Essentially, nothing can replace the noman of an individual person, and when that person dies the noman is also lost. Now, pigs have very little noman in this sense. They are recognized to have habits and drives, as we might say, which stand as their noman, but they share little of the human noman. Yet it is precisely pigs that are used to substitute for human life when a death has occurred. There is therefore a category shift from a body/mind entity to a different bodily entity, the pig, and essentially this is because the pig can either be eaten or itself used as wealth to reproduce life. When shells are further made transactable against pigs, there is a further shift toward the abstract, into the level of objectified signs. Little wonder then that Hageners both saw shell-moka as the activity that produced most objectified prestige and easily switched from shells to cash in the colonial period. Cash in turn has led to the possibility of the recodification of the human body in commodified terms.

Evidence of such continuing processes of recodification can be found in the intrusion of new language expressions into the Melpa language over time. In mid-1994 the term *jelas* ("jealous") was on everyone's lips, expressing the idea of envy of material wealth. In mid-1995, among the Kawelka and the Mokei groups, the Kawelka were expecting the Mokei to make a "demand," that is, to set a price for the death of one of their young men killed in a tavern brawl with young Kawelka men. This was referred to as though it were a matter of course, yet in fact it was an innovation. In compensation payments made in earlier years no such stage had occurred. It was simply understood that as much as possible would be raised to appease a victim's kin and make prestige for one's own group. The advent of a concept of "demand" marks the onset of actuarial thinking about the value of a life. In the event, the Mokei did not deliver a demand of this kind but produced a suggestion more radical still. They asked for land instead of wealth as compensation, basing their request on an ancient myth by which the two tribes were once paired as allies. Such a final recodification brings us full circle and makes the Melpa strangely Enga-like at this point in their history. It happened that the Mokei suggestion preceded by a short while the announcement that the Papua New Guinea government favors the introduction of universal land registration, a move that would make land more of a capital resource. The government's policy in turn was influenced by the World Bank. The Mokei in a sense anticipated at their local level the World Bank's global thrust, but they did so in a local context of a killing and compensation for it. The Kawelka did not accede. They paid a large compensation (150 pigs, K26,000, and some extra items), but sketches of future history had been drawn in the air (see further chapter 11).

Land, the ultimate locus of the embodiment of the person, had itself become potentially a sign. Michael Herzfeld's concept of the semiotic movement from indexicality to iconicity is also relevant here. A movement from an embodied action or state as indexical of social relations to an objectified use of this action or state in a wider context where it becomes an icon is characteristic of shifts that occur in transitions from the local to the national level (Herzfeld 1992:107). An index in this sense points to immediate social relations, as when close female siblings call one another "sister." An index becomes an icon when it is lifted out of its original context and is used to denote another level of relations, as when "sisterhood" is used as a marker of general female solidarity within a political movement. In the examples here a similar movement can be discerned. Localized persons can be substituted for by localized pigs (seen conceptually as home-grown even if some come from outside). The pigs are almost indexical in this regard of the social relations involved. Shells came from the outside, they were traded in from long distances, and were therefore iconic in their local effects. When shells were replaced by money (bearing the queen's head and subsequently Papua New Guinea's own national symbols appropriated from local usages), the national entered into the local. Land, however, remained local; but if land enters into compensations, implicitly substituting for cash, land too will acquire a national level of meaning and will lose its immediate indexicality. The Kawelka resisted this in 1995. Their perception that it might happen entered into their fear that their world was indeed about to end, as fundamentalist Christians had been saying would happen in the year A.D. 2000 (Stewart and Strathern [eds.] 1997; Stewart and Strathern 1998a).

In this chapter we have been concerned with the achievement of compensation as a means of settling disputes. We looked first at arguments regarding feud as a ritualized alternative to war and compensation as a ritualized alternative to feud. We then made a comparison between the Melpa and their neighbors the Enga, showing how feud intergrades with war. Compensation payments in both cases are the means of stopping conflict, but the transmutation of such payments into moka or tee exchanges represents a further stage of political evolution, one that has in turn fallen into decline as a result of state influences. The upshot is that compensation is coming to be seen by some people as part of the problem, not of the solution to issues of violence. A forerunner of the contested issues regarding compensation in the 1990s is found in fact in the events of the 1960s detailed in the preceding chapter (chapter 7).

It is of interest here to note that the Papua New Guinea Law Reform Commission revived in 1995 a 1975 brief to suggest new legislation to govern compensation payments in general. In 1975, the concern was with the "excessive" size of payments for killings; in 1995 it was with the "excessive" demands of local peoples for compensation in return for the "killing" (or "nonsustainable use") of their ground by multinational mining companies, along with threats to disrupt mining activities by violence. Compensation and revenge, it seems, have moved from local to national levels of significance and back again (see also Toft 1997). We turn to some of these intertwined levels in the next chapter focusing on problems of crime and violence in relation to compensation practices.

NINE

Crime and Compensation

In the rapidly proliferating spectrum of contemporary political phenomena centering on the contested concepts of "ethnicity" and "nationalism" we can discern an underlying dialectic. States are created with the aid of these concepts, yet they generate within themselves oppositional contexts in which new fractal versions of political identities emerge, and these in turn challenge the status quo of the state itself. It happens, for a multitude of historical reasons, that this dialectic has recently been played out more obviously and more speedily in diverse geopolitical settings than during the preceding Cold War era. We are dealing in some instances with postcolonial and in others with postsocialist circumstances, but in all cases we see challenges to existing structures of control, the rapid and often violent recreation of these at different levels of scale, and the harshly disputed valency of rhetorics, "deep" or "shallow," employed as tools for mobilization and action. There is an interplay of mimesis and alterity, to borrow a phrase from Michael Taussig, which leads to a kaleidoscopic set of conclusions (Taussig 1993).

In such a turbulent scene, the insights and perspectives of anthropology, often forged in the analysis of nonstate systems, gain a revivified relevance and at the same time are now severely challenged at macro and micro levels. The etic and the emic, state and nonstate, seem to merge in a flux of events. Our task is to separate these levels or moments of perception and to recombine them analytically into processual models that can give us at least a moderate grasp on what is happening: if not prediction, then at least understanding. The approach to the problem must be historical but must also draw upon and recreate anthropological concepts having to do with structure and agency, collective memory and individual action, fusion and schismogenesis.

The Highlands of Papua New Guinea is a region where violence has emerged between groups since independence, where marauding gangs of criminals have gained a foothold in local communities, where guns have been introduced into fighting, and where linkages between the political center and supporting factions have led to the development of a variety of proto-structural violence (A. J. Strathern 1992, 1993b; Strathern and Stewart 1997b), feeding off both earlier indigenous themes of segmentary identity and boundaries and resources introduced since colonial times in the early 1930s. An earlier habitus of oppositional action by male collectivities has easily fueled the reemergence of fighting, supported by the introduction of firearms, and extending in scale beyond the levels of conflict that were seen in precolonial times. Guns in fact were seen as new weapons, to be taken up by the younger generation of men, giving them access to a leadership status that may be called the "hero-rascal," an unstable but persistent image of potential power at times harnessed for group purposes and at times operating anarchically outside of group contexts. In a further twist, episodes of violence have also become associated with times when elections to both national and provincial levels of government take place.

The theme of "law and order" has been prominent in the concerns of Papua New Guinea's government and its citizens and other residents since at least the time of political independence from Australia in 1975. This policy focus derives from the earlier colonial context and is particularly salient in relation to the Highlands region, where initial contact with the colonial power was still within the memory of older living people in the 1990s. Government for these people, as we have seen in chapters 6 and 7, at first essentially meant pacification, forceful or persuasive action by powerful outsiders who were perceived as imposing their will by magical force or wealth on the populace and punished those who disobeyed with imprisonment. Government thus began as something that was coterminous with law and order; indeed, government was referred to as "law," setting up the first historical layer of a rhetorical contrast with "custom," made by both Hageners and colonialists. "Law" in this sense is made to control physically violent behavior. Later it comes to be imbued with a ritual dimension: it is the way or order in which things are done that conveys a sense of power, order, propriety: actions such as raising or lowering the flag, pitching and striking a patrol camp, marching in line, obeying the rules of bodily disposition. Hence the combination "law and order," in both parts expressing the notion of control and the sanction of punishment by an external power. Stereotypically, pregovernment society is in this image seen as "lawless" and "anarchic." Law and order are entirely imported items, and "custom" becomes problematic.

It is from this semantic matrix that problems to do with crime and compensation have more recently emerged. Crime is defined as against the state, while compensation claims take place between groups on a customary basis but are also now made against the state. We will explore these two matters in series and in parallel as different creations against the backdrop of state formation. The context in both cases is the arena of segmentary politics on the one hand and the ethos of resistance to power on the other. First, however, we make some further notes on semantics.

CRIME AND COMPENSATION: DIALECTICAL TURNS OF MEANING

In the 1960s government was synonymous not just with law but with imprisonment. There was no indigenous equivalent in the Mount Hagen area for the idea of imprisonment. The word *kalabus* was adopted from pidgin English along with *banis waia*, "wire fence," and the verb in the Melpa language *kān ngui*, "to give a binding to," to handcuff. A noted local leader among the Kawelka Kundmbo clanspeople in Dei Council, Ndamba, described with remembered fear how he had once been taken away and placed into a large, deep hole dug within the government station, which was where prisoners were initially kept. His kinsfolk came and eventually recovered him, explaining that he had not taken part in the fight that had led to government reprisals. There was a similar large hole at the substation Mbukl in 1964, a physical reminder of how Australian government officers had handled their tasks: prisoners first dug the hole, then were kept in it. Ongka, in his autobiographical account, notes that he himself had one such hole made to "house" prisoners (Strathern and Stewart 1999b).

The actions most often punished in this way were those that could be detected easily and most obviously threatened "order." They were also those that often were considered either legitimate or to be expected in terms of local politics and that might be linked to the payment of compensation as a means of redressing physical injuries or loss of life. Since men were those most likely to be involved in physical actions of this sort, it was they also who first became initiated into prison life as an early kind of acculturative experience, learning the taste of brown rice and corned beef and to obey a meaningless set of orders surrounding their daily actions. Prison became like a kind of men's house, with an assured supply of food, and returning former prisoners suffered no particular stigma. What began as something very intimidating later emerged as a kind of interlude or as an initiation into white men's ways. Men who went to prison on behalf of leaders (declaring in court that they and not the leaders were guilty) were greeted with elaborate parties and festivities when they eventually came home.

Government took onto itself the function of retaliation for action but not the function of compensation, which was often left to the local people themselves to carry out as before (although at a later stage government officers did become in-

▸▸▸ *Ndamba, a leader among the Kawelka Kundmbo, gives some directions to helpers in a new garden at Mina, near Ngolke. A rolled umbrella stands beside him (late 1970s).*

volved in organizing compensation occasions). A disjunction between "law" and "custom" was set up at two levels: what law forbade, custom might enjoin (e.g., retaliation for violence); and what custom enjoined (e.g., compensation), law was indifferent toward (A. J. Strathern 1972c). In the 1970s, when the rhetoric of "development" had further penetrated discourse, compensation payments began to be criticized as "excessive," on the assumption that they absorbed too much time and wealth that should otherwise be devoted to cash cropping and "business." Compensation, as an example of custom, became problematic and contested. The idea of setting up laws to control compensation emerged from this context. "Excessive" compensation, set up in custom to combat or redress "wrongs" ("crime"), was thus itself classified as a potential "crime."

Broader Definitions of Crime
The conflation of the roles of policeman, government officer, and magistrate which existed in the status of Kiaps (government officers) in the 1960s ensured that there was *no* perceived separation of law and government in the eyes of the Hagen people. People could be punished for a range of actions beyond the

context of violence, for example, for failure to pay taxes or perform compulsory community service, or for sexual actions defined in Native Regulations as incest or adultery, or for illicit actions of theft. As the concerns of government broadened, so did the definitions of what constituted crime, and the scope of centralized control grew more marked. After independence in 1975, village courts were created where customary ideas and practices were supposed to come back into play, with variable success. In the context of these courts, custom and law met for the first time. Customary rules were applied but were supported by the sanctions of law. Custom was made more rigid and codified and became more like law: hence the hybrid term "customary law."

In none of these contexts did "crime" take on an aspect of "resistance to the state." But this aspect definitely did emerge in later contexts: first in tribal fighting and second at a higher level in secessionist movements, most notably in the island of Bougainville (see May and Spriggs 1990; Wesley-Smith and Ogan 1992; Strathern and Stewart 1997b). If we recall that both government and law began as pacification, it is apparent that in the conflict between central government and secessionist groups the wheel has come full circle: we are back to pacification and a new contest about the contexts in which acts of violence are crimes. In the Bougainville revolution, which began in 1988 over disputes about the presence of a large mining company on Bougainville island, acts of resistance to the central government of Papua New Guinea were seen by the revolutionaries or local "nationalists" as "legitimate political acts" but were defined as "crimes" by their opponents, while forceful acts of suppression by the government were defined as "legitimate" by those who carried them out but as "atrocities" by the local people. The example is at the extreme end of a continuum that stretches between acceptance and rejection of outside power as a means of controlling local actions. Police raids on the homes of tribal fighters in which goods are confiscated, kinsfolk of suspects are taken away as hostages, houses are burned down, or fighters themselves are fired on with tear gas and rubber bullets and (allegedly) seized by hooks dangling from police helicopters, all participate in the same ambiguity and produce attitudes that range from fearful compliance to defiant resistance that begins to focus as much on the police themselves as on the local enemies (see A. J. Strathern 1993b). In one province, Enga, which experienced some of the most severe problems of fighting during the mid-1980s to 1990s, police mobile riot squads, equipped with shields and tear gas, have become classified as another kind of clan that intervenes irritatingly in battles between indigenous clans and may have to be eluded or driven off before serious fighting can proceed. The introduction of firearms by clandestine means into this context has led to shoot-outs and standoffs between police raiders and local fighters, sometimes leading to the withdrawal of the police in the face of superior fire-power on the other side (A. J. Strathern 1992). Such more powerful guns are usu-ally declared to have been stolen from the Papua New Guinea (PNG) Defence Force by local army career officers who have come home on leave or when dis-charged. In the final turn, when an emergency or curfew is declared by the na-tional government, Defence Force soldiers are called in as a backup to police action, a device that was at first rejected as unconstitutional but later permitted when it involved personnel from the Australian army seconded to assist PNG police. One context in which this has been permitted is that of elections to the national Parliament. Another is in the struggle of the national government to contain the activities of urban and rural gangs. Superior weapons and instru-ments are seen by the people as the key. In 1991 they declared that as long as the Australian soldiers with their *kampas* were there, the gangsters who infest highways and stage holdups would be controlled. By kampas they meant the telescopic sights used with long-range weapons to blast gang members out of their hiding places in clan territories. Subsequently, the PNG police have been left to deal with these problems on their own. The Highlands Highway has been declared officially unsafe in certain sections, especially by night (Stewart and Strathern 1999b). In Enga Province a Reservist policeman was killed in an attack on a party of police sent to investigate a murder in the Laiagam area in May 1998, and the then police commissioner, P. I. Aigilo, condemned the killing as an act of "savages" who do not know the value of human life.

Gangs and Guns

Gangs are a fairly recent phenomenon in postindependence Papua New Guinea. They emerge in both rural and urban settings but essentially develop out of urban experience. Their leaders are often well educated and have been exposed to West-ern-style media, encounters with expatriate criminals and deviants, and prison life, where they learn how to commit crimes more efficiently from more experi-enced inmates. Typically such leaders are highly mobile and move from one town to another or back into their rural homelands in a constant effort to find new op-portunities for crime and to stay ahead of the police. They break into buildings in coastal centers, stealing goods and often appropriating the guns of security per-sonnel, depart in stolen cars to the interior, take some of the proceeds, and fly down to the capital town Port Moresby to buy more ammunition from (stereo-typically) Chinese traders. The national government later attempted to control this trade more firmly by instituting baggage checks on internal flights run by the national carrier Air Niugini (but not on those run by smaller operators) and by initiating a bill to allow them to control the movement of people from place to place in the country. In their rural hideouts they may occupy barricaded sites in dense thickets of trees and undergrowth (analogous in a sense to indigenous cult sites as foci of power) or build caves underground in which they store supplies. Leaders are thought to have swift vehicles that can outrun the police cars. They are said to perform extraordinary feats of combat and to be remarkably swift and surefooted. The source for much of this imagery is videos and comic books; indeed, comic books are seen as manuals of magic. The gangster leader in general tends to take on the aura of the "hero-warrior," a type of tribal fighter that emerged in the 1980s after the introduction of guns into fighting and remained popular for some years, though overtaken in the mid-1990s by the turn to Christianity.

It is apparent that in this local imagery, gangsters are envisioned largely as stealing from or robbing outsiders, actions that are not regarded as reprehensible by their fellow clansfolk, and they are seen as sharing at least some of their wealth with their kin and affines in return for the security these provide. The same individual may indeed be both a gang member and a tribal warrior on separate occasions. Gang members first taught local people how to construct homemade guns and how to improve them over time, as well as being conduits for the trade in guns between coastal and Highlands locations. They specialize in break-ins, car thefts, highway robbery, and murder when necessary or as hired assassins acting on behalf of corporate political or economic interests. Although their actions are driven by self-interest and are not in themselves direct forms of resistance to the state, they tend to be involved in activities that do threaten the state indirectly, by causing insecurity, by distributing guns and teaching others how to use them, and by disrupting the allegiance of rural populations to government. They are like sorcerers or witches in the local political arenas, shadowy figures of power who disrupt formal structures and liaise between persons who otherwise have no contact.

In terms of the present theme, while the national government defines gang actions unequivocally as "crime," the attitude of local peoples is less clear. In some perspectives gangsters are seen as "heroes," albeit ambivalent ones. They are tricksters or mediating figures, agents of volatile transformation and forced redistribution of wealth operating beyond government control as tribal warriors also attempt to do. In a further twist, they may become the henchmen of particular politicians and contribute to processes of inducement to voters by offering bribes or to coercive acts of violence before elections and reprisals following them. Politicians themselves have begun to complain about this situation to the media, suggesting that a developed political "mafia" consciousness has come into being. In 1999 matters took a more serious turn within the Hagen local groups, since young men increasingly began to defy their own clan leaders and to commit crimes of violence and theft within their own groups.

ELECTORAL VIOLENCE

Elections to a national assembly in Papua New Guinea began in 1964. Since then a fairly complicated political structure has been created, with two major tiers, at national and provincial levels. The most intense competition focuses on the national elections, which take place every four years. In the years since 1975 expectations of violence surrounding both national and provincial elections have escalated to the point that it is clear that some form of violence is now a usual accompaniment of the voting process. This was particularly evident in the 1992 elections and subsequently the pattern has continued (A. J. Strathern 1993c; S. Dinnen n.d.; see also Ketan 1996, 1998). We take here some points that emerge from Dinnen's detailed analysis.

As Dinnen notes, "The tenuous purchase of centralized authority enhances the already considerable autonomy of more parochial sites of authority comprising, for example, enduring Melanesian social units such as the phratry, tribe, clan and sub-clan" (Dinnen n.d.:9). It is this same scenario of the local group vis-à-vis the state that pervades, as we have seen, the arena of tribal warfare, and also the arenas of elections and demands made against the state. To begin with, Members of Parliament, in the Highlands at least, represent electorates that transcend their own social groups, yet invariably their base of support remains their own group and to its members they owe their biggest obligations. This sets up ambivalence and distrust between the groups that elect the same member. It also creates even greater tension between the groups associated specifically with rivals for election and because of the congruence of indigenous and introduced lines of political cleavage it is overdetermined that contemporary politics should be perceived at least partly in terms of indigenous structures and values. These values invariably include an emphasis on gift-giving as an important basis for social relationships, and hence in order to be elected, and later reelected, a candidate must be able to distribute material benefits, a need that has actually been facilitated by the practice of granting relatively large amounts (up to K300,000) of discretionary funds to national politicians for use in stimulating "projects" in their areas. This pork-barrel form of politics in turn makes the position of politician more worthwhile, increases competition for it, and enlarges the frustration of defeat. The "politics of patronage" (Dinnen n.d.:11) and the likelihood of electoral violence are reinforced strongly by these factors.

The 1992 elections were preceded by newspaper articles predicting violence and by government moves to forestall it. The acting police commissioner at the time, Bob Nenta, who is from the Mokei tribe in Mount Hagen, was in charge of finalizing police plans for the Highlands region, and some provincial commanders authorized preemptive raids against villages suspected of holding firearms (Dinnen n.d.:16). Bans or restrictions on liquor were generally in force. (See Iamo and Ketan [1992] on the general issue of the relationship between alcohol consumption and violence in the Highlands.) The distribution of cartons of beer to supporters was a standby for Highlands politicians in the 1980s. In the 1982 elections Iambakey Okuk, a Chimbu politician, was rumored to have given out ninety thousand bottles of beer (twenty-four bottles per carton) in his campaign for reelection. Beer and alcohol sales have mostly been banned in the 1990s, but electoral violence continues (Ketan 1998). In Simbu province, the provincial government bought guns for its police. A total of fifteen hundred police and army personnel were to be deployed in the Highlands alone, at an estimated cost of K2 million, to protect polling booths and quell disturbances. The army's involvement was to be "symbolic," showing force of weapons and communications as a backup to the police. Police and army were to be a conjoint demonstration of state power.

Dinnen gives a detailed enumeration of violent incidents and their control before, during, and after polling. Violence was sometimes precipitated by heated exchanges between candidates with loudspeakers backed up by volatile masses of excited supporters. Threats of violence were used to dissuade from or persuade people to vote. Supporters themselves clashed in places in a manner reminiscent of tribal fighting. During and after the voting process, polling boxes were at times interfered with. For example, "eighteen ballot boxes containing votes from the Lumusa area in Western Highlands were burnt by villagers allegedly protesting over official failure to meet their demands for an electoral boundary change" (Dinnen n.d.:21). And twenty-eight boxes transported from the Southern Highlands were hijacked in suspicious circumstances suggesting police collusion. The hijacking was carried out by an armed gang near Nipa, a noted trouble spot where a government high school had earlier been burned down in a fight between two clans, and twenty-one of the boxes were destroyed while seven were returned after being tampered with. The sixteen police guarding the boxes appear not to have been able to prevent the incident from occurring.

Immediately after the polling, threats of violence by losing candidates and their opponents were rife. Police guarded telephone installations threatened by sabotage. Businesses restricted their hours and lost money accordingly. (Mount Hagen has often been the scene of election-induced vandalism.) Boisterous crowds greeted the news that a Mount Hagen politician, Paias Wingti, had been elected prime minister by the newly constituted Parliament. Government workers and teachers in both Western and Southern Highlands were unable to carry out their duties because of threats and skirmishes between disgruntled groups.

At a local level inside the Dei Council area the pattern of violence followed lines of cleavage known in advance. The candidate from one major tribal coalition, Melchior-Pep (who was also the sitting member), was pitted against a contestant from the rival coalition, Reuben-Parua, son of the previously long-standing MP for the electorate (A. J. Strathern 1970, 1976) along with six other candidates. Melchior won but was soon arraigned on charges of corruption, and Reuben later won in the by-election that followed Melchior's conviction. During the main election vehicles of candidates were attacked by supporters of rivals, and after it there was a fatal shooting of a security man employed by Melchior's people. He lived on territory belonging to the group of a candidate from a rival bloc, the Kentipi, and it was assumed that he was shot in reprisal for voting for his employer rather than his hosts. Fighting resulted, which was concluded by a peace settlement on July 27, 1992 (Ketan 1996; Dinnen n.d.:24).

Incidents of this kind all indicate the same recurrent features: the dense interweaving of violence with electoral activity, fueled by the material and symbolic-historical importance of the elections. They indicate that the processes of modern politics and government lead to problems of stability for government. Clansmen recognize that they have an important stake in government as a source of benefits for themselves, but this does not produce a respect for the symbols of the state; rather it increases their willingness to undermine the legitimacy of those symbols as a part of the very process of contesting for access to power. Violence in the democratic framework threatens to destabilize the framework itself because the political process leads to such an outcome. This is the process that has been characterized previously as "disintegrative integration" (A. J. Strathern 1993d). By this is meant that the linkage of local groups and factions to persons who exercise power at the center of government both causes an ongoing stake in and thus allegiance to the state and further leads to an increase in jealousies, tensions, and hostilities between factions at the local level. These processes are likely to be found widely as precursors of the collapse of state into nonstate politics.

A striking example from Enga Province west of Hagen, which has long experienced severe problems of intergroup fighting as well as highway crime, shows how issues of electoral results may further become entwined with issues of compensation. The example comes from the Tsak Valley in 1982, an area containing several political units and a population of about ten thousand. At an election a section of one tribe, A, tried to support a particular candidate and later a young

▸▸▸ *At a funeral ceremony,
guests have brought in piles of
food to sympathize with the
mourners, including cartons of
tinned meat and bags of rice as
well as plantains and sweet
potatoes (Dei Council, 1982).*

girl of tribe B was found dead on A's land. In an extraordinary move, tribe B now "demanded the votes of tribe A in compensation for the girl's death" (Mapusia 1987:58). Tribe A refused, tribe B then attacked and killed a prominent leader, and the battle escalated, causing several deaths and much destruction of houses and garden crops over several weeks. Intervention by a mobile riot squad of police did no good, and the war ended only through the later peaceful mediation by the provincial police commander, followed in 1985 by compensations for the deaths. The sequence of events is fairly typical, but what is remarkable is the entrepreneurial way in which *votes* were first demanded as compensation for a death. We now turn to further problematic arenas involving compensation. (On the wider context of problems in Enga Province, see Meggitt and Gordon 1985; Wiessner and Tumu 1998; Wormsley and Toke n.d.)

COMPENSATION: CLAN VERSUS STATE

We have mentioned earlier the question of "excessive" compensation. This issue arose originally because of the inflation in compensation payments that began in the Highlands from the time of European penetration in the 1930s. All forms of ceremonial payments increased in size because of the initially increased availability of shell wealth brought in by the Australians and secondarily because of the increased scale of groups involved in disputes. Problems of scale eventually led to unmanageable difficulties and a breakdown in exchange patterns, followed by resurgence of violence (A. J. Strathern 1974). These problems were exacerbated by rivalry over cash cropping and agricultural development and by the availability from the 1980s onward of firearms via gang activities. Problems of scale have since continued to produce contortions in the logic of compensation payments and at the widest level have led to clans contesting directly with the state and converting their contests into formal political activities, thus again straining the framework of legitimacy. Problems of scale need to be specified here more exactly. In the first place, the size and range of groups involved in conflict increased as a result of heightened social contact in the Highlands. Units and categories were set up that had no internal political unity and could not function effectively for the giving and receiving of payments. Still less could they convert unilateral payments into ongoing reciprocal exchanges over time. A different problem of scale occurs when a clan makes a demand against the state on a basis of "segmentary equality" with it rather than with a recognition that it is itself a dependent unit within the state.

An early paper by Paul Sillitoe about the Nipa area ends with a brief case history that points to the dilemmas increasingly experienced nowadays. The dilemmas in fact emerge from what historically has been a creative attempt to encompass and control change through stretching the fabric of their customary practices. Sillitoe writes:

> In late 1977 . . . a Mendi man employed on Nipa station was killed in a brawl by a Wola man. The people living in the Nipa area feared a revenge killing on them, especially as their aid post sent serious medical cases to the hospital in Mendi, which would present their enemies in Mendi with a perfect chance to exact vengeance. As a result many of them contributed wealth . . . toward an exchange which was the largest ever witnessed in the area. It involved far more people than a traditional event would have done, and so was considerably larger. They handed this wealth over as a group, as the people of the Nipa region, to another group vaguely defined as the Mendi, who shared it out among themselves. (Sillitoe 1981:80)

Sillitoe notes that the implications of such events are not the same as smaller scale events in the previous regimen because the participants do not know each other well. The point is well taken; however, the scale of payments had probably been growing since the 1930s, so that the process is not discontinuous entirely.

Stillitoe predicts that the state will generate a hierarchically based order that is incompatible with equality between horizontally ranged units. This prediction has become moot since the horizontally ranged units have not fully accepted hierarchy but have rather inserted themselves into the process of competition for power made possible by the centralizing function of the state and have also been able to oppose the state over local issues because of the relative weakness or ineffectiveness of the police.

Further, as the scale of events rises, it does so pari passu with the creation of new, larger horizontal entities such as are expressed in the terms *Nipa* and *Mendi*. Categories that began as neutral administrative labels invented and applied by outsiders for their own convenience become imbued over time with political meaning through the symbolic construction of events in a world defined by the possibilities and realities of violence. In 1991 this cultural logic was extended in a further direction in the Southern Highlands. A Nipa man was struck down by a government vehicle driven by the assistant director for education in the administration in Mendi, a man who was actually from the Koroba area that links the Huli and Duna areas together north of Nipa. The Nipa man's relatives demanded compensation not from the Koroba people but from all the schoolteachers employed by the government in the Southern Highlands and prevented education department vehicles from traveling on the connecting highway between Mendi and the Huli-Duna area until such compensation was collected. The schoolteachers felt consternation, fear, and puzzlement. Should the government pay? Should they all contribute? What kind of super-clan was being forcibly created here? Province and district-wide education services as a whole were meanwhile totally interrupted. Cultural logic had again strayed beyond its current bounds, and the outcome was unclear.

What is of particular interest here is the attribution of a nonhierarchical clanlike identity to a section of the government. Rather than hierarchy imposing itself, equality is being asserted as a means of nullifying hierarchy. But this nullification is genuinely in contradiction with, incompatible with, the bureaucratic organization of services which the people want. The Nipa people, it may be recalled, also burned down their own high school, nullifying their own access to services provided in it. It is likely that they did so as a part of disputes about land ownership and compensation for land demanded from the government.

Similar cases abound. In Pangia, for example, a local landowning group demanded compensation from the government for a small piece of land on which a water pump had been installed to supply the local high school, and when no funds were made available they prevented access to the pump, making it difficult to run the school in a hygienic and acceptable manner. The school was closed and reopened as the dispute waxed and waned. Every ex gratia payment made by government under rubrics of this kind increases the likelihood of further disputes on parallel lines. (Exceptions exist. In early 1994 the then national minister for lands, Sir Albert Kipalan, persuaded his fellow Enga tribesmen to allocate some land in Wabag town for an extension of the high school there without a demand for large compensation. This example shows the positive role that a prominent and committed politician can play outside of the immediate nexus of patronage.) In 1999 the Western Highlands provincial government began warning people not to make claims of this kind or they would not qualify for government services.

The issues emerge more sharply in arguments between local landowners and wider regional bodies with reference to mining rights. At Iagifu in the Southern Highlands, Chevron developed a huge project to tap oil, with a 159-mile pipeline to the coast, access roads, an airport, and local development projects to help the people enter into ancillary businesses and to provide schools. Supposedly, the company spent $1 billion, of which $45 million has been for local amenities, with an emphasis on "ecofriendly" operations. Local tribal groups complained bitterly of environmental destruction, however, and, most significantly, demanded for themselves a very large portion of the royalties from the project, denying spin-off effects to other groups in the province or the country as a whole. They were prepared to back up their demands with physical action. Sosoro Hewago, a local leader, declared, "All the money, or no oil—it's that simple" (as reported, at least, in the *Wall Street Journal* for June 9, 1992, but see also Knauft 1996:95–104). The Papua New Guinea government was very reluctant to intervene in any forceful way to control either the people or the activities of the company, and the result in 1992 was a stalemate. Our purpose in citing the case here is to point out how a local group in effect treats the company or the government as a rival clan, denying hierarchy. The ultimate denial of such hierarchy came, of course, in the Bougainville case, also sparked by the issue of mining problems: the Bougainville Revolutionary Army (BRA) unilaterally seceded from the state, halting mining operations altogether and nullifying both hierarchy and their own potential returns from it. This particular instance does not mean that the BRA treated the government as "just another clan" because the BRA itself is a multiclan regional entity. It does mean that BRA leaders saw themselves as coordinate and equal in power to the PNG state rather than being encompassed by it. Highlands clansmen similarly realize that their clan is not exactly on a level of structural parity with the national government, but they do think of themselves as possessed of a sovereignty equal in some contexts to that of the government and therefore capable of being mobilized as a source of opposition to government plans. They thereby privilege their local clan "citizenship" against citizenship of the wider state, at least in certain arenas of conflict.

CONCLUSION: THE DIALECTICS OF LEGITIMACY AND NATION-MAKING

These case studies of crime and compensation show the shifting spheres of political legitimacy and definitions of "law and order" in contemporary Papua New Guinea. The contests result in one sense from the integration of local communities into wider sets of political relationships. Resources that are made available through such relationships then become the object of contests which both disrupt the legitimacy of central authority and are a product of the very structure that they subvert. At local levels, an increasing scale of segmentary horizontal relationships also leads to severe problems as the level of violent interactions and the intertwining of contemporary politics with revivified and reshaped tribal categories produces a continuing set of dynamic probabilities of chronic conflict. It is in such a volatile arena that the old, colonially defined, problem of law and order becomes transformed into a struggle for resources phrased in terms of political identities. In a sense, custom (seen as a dynamic expression of identity) has resurged against law (seen as a static expression of control). The outcome of the struggle will necessarily involve the creation of a new order based on antecedent disorder, but what that order is to be is not yet apparent. It may have to be in some ways the reverse of the current processes: instead of "disintegrative integration," then, "integrative disintegration"? By this term, we mean to signify the possibility of creating more genuinely self-sufficient projects at local levels that would lead areas to redevelop trading links among themselves and thus lead to integration even without the coercive intervening structure of state control. To date, however, there are no signs of such developments, at least in Hagen, although among the northern coastal Tolai people an entrepreneur has supposedly recently opened a trading bank based on the old nassa-shell currency there rather than on the Papua New Guinea kina.

In contrast to the situation in many other places around the world which are experiencing political upheaval, the case of Papua New Guinea does not show a pattern that results directly from the historical interests of superpowers. Those powers, if anything, are probably more concerned with the future of PNG's western neighbor, Indonesia, especially in the wake of events of 1999, including the new situation in East Timor. Nevertheless, international capital has had much to do with the creation of circumstances that have led to the greatest problems in the spheres of mining and logging. In the Highlands the reemergence of tribal fighting has also been influenced by the expansion and distortion of political groups and their entwinement with competitions for electoral offices; but here local circumstances increasingly intervene in the processes that take place. Similarly, the development of gangs is certainly to be seen as a longer term outcome of capitalist-induced change, but the involvement of gangs with local clans was by no means an automatic or predictable outcome. It arose in a context of opportunism associated with the problems of intergroup fighting. Gang members have double identities which they use as they see fit. It is precisely the dense interweaving of factors that makes it very hard for Papua New Guinea's government to find viable solutions to the problem of violence. Here what is at stake certainly is shared with other cases worldwide: the possibility or impossibility of combining freedom with democracy. Anthropological analysis can contribute in a very marked way to this most vital of issues because it *begins from* a close understanding of locally based issues and can thus strategically study the interconnections between these and wider structures of power and influence.

Another important matter is when does ethnic identity come into play and with what results? In Papua New Guinea only the Bougainville secession case has come to be identified as "ethnic" in character and only in association with other primary economic factors. The other conflicts we have discussed verge on "ethnicity" only at their widest levels, for example when all "Hageners" are notionally ranged against all "Mendis" as a result of deaths and disputes over compensation. The mechanism for this kind of ideology to emerge is clearly present, however, and it would take only an escalation of incidents for it to crystallize. Conflicts between clans and the government could also take on this character. The intermingling of people from different areas also leads to conflicts as well as to friendships. Policy issues are set rather starkly here. If the Papua New Guinea government were ever to control people's movements to the extent of preventing contact and intermarriage between language groups or provinces, the stage would be set in a retrograde manner for the creation of ethnic groups and conflicts between them over time. The government must therefore seek, as many national governments do, to make national-level identities strong enough to counterbalance local ones, as well as sufficient to counteract the "Coca-colonization" of global influences. Both economic "infrastructures" and cultural "superstructures" will be indispensable in such an exercise of nation-making.

Anthropologists have only recently begun explicitly to examine the processes of nation-making at a cultural level in Papua New Guinea. Robert Foster, in an important pioneer collection of studies focused on the Pacific generally, points out that political elites in postcolonial states in this wide region have "generated a steady discourse of Custom and Tradition that seeks to ground national distinctiveness in definitions of indigenous ancestral ways" (Foster 1995:1). The preamble to Papua New Guinea's Constitution definitely attempts to do this and to mold together indigenous and Christian values. State agencies of course do not monopolize the discourse; the arena is contested and crosscut by the voices of the national Parliament versus local leaders. Nation-making discourses today also do not solely rely on the rhetoric of modernization that pervaded capitalist discourse in the 1960s. Instead, Foster notes (in the tradition of Benedict Anderson) that the nation is posited as "an imaginative construct that constitutes persons as legitimate subjects of and in a territorial state," and imaginations are seen as plural, not singular, in form, particularly with respect to what is defined as being "in the national interest," a phrase that emerges crucially in the Papua New Guinea Internal Security Act. Nations may also be constructed by means of narratives or stories, which may further be in a competitive relationship with one another in the struggle to establish a hegemony: school textbooks and rituals and control over media programs are obviously significant here. The "individual" may also have to be constituted as a "citizen" over and against other forms of identity. Foster refers to this in the context of capitalism as the creation of "possessive individualism," although this is not the only element involved in the social-symbolic construction of the citizen, since people may also define themselves in communalistic terms as Papua New Guineans in opposition to individualistic ways of living.

Foster deftly covers many of the cultural themes that can be found in the media nowadays in Papua New Guinea. What is perhaps missing from his account is an extended analysis of the role of state agents in promoting their *power* through the politico-legal structures they control and how the ideology of "the nation" thus comes to be contested. The struggle over the continuing existence of provincial governments indicates this arena of conflict, as is shown in the discourse of statements that continue to appear in the *Papua New Guinea Times* newspaper. For example, the chairman of the National Constitutional Commission, Ben Micah, wrote in the *Times* of May 12, 1994, that he wished "to honor an undertaking I made to the people of Papua New Guinea" and that he is "now pleased to announce to the nation" decisions of his commission (*Times*, pp. 30–31). In the same issue, the Papua New Guinea Telecom Workers' Union published a criticism of a decision by the government's minister for information and communication to grant a broadcasting license to a private company, PANSAT, in which the minister was accused of selling the nation's birthright and *sovereignty* to a "foreign multi-national giant" (p. 34). These examples, which could easily be replicated, demonstrate very well Foster's point that the discourse of "the nation" is highly contested, while the idea of the nation is just as highly prized. Agencies that subscribe to the nation as such may of course oppose the

▸▸▸ *A woman decorates her pig, which is to be given away in moka, with red ocher around its eyes (1980s).*

government on grounds that the government is compromising the nation and therefore endangering the state. We have earlier seen similar contests over the meaning and appropriation of the colonially inspired term *law* (Strathern and Stewart n.d.b.).

Crucial to the historical outcome of all these debates will be the roles played by the PNG Defence Force. Rumors of army coups circulate from time to time. The country's first cadre of ministers, in Michael Somare's early government, was well aware of the danger and sought to limit the size, capacity, and internal role of the army. As the problems of law and order have grown, however, so recourse to the army has also increased. It is obviously just a further logical step to imagine the army actually taking over in some alleged version of "national interests." What will guard against this event will be continuing to ensure that the army is not dominated by any one ethnic category and ensuring that political offices are spread widely among the country's provinces. Interestingly, the weakness of party politics so far in Papua New Guinea at least partly facilitates this need because governing coalitions can maintain majorities only by offering ministerial portfolios widely. At the same time, this makes coalitions unstable, weakens government in its policy-making capacity, and makes votes of no confidence more likely to succeed. Paias Wingti's action in "trumping" the system in 1993 by

▸▸▸ *Two women, in full decorations for a moka dance, wearing eagle feathers, marsupial furs, beads, crimped cordylines, pearl shells, and armbands. One beats an hourglass drum, the other holds a cigarette (1980s).*

resigning to avoid such a vote and then being reelected without a general election was in this sense a highly creative one and did indeed avert an electoral crisis. Bringing back rebels into the fold and the continual reconstruction of working majorities seem to be the only viable courses of continuing pragmatic political action of Papua New Guinea for the foreseeable future, if democracy is to survive there. Exactly the same improvisations are demanded from leaders at the local level in their own clan and electorates, but increasingly they must accomplish this with monetary gifts that partly coincide with, partly replace, the old moka exchanges. In the next chapter we look at attempts to mediate disputes generally in these local contexts by using new and old versions of practices of "confession."

TEN

The Embodiment of Confession

This chapter explicitly seeks to set out a relationship between practices of "confession" and the payment of compensation in Hagen. Links between these two topics, confession and compensation, have not been a prominent feature of the literature to date, and discussions of confession itself are not very common (Michael O'Hanlon's valuable treatment of both themes is cited later in this chapter) although the theme of concealment versus revelation is often alluded to (e.g., Merlan and Rumsey 1991:224–226 and Bercovitch 1998). One author who has made an explicit connection between these topics is Laurence Goldman in his *Talk Never Dies* (1983), a study of the Huli people of the Southern Highlands Province in Papua New Guinea. Goldman, working from within Huli linguistic usages, points out very clearly the parallelism set up by the Huli between disputes, breaches of norms in the group, and bodily sickness and the concomitant idea that compensation has to be paid in order to heal both social and physical wounds. It follows that the body may be its own witness, may itself reveal hidden truths. The Huli stress on this idea may have muted the significance of verbal confessions or revelations of wrongdoing. From the Huli example, however, we can suggest a general point that should hold at least in other Highlands New Guinea cases: the payment of compensation for killings, wrongdoings, insults, or physical woundings must depend on a viable attribution of responsibility. In some cases such an attribution will be self-evident, in others problematic. When it is problematic, a verbal confession may be sought, but if that is impracticable, unlikely, or difficult to obtain, the final "backstop" of any system is likely to be the human body itself. Hence a logical relationship always potentially exists between compensation, confession, and sickness. A reexamination of the New Guinea literature in these terms would likely prove to be rewarding but cannot be undertaken here. Such a reexamination would take into account the various logics of divination in relation to sorcery and witchcraft and compensation or revenge issues that flow from such logics. Here we proceed with our more specific examination of changing historical contexts in Hagen.

WHAT IS EVIDENCE?

What constitutes evidence for wrongdoing? Considerable stress is placed on the idea that the investigators of a case should bring accused persons to the point that they themselves declare what they have done. The admission of responsibility is therefore taken as an ultimate form of evidence. It is also evidence of willingness to undertake the steps to put matters to rights, insofar as this is possible. But there is a further point to this drive in investigatory practice. If a confession is not made, either the accused or the investigators can ask that divination take place and the results of the divination will be expected to show in a direct, nonverbal embodied form. If the accused lies, either he or she will get sick, a child will, or fellow group members will experience sickness and misfortune. For this process to be set in motion, the accused must verbally deny the charge, then undergo the divination or oath-taking. The results are expected to be "written on the body." The body thus becomes a repository of truth beyond words. But it is equally significant that verbal action has to be involved. These two components, the verbal and the nonverbal, constitute vital different aspects of personhood, to do with agency on the one hand and substance on the other. Responsibility is linked to verbal statements, to acceptance or denial of facts. The body then acts as a passive but powerful register of the consequences of exercising human agency.

The idea of "confession" involved here is one that has, therefore, a deep foundation in Hagen notions of personhood and truth. Contemporary notions are also inflected by Christian concepts, which have been taken into Hagen repertoires of thinking and blended with ideas concerning the workings of anger and shame, which are also at issue in questions of confession in disputes. An absence of confession leads to sickness, by two different pathways: a guilty person's failure to reveal what he or she has done can cause sickness to kin or also to him or herself; equally, a person who is *popokl*, angry/frustrated, with others may cause sickness to him or herself by not revealing the source of the frustration. It is this context that has been interwoven with Christian ideas to produce a new constellation of practices, while the basic logic remains the same.

Confession logically precedes restitution or the payment of compensation. We have seen, however, that a context of embodiment may act as a "back-stop" for evidential proof in a given case. By the same token, then, the act of paying compensation can be regarded as an admission of responsibility although it may sometimes occur without any such admission. We therefore look first at "confession" and then at "compensation" as two contexts in which the same principles are evident. Verbal statements, as declaration of agency, reduce ambiguity, but as denials they may be untrue. Nonverbal actions can also constitute statements but can be given variant interpretations, increasing ambiguity. And all of these processes also shift their forms in historical time.

First, however, we need to show empirically that there is a stress on both fact-finding and confession in disputes.

Two Cases: "Tell Us What You Did"

We adduce two cases to show the determined lengths to which investigators may go in attempting to make recalcitrant suspects declare their supposed guilt. Both cases are drawn from dispute contexts of the 1980s and have been reported on at greater length elsewhere but without a stress on the points at issue here regarding personhood, agency, and the embodiment of truth (A. J. Strathern 1993b:chaps. 3 and 4). Both cases also took place within the general ambit of relations between one group of people, the Kawelka, living at Kuk, and their immediate or more distant neighbors. The disputes were heard outside of the formalized context of village courts where appointed magistrates hear cases in accordance with introduced procedure while following custom in whatever way they choose to do. The disputes here were therefore handled in moots, where there was full community presence and the broadest invocation of factors and knowledge. In the second case the agency handling the case was a Trouble Committee set up with government sanctions behind it, but the committee members operated along with others and behaved essentially as a form of moot gathering.

Case 1: The Wandering Pig

In this case, a man was accused of stealing the pig of another man by finding it in a garden space belonging to the pig's owner, tethering it, and then secretly returning to fetch it and take it to his home. K., the accused, agreed he had tethered the pig but denied he had removed it or that it had gone to his place. The pig's owner, M., pointed out that the footprints of the pig had been recognized, headed in the direction of the accused's house, at the place Kuning. Investigators strongly suggested that this implied K.'s guilt and also hinted that the mere fact he had tethered the pig made him guilty of an offense ("unlawful restraint of a pig"?). They established that K. had been playing cards in a local men's house up till a certain time on the evening of the supposed theft and that he had left alone and could have collected the pig and taken it home in the dark. One investigator, Ru, related to K., noted: "If you thought that the pig was wandering around and you didn't know who its owner was, then say so. . . . You are not a small boy that we can force you to reveal the truth." A local magistrate weighed in as a by-stander, saying that the protagonists were both leaders and the facts should be revealed quickly. The owner, M., said K. should reveal whether he took the pig in anger, that is, for some reason. Another magistrate was sarcastic: "So, you thought that M. is your brother, so you tied the pig up for him without a thought to steal it. And later the actual thief broke in to the area, found it, and stole it. . . . Someone else stole the pig, and you, an innocent man, are sitting here under the sun." An observer pointed out that if the facts were not revealed, bad feelings would continue. The second magistrate continued with his sarcastic tack: "This pig was in your care, and you might have secretly tipped someone off. Or else maybe the pig itself wanted to get you into trouble, so it followed you into your area." Other observers argued that people should live peacefully together on the land and suggested that K.'s kin would be happy to contribute to pay for the pig going astray. K., however, adamantly refused to admit any guilt and declared that he was prepared to take the matter to an outside court. Because of his intransi-gence, the matter was dropped. The pig, meanwhile, reappeared.

All kinds of personal and community pressures were applied to K., but he was not threatened with a divination ordeal, probably because the pig turned up in the nick of time.

Case 2: Who Stole the Car?

This case concerned a violent attack on the Kawelka leader Ongka by a set of young men of his own group. The young men suspected that Ongka's son Namba had informed on them after they had stolen a car belonging to the local Depart-ment of Primary Industry Station. The case occurred in two phases. In the first, the young men were interrogated about their reasons for launching their attack. Two levels of process were involved. One was to establish that they had in fact stolen the car. The second was to get them to substantiate their claim that Namba had informed on them or to abandon it, leaving them without even a flimsy excuse for making the attack. Their own words in making the attack incrimi-nated them on the first point. On the second, one of them had reported to the others on seeing Namba in conversation with the station boss. Meanwhile, the car, like the pig in case 1, had been recovered. Ongka said he knew nothing about the car or where the thieves had hidden it (in another Kawelka territory, from which they had migrated back to their original place at Kuk). Namba said he had said nothing to the station boss about the car. An investigator asked if anyone had seen Namba's lips moving to pronounce the word *car* as he spoke to the boss. It was admitted that this was not so. The inquiry here was minute, exhaustive, and is to be explained in terms of the fact that if the attackers were mistaken in their ideas they had no excuse whatsoever for their hasty and violent actions. Interestingly, they did not fabricate evidence, nor did anyone think to ask the station boss himself. The focus of the investigation, ostensibly centered on a minor set of facts, was in fact on intergroup relations. The attackers were rendered culpable and threatened with arrest and being taken to court. They and their kin acceded to the payment of compensation (admitting not only the attack, which was evident, but their total culpability), which was followed by the cooking of pigs and a shared feast to restore relations between the group segments involved. The minute attention to facts and the invitation to the attackers to say why they did what they did and to admit they were mistaken were both aimed at reaching the possibility of reconciliation. Neither Namba nor the accused was asked to take a divination test. No one was therefore expected to get sick.

Both cases show an impressive forensic and rhetorical ability by investigators, appealing to a wide range of "personhood notions." Neither case proceeded to the level of invoking the body as a repository of truth, but the stress on achieving reconciliation was in line with doing so, since hostility and anger can always lead to sickness and further trouble.

FORMS OF DIVINATION: LANGUAGE AND EMBODIMENT

In cases where verbal investigations have not revealed the truth, there can be resort to divinatory practices. As we shall note in the next section, these have now been largely replaced by holding the Bible and swearing by it, but the logic involved is exactly as it was before. This logic reveals a relationship between language, truth, and embodiment.

The standard form of swearing as a divination is for an accused person to take hold of a sacred plant or object associated with the origins of his or her group and make a declaration of innocence, invoking the power of the object to cause death in the case of lying. It is thus an act of literally taking one's life into one's hands. The object is the group's *mi,* the source of its life; it is "laid down" from the times of origin when it was first shown or revealed to an ancestor as the means to increase the growth of the group. It is that which is permanent, *tei mel,* "laid down" for all time. The ancestor also took possession of it by holding it (*ömböröm*), just as a descendant who swears by it must do. People regard the mi with respect and do not lightly undertake to swear by it in this way.

Ongka, in his autobiography (Strathern and Stewart 1999b), tells of another test that was used in the past. People suspected of killing someone by sorcery were invited to take part in a firethong divination. They would say:

"I wonder if you'd like to come up to our place for a little ceremony?" The suspect answered directly: "I didn't kill your man, why are you asking me this?" "Oh, we're embarrassed, it's just a little thing like a bird's song or the feces of a spirit, don't worry, it's nothing big. We're eating food together with you, and one of our children has fallen sick, so come up and we'll try the firethong divination."

The suspect's people argued about whether to go or not, but eventually they went, preparing themselves for violence. The hosts brought out a hardened firethong and a tinder of *kuklumb* leaves and invited them to try it. At first they declined. At length, a big-man would come forward and say, "If there is trouble, we should not fight or kill in revenge, we have pigs and shells with which to pay compensation. Just try out the firethong."

He made the talk "cool" in this way, and one man came forward to use the thong. If he successfully made fire, he went free, for he was accounted innocent. Perhaps he had cooked a pig as a sacrifice for his own ghosts and obtained their support? But if fire would not come or the thong broke, they would exclaim, and set upon him at once. (p. 58)

The logic involved here is that the creation of fire is a sign of benign influence and goodwill. The aggrieved spirit of the dead would prevent the fire from coming. A similar ritual is performed at the beginning of a sequence in the Female Spirit cult, when a fire is lit to heat the stones for earth ovens to be used in pork sacrifices. If the fire does not light, the performer of the ritual does not have the right bodily condition, and this can result from dissension within the group involved.

Fire is instrumental in cooking, and the same logic of the "raw" versus the "cooked" is seen in the case of the taro divination, which was performed in the past. Suspects of thieving or sorcery were asked to select taro corms, which were placed in an oven for baking and later removed. Whoever had a taro that was not properly cooked was held to be guilty. Angry spirits had prevented the corm from cooking so that the guilt was revealed. By the same logic nowadays rice that is cooked for someone but has sorcery stuff in it is held to be hard to cook properly; it tends to remain "raw." Improperly cooked rice is therefore by definition suspect. In these instances the taro or the rice becomes the vehicle that embodies the true situation—that a declaration of innocence is false. In extreme circumstances the mi itself may be burned by fire. If this is accompanied by an untrue declaration, the one who swears falsely will swiftly die.

The relationship between language and embodiment here is interesting because the two are conjoined. A verbal statement is tested by an embodied act.

As we shall see next, for the Melpa the verbal and the nonverbal form a communicative continuum.

"Confession" and Christianity

"Confession" as used so far is a gloss for the Hagen or Melpa phrase *nemba mot ndui*, "saying, to make evident." Things that are not said but become evident by showing themselves, as sickness shows in the body, are referred to as *mot ninim*, "it speaks *mot*." What we would call "nonverbal" is thus encompassed by a verb of "verbal" action in Melpa, an interesting point that shows the communicative locus of the verb *ni*, "to say." Things "speak *mot*" when they are not covered up or occluded, as stars that shine when they are not obscured by clouds and are said to be stones, *ku mot ninim*, "a stone speaks *mot*." The overt onset of an illness does the same: *rukrung pepa ekit omba mot ninim*, "it lives inside and comes out and speaks mot/reveals itself."

The dramaturgical image-schema of concealment versus revelation is basic to contexts both inside and outside of conflict situations. In the Female Spirit cult dancers mass behind a tall fence and then burst as if newborn into the midst of a huge throng of spectators who have been eagerly awaiting their arrival (Strathern and Stewart 1997a; Strathern and Stewart 1999d). The dancers for a moka prestation prepare themselves privately and individually and then mass together to show themselves on a ceremonial ground. Moka gifts themselves may be likened to a snake as it appears at the edge of a brushwood covering: its head may be visible but the length of its body and tail are not. This refers to the time when people are still collecting pigs for the gift and have not yet revealed how many they have. The revelatory pattern involved is that which Roy Rappaport refers to in relation to Maring ritual: it is epideictic and it converts analogical into digital signals (Rappaport 1968, 1999). Things that reveal themselves may therefore be good and favorable as well as unfavorable. "Speaking mot" is also a strongly performance-orientated term. Things come into existence when they are *shown* to do so, as a matter of clear evidence.

In dispute contexts revelation may come from various agents: from accusers who finally show some piece of evidence they have, or from the accused who decide to tell, or from witnesses, or from spiritual powers whose presence has been invoked or whose evaluation has been elicited. In all of these contexts revelation means resolution of the issues in hand and the possibility to move to a phase of settlement in the discussions. Also, revelation may in turn mean that an unpleasant consequence can be averted. For example, if a person accused of stealing a pig stubbornly denies the imputation, the aggrieved and suspicious accuser may take a clandestine reprisal and secretly steal a pig of the accused, provoking an escalation of conflict between them since the accused guesses from the timing what has happened. Or if a man has had illicit intercourse with a fellow clansman's wife while she is secluded in a menstruation hut and he falls sick, it is held that he cannot possibly recover from the sickness unless he reveals what he has done and thus enables a purification ritual to be held on his behalf. The menstrual blood must be sucked from his body at certain points through pieces of sugarcane skin and spat onto heated tin drums to neutralize it. If he fails to reveal the situation, the pollution will reach his brain and dry it up totally so that he dies. Since the action of committing adultery with a clansman's wife is considered to be an offense to shared ancestral spirits in the clan, it is a matter of shame and thus may be concealed. An episode of sickness is likely to be the only event that will induce the man to overcome shame and reveal what he has done because the sickness shows on his skin and draws comment from others, eventually eliciting his confession and a ritual of reconciliation with the spirits and his kinsfolk through a pork sacrifice.

The context of sickness is the one in which a term such as *confession* comes closest to being an accurate gloss for the Melpa term. Sickness events are heavily loaded with moral significance in Hagen. Sickness may result from situations of conflict that precipitate anger/frustration (popokl) between people. The relationship between sickness, anger, and revelation is certainly an example of a perduring cultural form or image-schema in Hagen social thought, and its resilience is shown in the fact that it has been a matter of everyday experience in fieldwork since 1964. It has, however, undergone a metamorphosis since it has become intertwined with introduced Christian ideas.

In the original indigenous system, as far as can be ascertained, sickness was an expected result of popokl, and would be experienced by the one who was made popokl. It was legitimate, indeed necessary, to express one's popokl in order to gain redress. Concealed, it could be lethal. A male wrongdoer also ought to confess, though not out of popokl, in order to prevent, for example, pollution sickness to his own body or to enable a sickness of his wife and children to be cured (A. J. Strathern 1985; Strathern and Stewart 1999c). In one such case a man failed to reveal that he had sex with his own mother-in-law, and all of his children and his wife were affected by a sickness (scabies) on their skin. Revealing the cause of an event or condition, then, whether to deal with anger and its threat of sickness or to admit to one's own wrongdoing, is considered essential to righting whatever wrong is implied by the event or condition itself. The expression of popokl is therefore legitimate; its concealment is not.

These ideas about popokl began to change with Christian influence from at least the 1960s onward. In the Christian viewpoint, anger, which may be associated with acts of retaliation and revenge, is not considered legitimate, and institutions that are seen as regularly leading to anger are therefore questionable. Polygyny and moka exchanges are cases in point. In the 1960s Lutheran and Baptist missionaries argued that Christians should not get too involved in moka exchanges because these tended to produce anger. The term *ararimb* was used instead of *popokl*, but it is uncertain whether this was a new coinage at the time or an existing variant term. The state of anger/frustration was considered to be undesirable, equated with sin. Confession and removal of anger/frustration were seen as necessary before people could take part in the harmonious ritual of communion. Hence it was the state of anger itself, rather than the actions of others that provoked it, that was seen as undesirable and in need of correction.

Similar changes may perhaps have occurred in Santa Isabel in the Solomon Islands, where Geoffrey White remarks on the fact that divulging transgressions in Anglican areas to the priest had taken the place of public "disentangling" discourse that could lead to further "entanglings." White also notes that the Anglican bishop had encouraged confessions of the private type and discouraged public moots (thereby playing a hefty role in social change). A cultural practice was maintained at one level, then, and subverted at another (White 1990:93).

In Hagen Christianity itself was seen as *min-nga kongon*, "work of the soul" (the part of the person that survives death and can go to heaven or hell), and confession was therefore seen as setting the soul in order and in a good relationship to God. The concept here is subtly altered from the older indigenous context, in which anger had nothing to do with the soul (min) but was experienced in the noman (the mortal mind), and conflicts had to be settled by removing anger from and aligning the minds of people. The revelation of anger and wrongdoing therefore had to do with ongoing social relations, not with the relationship of the person to God, the future residence of the soul, and its individual immortality.

In the Catholic religion regular forms of "confession" are practiced. The Melpa, however, do not call this Catholic act by the term *nemba mot ndui*, because the information does not become public and does not stimulate acts of social retribution or rectification although it does prepare the person for communion. Nor is such confession seen as a necessary prophylactic act needed for the success of a future enterprise or to forestall a disaster or to pave the way for an atonement of a public kind. In times of fighting, men are supposed to gather in cult places and reveal any wrongdoing they have been guilty of in relation to their clansmen to forestall the withdrawal of ancestral favor. Conflict and disharmony, secret wrongdoing, undermine the subtle ties that bind men to the ancestors and the protection these afford, and so any man who has done wrong is exposed to being killed by the enemy: hence the public revelation followed by sacrifice. It is most serious when men hold the mi or sacred cordyline (in the case of the Kawelka) and declare that they have done no wrong because if they lie the mi will destroy them at some later point. Here again, a subtle change has recently been slotted in. Instead of taking a cordyline leaf, people of either sex use the Christian Bible to swear on, explicitly commenting that they have seen this done in courts when disputes are adjudicated and the Bible is like a mi, which can function in the same way for all groups provided that those who swear by it are Christians. Here the "swearing" can also be called *nemba mot ndui*, to make a public statement, to stake a claim to the truth publicly. The Bible is also a sacred emblem that can be shared by both sexes and across group boundaries, so it fits with contemporary conditions of life. In another sense, it makes or creates a new kind of group, just as the revelation of the mi in the past is supposed to have marked a new group identity.

In the context of sickness, Christian ideas have also somewhat altered the notion of confession. The newer charismatic churches (such as the Assemblies of God) greatly favor the idea of prayers for healing the sick and use this emphasis as a recruiting device. Sickness, seen as a result of anger, is described as a "heavy" thing (*mbun*), whereas, in indigenous practice, it is a legitimate protest against wrongdoing. In Christian ideas, as we have seen, anger is also a sin and therefore the sickness is in a sense itself a kind of wrongdoing. Confession of anger removes it and is held to relieve the associated sickness or the threat of becoming ill. A small sacrifice is usually performed, although never said to be for ancestors. Prayers are said earnestly over the sick person to remove the power of the Devil and to instill the power of Jesus to heal. A dualistic battle of good versus evil is thus set up. The logic here is that of the indigenous system turned ninety degrees. Sickness, produced by anger, is seen as sin rather than as a protest against wrongdoing. The sick person is urged to cast out anger and in effect to turn the other cheek, not to seek the revenge actions that ordinarily might follow from anger. The aim is to put to rights the state of the sick person's min as well as to call on Jesus to heal the actual sickness. Sickness as a source of heaviness (*mbun*), then, is seen in this revised schema as resulting from anger, as before, but the cure is differently conceptualized. In cases when the sick person has a grievance against a fellow member of the same church congregation, there will be a meeting to discuss the problem (in the case of Lutherans, this is known as a *sutmang,* apparently a Kâte word introduced in the 1960s by coastal evangelists from Finschafen). Community action follows, therefore, as before, but the ancestors are not made a part of the process, and prayers to God and Jesus are directed toward healing the sick persons and also to changing the hearts of those who have wronged them. Exchanges and pork sacrifices are not made essential to the process, though it is notable that revealing the causes of feelings or the facts behind the scene is still thought to be important, indeed essential.

Many times during our 1997, 1998, and 1999 visits to Hagen we heard from people that when something unfortunate had happened to them it was caused by their own wrongdoing by not adhering to the teachings of the church and letting popokl block the granting of forgiveness to others. A case in point occurred when one of our female informants, M., explained that her husband, R., had "broken" her house in a drunken rage on grounds that she had stolen some coffee beans of his and that he would not repair the structure or build another house for her because of the popokl between them.

One way in which the adherents of the charismatic churches relieve the pressure of their concealed popokl is through witnessing (standing in the church in front of the congregation and confessing). This action is especially important nowadays when many Hageners declare that the end times may be close at hand and the year A.D. 2000 will herald the return of Jesus at which time those who have confessed their sins and asked for forgiveness will be favored for salvation while those who have not done so will perish in the consuming fires ignited by the Antichrist (Stewart and Strathern [eds.] 1997).

The act of witnessing in the congregation privileges the Christian church in which the words are spoken, thereby strengthening the power of the religion within the community of church adherents and thus strengthening that community itself. Its functions are thus similar to those of "confession" in the earlier indigenous sphere.

The charismatic Catholics in Hagen have taken the act of voluntary witnessing one step further. When rumors circulate that a person has fallen from his or her faith in God through "wrong" actions, the religious community gathers at the home of the person and holds a fellowship meeting that lasts throughout the night and into the early hours of the morning, during which Christian hymns are sung to the tunes of traditional songs while drumbeats set the rhythm. We might suggest that these songs are a means of communicating more immediately with the heavenly (and perhaps ancestral) realms from which the power of the Holy Spirit is evoked by their ritual actions (Stewart and Strathern, 1998a). The words of the hymns are sometimes in Melpa, but sometimes also of an unknown provenance, akin to "speaking in tongues."

This section has shown the continuing significance of "confession" though within a changed moral configuration of practices.

"Compensation" and Its Embodied Concomitants

In the context of the above discussion, the payment of compensation for a killing can be seen as a nonverbal form of the "confession" through acceptance of responsibility for a death. Moreover, there is a link with the body, since compensation is thought to have a healing quality when it is paid for the infliction of a wound. We can set up the following scheme:

Verbal admission————> Social reconciliation
Compensation————> Bodily healing

When the compensation is for a killing, the "healing" is displaced: the life removed cannot be restored, but new life can be created in its place by the use of wealth.

As with verbal confession, however, there has been an historical shift in the meanings of compensation over time. This can be deduced from the fact that *compensation* itself is a term that has entered the indigenous Melpa vocabulary in the last five years or so. Its use coincides with a shift in both consciousness and practice, from an ethos of bilateral exchanges leading into moka exchange sequences to one of unilateral payments not articulated into any wider planned concatenations or forms of reciprocity between groups. Correlated further with this pattern is a shift from the practice of sending "solicitory gifts" in order to receive a large payment for a death, to one in which the victim's group presents a "demand" to the group of a killer that they are then required to meet or to meet as nearly as possible, as observed in 1995. The ethic of exchange that underpinned transactions in the past has gradually been supplanted since the 1980s by an ethic of payment that corresponds generally to a commodified pattern. Here we explore the history of commodification of the person and its intersection with practices of compensation for killings over time.

Complications of the Person: Commodification and Violence

In the precolonial social system, violence was always the ultimate sanction of relations between persons not tied closely together by kinship or affinity. In certain contexts, physical violence was an automatic reaction to provocation, as much an intrinsic expression of group identity as a calculated strategy of reprisal. In this context it was linked to the concept of popokl, deep-seated anger/frustration, which, if not revealed or acted upon, will result in the sickness of the person who experiences it. Between those categories of persons who were defined mutually as *el parka wamb,* "Raggiana Bird of Paradise people," or major traditional enemies, a permanent state of popokl was expected to hold, and large-scale compensations were not generally held between them. Raping of women in warfare and the mutilation or burning of the bodies of male enemies at the boundaries of their territories marked this basic attitude to the body of such enemies: the practice was to destroy them, spoil them, render them worthless, and thus insult their living kin. Between "minor enemies," however, it was expected that compensation would be paid for killings and reparations made to allies who gave assistance in fights. Intermarriage took place between these minor enemy/ally categories, there was a sharing of "blood" as a bodily substance between them, and an arena in which transactional exchanges of wealth as substitutes for blood was preserved. There is a common ideology among the Melpa of Hagen and the Duna people of Lake Kopiago in the Southern Highlands Province that when a dispute occurs between two people and one party is wounded, the wound will not heal until compensation is paid. The wounded party will say, *nanga mema pindi:* "replace my blood!" (or "fasten my blood"). This is a frequently heard demand in dispute encounters resulting in physical violence in Hagen. The claim made is not for blood to be replaced by blood, however, but for a cathexis to be enacted between social relations and bodily condition that amounts to a ramified set of embodied practices in Hagen culture. The demand is in effect for a payment of compensation in wealth goods (pigs, pork, valuable shells, money), and this payment is itself thought not only to ease the hurt feelings of the one who has been assaulted but also in effect to stanch the flow of blood from this body and restore its balance within that body. Once an agreement has been made to institute social accountability, the wounded person can begin to recover. The value of the body here depends on relationship, on shared substance, or the transacted substitutes for substance. Within this sphere, then, the body gains its value, and that value is defined socially, as an expression of the value of the ties that bind persons together. The value is thus communalistic and founded on the embodiment of sociality.

In colonial times this sphere of embodiment was extended to pockets of previous major enemies, via intermarriage and the alliance-seeking activities of bigmen. Precolonial practices preserved their meaning, stretched into a larger arena, and were supported by pacification and an influx of shell wealth. The Melpa remained in control of their own definitions of the value of a body because shell wealth operated only in their own system, even if it came from outside and even if the supply of shells came from colonial sources. With the shift to money, accelerated around the time of Papua New Guinea's national independence, this local independence was eroded (Strathern and Stewart 1998d). Shells were abandoned when the people's attention shifted to money as a scarce valuable, and at the same time people were drawn increasingly into activities that could secure for them a monetary income. Coffee grown on clan land also gave that land a monetary dimension and thus gave a new meaning to old acts of destruction in warfare: enemies concentrated on slashing down coffee trees and hacking trade stores to pieces as well as the earlier practice of burning down dwelling houses. Cash-cropping practices also brought a dynamic shift in gendered roles and status as women were able to acquire wealth in ways not previously conceivable. This money flows readily into compensation payments. With the introduction of education, younger men and women entered the nexus of business and politics, funneling cash back into their home areas as a means of building political factions to secure election to positions in the introduced governmental system, an arena suppressed in colonial times. Money became a dominant component in moka gifts between allies, but transactions in it between major enemies halted, along with the regrowth of political competition between them. Such political blocs became the basis for the major factions in the new political system. The colonial expansion of the precolonial system fell to pieces, revealing again the edges of identity and hostility along which the value of a body or person was nullified. Major battles, which took place in the latter half of the 1980s, occurred between these major enemies and were deeply exacerbated by the introduction of guns, making it possible to kill many people and to do so without even knowing who they were. This situation is also complicated by the consumption of alcohol, leading to heightened violent encounters. The scale of these killings further made it difficult even to contemplate making compensation payments to cover them.

In addition, new layers were added to the arena of compensation payments at large. Members of language groups that previously had lived separately now dwelt side by side in resettlement areas laid aside for cash cropping and available to land-short farmers in the wider region. Disputes and killings between these persons tended to escalate rapidly, bringing in large numbers of kinsfolk or co-ethnics on either side. Identities were "blown up," without the mechanisms to mediate between the parties (A. J. Strathern 1992). Claims for compensation were enlarged and the amounts demanded purely in cash or with notional stipulations of numbers of pigs, which obviously could not be met. Most significantly, a pattern of killings of prominent businessmen and politicians began to make itself felt. In two cases that became widely publicized in the national media, leaders from the Enga language area west of Hagen were killed and the killings traced to gangs or hired assassins from the Hagen tribal groups. The amounts demanded for these deaths skyrocketed and were based on a kind of actuarial, future-based assessment of their individual worth, running into figures far beyond those collected for the settlement of interclan disputes in the past. This shift indicates how new definitions of value have intersected with the "individual" side of the concept of the relational-individual but also with the relational side, since elite persons are thought to be of value to their clans.

The inflated demands were at this point met by markedly deflated offers on the part of the Hageners (Melpa). Although millions were being demanded, only a few thousand kina were collected. Where amorphous collectivities of co-ethnics faced each other, and the blame or responsibility for the killings could not unambiguously be attributed, compensation could no longer retain its precolonial structure of meanings. The individual values of the bodies of the two prominent Engans were linked to an ethnic, not just a group, identity, replacing the old fusion of the big-man and his group with a new monetary-based equation. Such huge demands for payments were focused largely on men who had attained prominence in the introduced capitalist system, and the payments for their deaths thus became categories of payment in an indigenized capitalist nexus rather than in a capitalized indigenous nexus as before (compare Levine 1999 on the genesis of ethnic identities in contemporary contexts of embodied practice).

Even in contexts where businesspeople or politicians were not involved, the destruction of trust between groups was such that the form of payments altered. There was no possibility to create interpersonal networks between individuals as a means of underpinning and prolonging temporally the effects of wealth transfers. Instead, groups nervously confronted one another, weapons at the ready, handed over payments en bloc while watching for treachery, and left rapidly. Needless to say, such events could not produce peace. The threat of assassination by hidden gunfire to a great extent lay behind the collective fear and unease displayed on these occasions and enormously curtailed the effects of the indigenous oratory, which was designed to form a bridge between groups and signal their consensus (see chapter 5 on this form of oratory).

Only one context was preserved from this progressive degeneration of the compensation system: ally payments made with pigs. In the first half of 1991 an amassing and disbursement of large numbers of well-grown pigs by the Kawelka to a diverse set of allies occurred in which all of them had lost men in helping the Kawelka against their major enemies in the previous five years. The pigs were either home-reared or purchased with money. In this context, traditional oratory and discourse prevailed. Pigs are not fully commoditized: their status as substitutes for human life remains intact because they have no place in the outside system other than as an occasional trading resource. The concept of "eating" and thereby achieving a satisfaction in the replacement and sharing of substance applies to them. The compensation, accompanied by the slaughter of many of the pigs, their consumption, and their implicit dedication as sacrifices to ancestral ghosts and those of the recent dead, succeeded in creating harmony between those involved. But this event, hard as it was to organize and extremely expensive for the Kawelka, still fell far short of neutralizing the major axes of future violence because the payments were made solely to allies, not to the major enemies with whom all scores remained unsettled. Rumors that killings of such enemies or by such enemies had been effected by sorcery and trickery or by assassinations in distant parts of Papua New Guinea kept alive the deep sense of enmity and suspicion in the region and the possibility of further violence in the future. Nevertheless, the planting of a Christian cross at the border between the Kawelka and the Minembi, by agreement of both sides, did stabilize the situation for peace.

From one perspective, major enemies remain major enemies and there is a state of permanent hostility with them. But this picture of "no change" has to be set against a background of kaleidoscopic changes in economy, government, and ritual. The processes were set in hand in colonial times. The commodification of land and wealth has sharpened oppositions between enemies, and the inflated "rates" of compensation have produced a breakdown in the flow of payments. Whereas the substitution of exchange for violence in the past produced an aura of security, nowadays people feel much more vulnerable in their bodies, especially with the advent of guns. Violence began again in the 1980s to define the edges of identity, destroying the substitution of wealth for killing, and defining an expanded arena of killing in which some bodies once more became worthless, while others attained a factitious or cargoistically inflated value in monetary terms. Christian campaigns in the 1990s have modified this pattern to some extent, but Hagen remains a place where people are ever conscious of danger, whether in the rural hinterlands of the township or in the town itself, where crimes of violence associated with theft became commonplace throughout the 1990s.

INDIVIDUATION, CONSCIENCE, AND COLLECTIVE CONTEXTS: TWO COMPARISONS

The introduction of Christianity into our analysis here prompts us further to set our findings into a wider comparative framework, such as is provided by Michael Hepworth and Bryan S. Turner in their general study of confession, or studies of deviance and religion (Hepworth and Turner 1982). These authors examine the development and impact of ideas of conscience and confession from medieval times in the Catholic church in Europe, through the individuation of conscience and the sense of guilt in Protestantism, and thence to the place of notions regarding confession and therapy in psychoanalysis. They discuss European witchcraft trials and compare them to confessions in other contexts, as for example the remark made by I. M. Lewis that a public confession of tensions can help to "restore social harmony in a ceremony where the village shaman gives expression to the consensus of the local community" (Hepworth and Turner 1982:39, referring to I. M. Lewis 1971).

Hepworth and Turner are concerned with confession only in the sense of the admission of wrongdoing, in the Christian religious context seen as sin, and with the place that such confessions have in bringing to a close processes of investigation, enabling counteraction to be instituted (e.g., incarceration, restitution, death), and in marking social boundaries of inclusion and exclusion. It is the last of these functions that is of particular interest to us here, although equally significant is the point that rituals of confession are supposed to lead to a reestablishment of the social order, as in the historical examples from Europe in which confessions of violence by "unruly knights" acted to constrain their violence and of sexual misdemeanors by female members of landed houses served to protect property interests. For Hagen it is obvious that confessions of forms of "theft" (of property or of sexual intercourse, for example) within the clan group served periodically to cleanse the group of suspicions of wrongdoing and generated the compensatory gifts and exchanges that were needed to restore group fertility. The mi was the very symbol of in-group morality in this regard. A voluntary statement of wrongdoing would thus announce the confessor as having transgressed social boundaries and equally as wishing to be readmitted within them. The mechanism for readmission was the payment of compensation accompanied by sacrifice to ancestral ghosts. (In the European context, in-group morality was also upheld, either through the rehabilitation or the stigmatization/extinction of the confessor.)

Confession in Hagen before the growing significance of Christian ideas thus reflected a collective context, but it also had an element that tied persons in an embodied fashion into that context, since it operated in tandem with ideas regarding sickness. Unconfessed, hidden wrongdoing leads to sickness that cannot heal unless a confession is made: the concordance between body and society is exact because social wrong leads to physical illness. Individual "guilt" leads to "self-punishment" in the body itself because the body is as much an expression of social relations as a physical unit.

Formulating the Hagen ideas in this way makes it possible to see how such ideas can be subtly altered, as we have argued, to bridge over the gap between indigenous and introduced notions of responsibility. It is necessary, however, to recognize the specific elements that must come into play before confession of a "European" type can appear. Hepworth and Turner formulate these (p. 67) as a theory of individual guilt, a moral order against which individual sins are committed, a system of authority that can receive and absolve sins, and a variety of techniques to deal with confessions. Notions of individuality and hierarchy are crucial here and operated differently from the relatively egalitarian and community-oriented ethos in the Hagen system, although the body in Hagen stood, as it were, both on the side of individuality and on the side of society.

There is another complication in the Hagen situation because "confession," in the sense of "revelation," making known what was hidden, could be used to point to another person as the wrongdoer and thus functioned as an accusation. Here the confessor placed him or herself inside the social boundary and declared the other to have transgressed it. The catch is that in both cases "anger" worked the same way: it could cause sickness unless revealed. Virtue and self-interest thus conduced to making one's anger known. As we have also seen, it is this context that has been somewhat elided by the Christian "interpretive turn," and this has left problematic the question of redress against wrongdoing. The Christian is supposed not to become popokl because now popokl itself is seen as sin. This Hagen twist on Christian ideas gives the confession complex today its particular hybrid quality because the rules of its contemporary discursive formation (in a Foucaultian sense as explicated by Hepworth and Turner chapter 4) are an attempted conflation of different thought-worlds through the selective alteration of points where they intersect, viz., in the relationship of anger/frustration to the body.

Introduced Christian ideas have, then, been partially blended in with indigenous Hagen notions, but only by a form of matching that simultaneously transforms both elements. It is interesting to compare this production of a third form from two originals (a reproduction with difference) with what happens when we compare Hagen ideas and practices with those of the Komblo people on the North Wall of the Wahgi, eastern neighbors of the northern Melpa-speakers, as described by Michael O'Hanlon (1989). O'Hanlon's exposition shows clearly that while Melpa and Wahgi (Komblo) ideas show a core of shared ontological propositions, their application to political life is somewhat different in the two cases. The comparison also shows that dominant features of the Wahgi appear in muted or secondary form among the Melpa. The Komblo are a formerly refugee group who were reestablished in their area with the help of allies. Understandably, they are much concerned about group solidarity, strength, historical viability, and possible threats to these. Like the Melpa, they consider that hidden wrongdoing will cause misfortune unless and until it is revealed and made a part of public discussion. The Wahgi phrase for this is *yu ne penem kele*, "throwing the talk into the open" (O'Hanlon 1989:66, 127), equivalent to the Melpa *nemba mot ndui*, "saying to make evident/revealed." At this level, Melpa and Wahgi ideas are identical. Both peoples also say that wrongdoing that results from anger within the group, or produces such anger, can cause harm to group members and their enterprises, as long as it is not revealed. This is simply a specification of context for the first level of ideas. From this point onward, however, the idea-systems show some divergence. The Komblo do not appear to have the Melpa notion that anger can cause sickness to oneself, an assertion that Melpa apply equally to both sexes. Rather, they stress the male sphere and the damaging consequences of anger between in-group males (O'Hanlon 1989:66, 149). Further, they are greatly exercised by the prospect of in-group betrayal, in which an angry man may give away secrets to an external group, through a pathway of matrilateral kinship, and this is held to result in misfortune, death, loss of fertility, and especially the loss of an ability to attract brides through epideictic displays of male finery and dancing in the *gol* pig-killing rituals. The process of betrayal may be preempted by a revelation of anger and presumably attempts to redress its causes; but if the aggrieved person proceeds to the point of betrayal, this is described by the Wahgi as *kum,* "witchcraft," a striking usage that linguistically parallels the Hagen term for witchcraft but seems to have a markedly different emphasis. In Hagen kum refers to cannibalistic witchcraft, stereotypically perpetrated by women married into a group, and serves as an antisymbol of proper external exchange relations (Stewart and Strathern 1997b; Strathern and Stewart 1998e). Kum in Wahgi serves as an antisymbol of proper in-group solidarity. Highly complex rhetorical claims are made in Wahgi around this theme. O'Hanlon (1989:131) details a speech made by a Komblo leader of the Kekanem clan, Kinden, in which he revealed that he had made kum against a neighboring group with whom he was angry and had magically enabled his cross-cousins in another group to outshine the others by rubbing grease into their skins and inserting plumes of his own into their head-nets (we may note here the strongly embodied context of this "laying on of hands"—and plumes). Later his cross-cousins ungratefully made boasts against his own group, the Kekanem, saying they were dying out for failure to attract girls. Kinden then withdrew his hidden support and revealed the talk (O'Hanlon 1989:133).

Kinden's actions would not be described as kum in Hagen. The processes, however, of switching allegiances in an interplay between matrilateral and agnatic allegiances are well known in Hagen as they are in Wahgi. Nevertheless, the emphasis in Wahgi on the theme of betrayal seems to be overwhelming by comparison. We may conclude that the Wahgi gol celebrates in-group male solidarity and male power in attracting brides through dancing and decoration. Threats to such solidarity are therefore the stuff of politics and the antithesis of "fertility" in this sense. In Hagen, by contrast, the aim of achieving and expressing intergroup alliance by a multiplicity of moka exchange partnerships was added to the imperative of group solidarity. Threats to exchange, symbolized in the image of consuming greed or kum, therefore were the focus of anxiety. It is not simply that individual financial capacities were involved (O'Hanlon 1989:130). There is/was a moral component as well, since the individual efforts to excel in exchange added up to a display of group status. For this reason, it is not surprising to note that in Hagen the same basic kinds of assessments of dance decorations and movements were made as in Wahgi: groups with dancers who moved awkwardly or had dull decorations were spoken of disparagingly as having internal troubles and as likely to lose a member of the group (*ti kawa ndomba*, "one will be cut down [die]"). Conversely, in Wahgi, a secondary discourse extolled the individual success of some dancers against others, as shown in the narrative by Kinden. The two cultural scenarios thus both contrast and complement each other in terms of dominant versus muted characteristics. And both stress the importance of revelation as a means of creating and altering the boundaries of social inclusion and exclusion, as Hepworth and Turner argue. This two-step comparison between Hagen ideas and Christian ideas on the one hand and Hagen and Wahgi ideas on the other indicates that significant transformations occur simply by the switching of one element or by its greater elaboration. Such an examination of cultural structures may help us to understand the processes whereby changes occur and how the universality of a theme such as confession is partnered by its local specificities.

We have followed the historical turns of practice in relation to confession and Christianity on the one hand and compensation and money on the other. Both confession and compensation form part of the wider logic of settlement by reconciliation in Hagen, a logic that operates best in within-group contexts. Confession may lead to compensation, and compensation is itself an equivalent of confession, a revealing of the truth accompanied by a corrective action in relation to it. The body is the ultimate marker of the validity of both: failure to confess leads to sickness, failure to compensate leads to bodily revenge, and a proper compensation heals the body that has been wounded. Verbal and nonverbal, mental and corporeal acts go together and conduce toward the same totalization of action and being. Ultimately, as we have also seen, both confession and compensation are about definitions of personhood. An insistence on confession makes the person as individual agent the focus, and agency is underpinned by social or relational substance, so that if agency fails, substance linked to spiritual powers takes over (cf. A. J. Strathern 1996; Stewart and Strathern [eds.] 2000). Compensation practices recognize the substitutability of wealth for the person, and contemporary problems over this reveal the incipient commodification of the person-body complex resulting from the effects of monetization in the economy at large. Concomitantly, a change in the focus of confession from communal inquiries to a more private statement made to God indicates a similar change, at least in the religious realm, of the definition of personhood, toward a new kind of individuation and therefore a new way of looking at body and mind. Nevertheless, in many ways we can see Christian ideas as transpositions of indigenous ones. Certainly, the potential contradictions between Christianity and customary ideas and norms have been at least partly mediated by such transpositions. Equally, the struggles to interrelate Christian and indigenous notions of personhood appear somewhat at a remove from the more blatant struggles for power in the arenas of politics and inter-group demands for compensation; yet in all of these contexts the tensions between individual and relational aspects of social activity are clearly revealed.

In the next chapter we look at these themes in a broader purview again, bringing together in a single discussion matters to do with the commodification of relations, the introduction of parliamentary politics and the state, and changing ideas of personhood.

► ► ► PART FOUR ► ► ►

CONCLUSIONS

Our studies and portraits of historical change in this book are to be seen as varying ways of approaching complex threads of history, of different colors and thicknesses. In our conclusions here, we emphasize two matters out of many: first, the impact on ideas of personhood of capitalism, democracy, and the state, all, however, realized only in local specificities; and second, the growing but equally complex significance of the indigenous appropriations of Christianity. Our observations and suggestions conduce toward a picture of change that suits well with the work of theorists such as George Marcus, who sees the ethnographic task as that of delineating in contemporary societies the co-occurrence of the global in the local (Marcus 1998:79–104).

ELEVEN

Money, Politics, and Persons

Theorizing processes of recent historical change in Papua New Guinea entails coming to terms with a triad of forces that we can identify as capitalism, democracy, and the state. These, of course, are broad terms, and we need to translate them into the specific forms they are taking in Papua New Guinea. Several authors have attempted this task, at different stages of the country's own development and of the development of anthropological theory itself. In terms of capitalism, some theorists (well exemplified by Amarshi, Good, and Mortimer 1979) have stressed dependency theory and Papua New Guinea's position on the periphery of capitalist influence, along with the development of the peasantry as a social class whose interests are potentially opposed to those of the urban bourgeoisie. "Big peasants" or "kulaks" are seen as the successors in capitalist mode to the big-men of the past. Papua New Guinea's Westminster-style democracy has provided avenues for such emergent leaders to enter into politics, and the emphasis on wealth and its distribution as a means of attaining and legitimizing political power has given a particular cast to the activities of politicians generally, who need wealth both to gain votes and to reward supporters. Such local imperatives have driven the national political machine to provide sectoral funds for direct distribution by politicians in their electorates, bypassing the public service channels. Democracy has thus been diverted into patronage, and strong policy-based political parties have not emerged. The state organization that underpins political and economic activities has accordingly failed to develop into a powerful force, and although the state is actively involved in the process of nation-making (Foster 1995) with the customary apparatus of the flag, festivals, rituals, and government speeches, its penetration at local levels has been patchy. In contrast, the influences of change in general have been pervasive, and anthropologists have been well to the fore in documenting these, particularly with reference to the theme of "globalization" and the difficulties of rural populations in achieving economic progress (e.g., Smith 1994; Gewertz and Errington 1995), colonial and postcolonial history (e.g., Brown 1995; Foster 1995), problems of social control (e.g., Meggitt and Gordon 1985), and the adoption of forms of Christianity (e.g., Barker 1990). One theme that has emerged from many of these studies is that of changing concepts of personhood and gender relations (see also Knauft 1997; Errington and Gewertz 1997; Gewertz and Errington 1998). The question here is whether notions of personhood, under the influence of forces of change, are shifting from a more relational to a more individualistic form (although both tendencies may be present in any given ethnographic case) (Strathern and Stewart 1998c). Our argument is that the combination of capitalism as cash cropping plus consumerism, democracy as patronage, and state influences that are both pervasive and yet weak in the frameworks they provide for everyday life has led to a peculiarly critical situation for the Hagen people, conducing toward a search for security and identity in the spheres of religion and ritual activity. We attempt therefore to understand some of the main ways in which extralocal forces have influenced and interwoven themselves into local community life in Hagen, recognizing that influences are simultaneously external and internal, extralocal and local. We attempt this assessment partly as a way of ordering impressions from a field visit in August 1997 and partly as a means of making a reassessment of earlier approaches to trajectories of change in Hagen and elsewhere in Papua New Guinea, especially the Highlands region.

The predominant paradigm of the Central Highlands societies, regardless of variations in their systems of kinship and locality, has been that they are based on the ideology and practice of gift exchange, out of which big-man patterns of leadership emerged, and that women gained recognition and respect through their work in the gift-exchange network. In the earliest conceptualizations of change this viewpoint was applied by Ben Finney (1973) and others to argue that big-men and exchange-based societies were preadapted to entrepreneurial business strategies introduced to them in the late phases of Australian colonial control. Highlanders were seen as secular, pragmatic go-getters, who would energetically transform themselves into cash croppers and merchants and eagerly adopt the modernizing model of society brought to them by the Department of Agriculture and the World Bank.

This optimistic model of development soon fell foul of several criticisms. Marxist scholars argued that underdevelopment and dependency were being foisted on the Highlanders in the longer run, and in line with this notion Diana Howlett, a geographer, proposed a model of "terminal development," development that could not raise the people at large beyond a certain economic level, attained through primary cash cropping of coffee. Other scholars also pointed out, from at least the 1970s onward, that the so-called 1970s "return of violence" in the Highlands following initial pacification in the 1930s and 1940s threatened to engulf and negate the effects of modernization and cash cropping. Marxist analysts were quick to suggest that this pattern of violence could itself be seen as a response to widening tensions caused by inequalities of social class and as forms of resistance to state control arising out of such tensions. Whether land shortage was at the root of violence became moot, echoing earlier debates about precolonial structures and patterns of warfare. It became evident over time that the expanding conventions relating to revenge for killings and the imperative to pay compensation in order to avert revenge constituted an arena *in themselves* that conduced toward the continual buildups in intergroup hostilities (Strathern and Stewart 1998b). Add to this the introduction of guns, the growth of criminal gangs, and the alleged alliances between politicians and men of violence, and it becomes clear that there is an overdetermining set of factors predisposing communities to insecurity and danger. While everyone continues to grow coffee and to be involved deeply in the cash economy, all are equally deeply involved in the quest for personal and collective security. Indeed, this tension between profit seeking and security seeking lies at the heart of people's daily struggles to chart a pathway for themselves.

What, then, of the roles of democracy and the state in this capitalist-contradiction-induced situation? Political elections have become an immensely important part of life in the Highlands, evidenced by the large numbers of candidates for office, high levels of material inducements offered to voters, and considerable outbreaks of postelection violence and recriminations, all patterns seen clearly in the national elections of June 1997 (see also Saffu 1996). The elections brought great disillusionment to those who paid large amounts of money, which they could not realistically afford, in support of candidates who lost. Thus the patronage sought at such a high price could not be obtained. Democracy, in effect, has been put to the service of expensively sponsoring a winner in elections, on the expectation that the winner will repay his supporters with patronage for jobs, development funds, and infrastructural improvements. The large sums of money placed in the hands of MPs for "sectoral development" amounting to three hundred thousand kina per annum per MP have directly caused this situation, and these funds in turn have been used to shore up the support of electors for the MP and of the MP for whichever temporary coalition is in power as government. The individual MP has become a "super big-man," creating a level of politics that has eclipsed or swallowed other modes of local political activity. But since there are always losers, there is a further built-in tendency for factionalism and hostility. This form of democracy does not, then, conduce to local stability.

Instead, it increases local tensions. The patronage involved is also intensely *local* and does not form an easy basis for the development of national-level identities and loyalties (see also Ketan 1998).

The relative weakness of the development of senses of nationality goes along with a predominant set of dispositions toward the state bureaucracy (see Otto and Thomas 1997). In colonial times people looked first to the colonial patrol officers, and later to their Local Government Councils, to produce benefits for them. The MP has taken on this mantle, and the more so in the years 1995–97 following the abolition of the level of provincial government as an intermediary between the people and the national Parliament and bureaucracy. There has been a corresponding overestimation of the importance of the MP's role, witnessed in the large amounts of money spent by and on supporters to secure the election of candidates, and an underestimation of the role of the public service or bureaucracy, which is seen as plagued by inefficiency, unresponsiveness, and "jobs for the boys." The state in this context is seen as either ineffective or as inimical to local interests, even though in a broader sense state-based influence is predominant to some degree in people's lives, through education, health, banking, and other services, some of which they have come to take for granted. (Other services which the people might rightly expect to be provided such as road maintenance and security are sorely lacking, as are supplies for health centers. Curiously, in these contexts people have come to look to mining companies for provision of these services and even in some instances to individual outsiders such as research workers in their area, who do not have resources to meet such demands.)

The state in its legislative and judicial capacity has also obviously affected people strongly. Beginning in the 1970s, there has been a series of legislative measures designed to bring into alignment state interests and the interests and concerns of individuals and groups at the local level. The measures that have most affected local communities have to do with social control and with land issues. Village courts were set up to provide communities with their own means of redressing certain wrongs involving custom, for example. Legislation to declare "fight areas" on an emergency basis and to provide the means of appointment of "trouble committees" to reach peaceful settlement of fights has strongly influenced the form of compensation payments for killings between groups. Also, village courts hear and bring to resolution some of the common disputes such as wife-beating cases, insults, failure to meet debts, and physical assaults in general. These have become much more unilateral, stipulated forms of transaction and much less a mechanism for developing reciprocal exchanges between the groups involved. Finally here, legislation to promote business groups and land groups has created entities that are neotraditional in appearance but in practice function much more as hybrid accessories to the interests of state and capitalist agencies and of powerful individuals within the neotraditional structures themselves. Ben Finney's 1960s coffee entrepreneurs are beginning to reappear as oil and gas barons with the discovery of such mineral deposits in the Southern Highlands and the payment of royalties to landowning groups. Groups that were founded in the 1970s in the Western Highlands Province with a mixed set of declared aims, including the promotion of traditional cultural forms, have all turned essentially into engines for local business (mostly plantation) development and also into power bases for local politicians. In the 1997 elections in the Dei Council constituency of Mount Hagen the winning candidate was rumored to have manipulated the voters' rolls so as to include a very large set of voters in his own area, which happens to include the biggest coffee plantation in the province and employs an extensive cadre of laborers. The MP himself, however, declared himself a born-again Christian and claimed that his support derived from his standing as a churchman of the Assemblies of God.

This example draws attention to a factor that has emerged increasingly in Hagen in the last decade: the importance of Christianity not just in terms of conversion and the abandonment of customary forms of religion but as a pervasive influence in community life generally, including politics. The supposedly secular Highlanders have suddenly been recognized as deeply bound into evangelical and other forms of Christian activities (Stewart and Strathern [eds.] 1997; Stewart and Strathern 1998a). Understanding the meaning of this apparent transformation requires us to abandon the earlier simplified stereotypes of secularism and to recall strictures made on these, for example, evidence that big-manship was also linked to ritual ideas and practices and that the Red Box money cult in 1968–71 in Hagen belied coastal/Highlands contrasts then prevalent in the literature (A. J. Strathern 1979–80; Stewart and Strathern 2000). Hageners have not become religious overnight. They have adapted themes that were of concern to them in the past and recast them dramatically in Christian idioms. At the same time, these idioms and the ideology that informs them genuinely subvert and replace aspects of their old wealth-oriented ideology in society, setting up complex contradictions that are now reflected in "world's end" forms of rhetoric.

Along with this subversion regarding wealth, there are powerful changes affecting gender relations. While men are taking on new tasks and finding altered ways to define their personhood, women who are prominent in the new churches are also discovering new arenas for their creativity and productivity. Women are also significant as workers and sellers in the cash economy, both of coffee and of vegetable crops. They attempt to modify polygynous practices and bring their husbands into the church and its teachings. Women as mothers who

▸▸▸ *Dedication of a partly completed permanent materials Lutheran church. A pastor reads out a prayer service before the seated community (Dei Council, 1970s).*

produce daughters that become brides are gaining increasing recognition in contexts of bridewealth. The production of the person through kinship is itself becoming commodified along with the recognition of women's roles in bearing and nurturing children. We argue that these changes are also indirect reflections of the triad of forces we identified at the outset.

In what follows we exemplify and follow up these generalizations with more specific local evidence.

LAND AND LAND GROUPS: DILEMMAS AND IRONIES AT KUK

The Wahgi Valley, where the bulk of the Kawelka people with whom we have been working live, is an area of very dense human habitation, in which large sections of clan land have been alienated since the 1950s for plantation development (coffee, tea) and considerable portions also have been taken for private leasehold development and for resettlement schemes used by immigrants from high-altitude areas that are periodically subject to famine through drought and frost (as was the case during 1997 with the effects of El Niño, Stewart and Strathern 1998b). The Kawelka returned to their present location, known as Kuk, from the early 1950s following pacification, after being driven out in fighting with the Mokei people around 1914. In the mid-1960s the administration purchased rights over large swampy areas adjoining the resettled Kawelka lands and turned them into an agricultural research station and a tea plantation operated by Manton Brothers, an Australian business family. The station's function was to experiment with types of tea for plantation use. The land purchased for the station had been swampy. It was now drained and sectioned neatly, solid roads were made between the sections allowing vehicle access, and casuarina trees and ornamentals were planted alongside the roads. Much later, in the 1990s and under the control of the provincial government, the station fell into disuse and disrepair. Its houses were colonized by local public servants and others, rents were not collected, it became a target for criminal activity, and a market with beer drinking and darts playing took over the entranceway into the old station precincts (Strathern and Stewart 1998d).

The Provincial Department of Primary Industry then seems to have effectively ceased to administer the station, and the provincial government itself was abolished by the national Parliament in 1995, after which no one appeared to take responsibility for the area. The neat interconnecting roads became choked with Phragmites canes, overgrown tea bushes were cut for fencing stakes, clogged ditches overflowed and caused swampy patches, and logging trucks entered these places to cut and haul away casuarina trees sold to them by individual Kawelka, in the process churning the roads into rutted quagmires. The Kawelka began re-colonizing this scene of decayed colonial enterprise, first by tethering their pigs in its fertile cane-covered recesses where they could not easily be identified, and later, from 1995 onward, by more openly claiming specific portions in which to plant both subsistence crops and coffee. In effect, the whole station has been remapped into sections that are notionally associated with segments of the Kawelka, facilitated by the station's own division into original drained blocks.

This informal process of reappropriation appears to have taken place without overt conflict to date. It has been prompted, however, by existing and emergent disputes over land uses in the areas retained by the Kawelka after the original "sale" of the station land. These disputes center on land used for coffee and thus removed on a long-term basis from the flexibilities of the cultivation cycle. The availability of former station land in this way has undoubtedly eased, although it has not entirely obviated, these intraclan disputes, which usually focus on those who are perceived as economically more successful than others. Such persons, in turn, have been prominent in the recolonization drive, sometimes actually moving their dwelling houses into the station area, sometimes building outhouses from which they can guard their growing coffee trees, since theft of coffee beans by nocturnal marauders has become a common hazard.

What is interesting here, and highly problematic, is the question of what tenurial rights will be developed over the station area. Legally, the government (i.e., the state) has never officially ceded its rights back to the Kawelka. Equally, to date, it has not contested the recolonization (see discussions in Strathern and Stewart [eds.] 1998). The Kawelka, for their part, have acted in such a way as to indicate that they never ceded their underlying rights to the station land in spite of the 1964 "sale" and that they do not need to approach the government for permission to make gardens there. The area was previously swamp, however, and was drained to create the station, so it is reclaimed land. Moreover, the informal processes of division that have taken place do not have any support in sanctions between the groups or between individuals. Once a pattern is set, it will become subject to inheritance and thus will fall under customary modes of division. For now, all practical arrangements are a matter of improvisation, but since in every case the subsistence crops are interspersed with coffee seedlings it is obvious that each gardener intends to secure claims for the future. Planting coffee is equivalent to "enclosing" a specific area for the foreseeable future and also "foreclosing" it against easy resumption by the government or by any business concerns, since heavy compensation would be demanded. These newly claimed areas thus are coming, through the planting of coffee, to resemble forms of freehold tenure such as R. Gerard Ward and Elizabeth Kingdon have remarked on for parts of Africa such as Malawi and Kenya (Ward and Kingdon 1995:30). Ward and Kingdon also point out a danger here for such hybrid forms of practice as they separate themselves from either a "customary" or a "legal-bureaucratic" form: that courts will not recognize the claims because they have no secure basis (ibid.)—including in "custom" itself. At another level, of course, the Kawelka are reclaiming both custom and history for themselves because they are asserting an overall right of "domain" over both their existing and the recolonized parts of the Kuk area, appealing here to the validating status of a stone landmark that stands in their territory (Strathern and Stewart 1998d). This conjunction of "domain" right and individual parceling of land in blocklike sections shows a patchwork combination of "premodern" and "modern" elements put together in a decidedly "postmodern" fashion. The state-formed landscape of the station influences the imaginative practices of the Kawelka, even as they retransform that landscape back into the shape of indigenous fields, enclosing regular areas in ways they do not follow outside of the station.

We may look at this case history briefly again from the viewpoint of our general theme. One of the purposes of the colonial Agriculture Department was to introduce people to the idea of individual cash cropping in coffee as well as to stimulate the corporate production of these crops, often by expatriate companies. In other words, a state organ promoted capitalism and its corollary, peasantry. The same colonial administration was pushed by the United Nations into introducing democratic and independent political institutions. This process gave people the idea of taking back power for themselves. Over time, this has led them to override a colonially established rule regarding land use and to take their own land into their hands again. Their political sense of themselves has led them to transcend the bureaucratic categories of the state. Representatives of the bureaucracy now have to consider what to do.

Analytically and theoretically, what we have here, as we have seen, is a hybrid situation. The station land was "bought" from the Kawelka, for tiny sums of money (rolls of shillings divided among subclans). The Kawelka have now reclaimed their land simply by moving onto it. If national-level interests were to suggest a reimposed alienation, they would be faced with demands for a very high price as unwilling inheritors of a colonial debt legacy. Capitalism's role in all this is clear, as is democracy's. The "state" and the "nation" are caught in postcolonial anomaly here, while local assertiveness has become very strong.

BRIDEWEALTH

The connections drawn so far between capitalism, democracy, the state, and land can be further elaborated through an examination of bridewealth fluctuations.

Bridewealth payments are intimately associated with issues of fecundity which extend beyond the fundamentally important reproductive capacities of a woman, encompassing her ability to use the land allotted to her by her affines to produce pigs and vegetables in addition to cash crops such as coffee. The dynamics of bridewealth payments are driven by various forces. We were in Hagen in August 1997 when reports of greatly inflated bridewealth demands were retailed to us as a major source of grievance. We were told that five to six thousand kina was a typical current rate, plus several pigs (each worth approximately five hundred to a thousand kina depending on the size) and nowadays various other items such as bundles of sugarcane, pandanus fruits, and bananas. (All of these amounts are greatly reduced if the prospective bride is marrying for the second time.) These items, including the money, must be collected by the parents of the prospective groom through requesting payments from kin and exchange partners who have some ties within the family's network of relations. Failure to contribute to the collection alienates one's relatives and exchange partners, making it difficult to approach them in future when a reciprocal contribution is needed either for a brideprice or for a compensation payment for a killing. With the decline of the moka system of exchange, bridewealth payments appear to have been placed in a new ideological framework which has been fashioned by the religious changes and alterations in gendered categories of prestige.

Moka exchange had been an integrating capstone for much of the social structure in previous years. It allowed the big-man system to exist, accompanied by polygyny, and it partially defined female personhood through the productive capacities of women to rear the pigs for moka exchange. With the decline of moka and of the prevalence of big-men, the underpinning of polygyny has been greatly eroded. The labor of many women for moka exchanges is no longer required to the same degree as in the past and the economy of keeping the separate households demanded by each wife can be ruinous nowadays.

The inflation in bridewealth may be correlated with a drive to keep marriages monogynous through a sheer lack of funds available to pay for a second wife and maintain the expenses of the two households required, but other factors are also involved. For example, the mother of the bride is given a much greater amount in the bridewealth payment than in the past. This may reflect a greater emphasis on the nurturing work of the mother in raising the daughter and a heightened awareness of the kina value of the mother's work. A parallel situation exists in the Duna area of the Southern Highlands Province of Papua New Guinea, where the payment to the bride's mother has increased greatly since 1991. Such increases further suggest that the notion of the value of the bride or of the mother has perhaps begun to be calculated in a new way; the proper size is determined by the need to honor the bride's mother, or else she would tell her daughter to walk away from the marriage negotiation.

Several male informants from Hagen provided another explanation. They explained that the increases were driven by competition for prestige among grooms who wanted to be able to boast about the amount that their family was able to raise and pay out to the bride's family, thereby demonstrating the abilities of the groom's family to convince kin and exchange partners to contribute large amounts to the payment and at the same time making a statement about the relative worth of the bride obtained. This competition carries different "financial" implications from those of the moka exchange, which was a highly regulated system of reciprocity that in principle guaranteed returns to people with an increment beyond their last "investment." The decline of the moka appears to have led to a shift into brideprice as an arena of competition for prestige, but individual brideprice payments do not lead to delayed returns "with interest" as happened in the moka. It is true that the circulation of high payments does help each group to arrange marriages and that the recipients of each payment are expected to raise a proportional fraction of it to give back as a return prestation. Nevertheless, the complicated dynamics and contingencies of historical conjunctures can mean that a given group or area is hard-pressed to meet its obligations or achieve its ambitions. Long-term inflationary trends in brideprice as well as other modalities of transactions could also lead to a situation in which the rates demanded and expected could not be sustained by the overall circulation of money through production and wage income, thus causing a reversion to lower rates. The upward trends have been in place ever since at least the 1960s. In the 1960s and 1970s colonial patrol officers complained that high brideprices were a burden that took money away from other uses. In the Dei Council area the Local Government Council repeatedly made rules limiting the size of brideprice payments, although these rules met with only limited success.

Several factors have combined to make the situation of the Kawelka difficult in the late 1990s. They are short of land and, as we have seen, have embarked on a new project of recolonizing former government land in a bid to increase their coffee production. In September 1995 they raised a large compensation payment of 26,000 kina and 150 pigs to the Mokei people for the murder of a young man in a barroom brawl. They had more recently spent large amounts of money and numbers of pigs in supporting the unsuccessful election campaign of William Pik for the national Parliament. Finally, their existing coffee crop was late because of the drought conditions and they were running short of subsistence foods as well, so that they needed money to buy food in trade stores. Under these circumstances, it was remarkable that some Kawelka families nevertheless instituted high-pressure campaigns to raise large brideprices and in fact instigated a competition for contributions in their fairly involute and overlapping networks of support. The effort produced a wave of grumbling and recrimination, especially among younger men, indicating that these men perhaps feel less bound in with projects of family and clan prestige than in the past (something other leaders themselves remark on): a sign of changing notions of personhood and aspirations toward running their own businesses or at least spending their own money.

This complex of historically induced factors shows the same bunching together of long- and short-term political and economic factors that we have found in relation to land. Cash cropping produces its own pressures on people and raises the monetary element in prestations, but because these depend ultimately on production, instabilities of demand and ambition arise. The result is a fluctuating process of negotiated rates for killings, brideprices, and political support that can cause severe difficulties for a given group. The whole process continues in the "customary" realm outside of the purview of the state, yet it is deeply influenced by the state's own actions over time (i.e., the introduction of cash cropping in colonial times and the postcolonial development of patronage-driven politics). In addition, we speculatively suggest, the hurried effort to arrange brideprices in 1997 may be a part of the wider struggle to control the behavior of younger people and to set the social structure "in order" before the expected "end times" (although this was not proffered to us as an explanation by any of the people themselves).

Another factor that may be driving brideprice payments upward is appreciation of the new roles that women have created for themselves through their enrollment in the local churches. Women are extremely active in holding fellowship meetings and prayer services in attempts to protect the land and its inhabitants from the Satanic forces that they believe are so powerful in bringing "negative" influences into their community. These church activities may have altered the relative prestige that women hold in the society, thereby partially explaining the increased amount of money paid in bridewealth. (This argument depends on the idea that such notions of value are embedded in Melpa bridewealth practices. Of course, other factors, such as the overall increased demands for money in the society as expressed between kinsfolk and affines, are also at work.)

RELIGIOUS CHANGE

Dramatic alterations in life patterns and expectations have arisen in Hagen since the 1960s. A means of coping with such changes that has reached powerful proportions is the belief that the world's end is close at hand (Stewart and Strathern 1998a, 1998c; Strathern and Stewart 1997c). This requires the day-to-day vigilance of those who consider themselves to be listed in God's Book and thus bound for salvation before the destruction of the earth. Each night when we were in the field in August 1997 we could hear the fellowship/prayer services being conducted in an effort to drive away "evil" from the community. On the last night in our field house this escalated to a new level when the house was circled by those praying and speaking in tongues. We were told that these efforts were meant to protect us and our house from thieves and rascals (gang members) who seek money and are jealous of what other people possess. This rhetoric of jealousy came into the area as the nearby town of Mount Hagen became more and more stocked with various goods that were not available in the past and which one could easily obtain if one had money. The actual term used for jealousy, as we have noted previously, here is *jelas,* a Tok Pisin term that functions differently from the original Melpa term *wölik,* which was applied specifically to competition between individual persons for scarce resources. With jelas the sense is rather that of generalized envy and anomie in relation to consumer goods available on the impersonal market. Money is in short supply because great quantities go out in brideprice payments, compensation payments, and for political bribes in attempts to get local politicians elected. Money is seen to be—if not the root of all evil—the force that stimulates greed and desire in people driving them into "wrong" actions. One of our main female informants, Mande, told us that a power exists in the ground itself

‣‣‣ *Young people lead a Christian Revival Crusade church service at Kuk (1997, Dei Council).*

called "ground place power" (GPP) (*Möi Kona Paua* in Melpa). This power is charged by the plethora of material goods available, which are difficult if not impossible for most Papua New Guineans to obtain. GPP is stated by some Hageners to be one of the main signs or markers of the return of Jesus that they say will occur first before the end times. Before the return of Jesus, the Antichrist is thought to be making an appearance on earth at which time he will mark all of his followers with a code number functioning much like a grocery store bar code. This number is often said to be 666, and the possession of it will allow its holders to purchase goods in stores. Joel Robbins has described the same idea among the Urapmin of Sandaun Province, Papua New Guinea (Robbins 1997, 1998). Those who are Christians and refuse to take this number will be unable to purchase items because their money will be useless. This fear of finding oneself in a situation where money in hand is insufficient accompanied by the perception that those who do have sufficient money have obtained it by polluting, Satanically influenced means (theft, prostitution, and killing) finds its culmination in the end times scenario (Stewart and Strathern 1998a).

One might equate GPP with a plague that is seen to be spread widely, replacing what we have termed "ground fertility power" (GFP). GFP was generated through the creative interactions of people with the soil such as through gardening, rearing pigs, and conducting fertility rituals (Strathern and Stewart 1997a, 1998a; Stewart 1998). GFP was a resource that was renewable through ritual practices such as the Amb Kor (Female Spirit) cult ritual in which men and women worked together to ensure that the power derived from the Amb Kor would penetrate the soil and bring health and fertility. The Amb Kor ritual is no longer observed. Unlike the Red-Box money cult (A. J. Strathern 1979–80, Stewart and Strathern 2000), which was said to have been brought by Satan and came to nothing, we were told that the power brought by the Amb Kor was very real and not that of Satan. Her power is seen to be simply no longer a viable option to be tapped into now that God has been introduced to the Hageners along with the notion that the world as they know it is ending or, as the Duna say, "the ground is finishing."

These notions of the world ending and the ground finishing have taken on a more immediate sense of reality with the devastating effects of the recent drought and famine in the Highlands. This loss of fertility is correlated with an increase in witchcraft accusations. These witches (*kum koimb*) operate in a terrifying way. They eat the inner parts of a person and kill him or her, or instead they turn their victims into cannibals who then seek out humans to eat. The core idea in these notions of witchcraft among the Hageners as well as among the Duna people is that of *greed* or the desire or capacity for consumption. As the millennium approaches and the "faithful" are watching for signs of the world's end in the year 2000–2001, the increase in kum activity is taken to be a positive indicator of the end. This cannibal witchcraft activity might well be perceived as signaling the end because it is the antithesis of various aspects of fertility rituals which aim to create life (Stewart and Strathern 1997b).

The notion that greed and excessive consumption are inappropriate forms of behavior for humans has a long tradition in Hagen and Duna society but is now further fueled by notions of GPP in which material goods are causing increased greediness and a desire to consume which in some instances can be satisfied only by the acquisition of money through criminal activities (Stewart and Strathern 1998a).

Witches are also often seen as operating in groups much as gangs do, and their leader is said to be a queen of the witches who lives in the neighboring ethnic area of Simbu, in the province east of the Western Highlands on the Highlands Highway. A not very deeply veiled animosity toward the Simbu is thus expressed in this image. In fact, with the collapsing of various boundaries and spaces between different ethnic groups in Papua New Guinea because of the greater ease with which people can move about, new arenas of multiethnic conflicts continue to arise.

▸▸▸ *A pastor, standing on a dais, makes prayers before wealth items assembled for a large compensation payment to people of Enga Province after a co-wife killing. The Papua New Guinea flag stands by the dais and the loudspeaker equipment, along with a horse that was included in the payment (Wurup, 1998).*

A Runaway World? Multiethnicity, the Collapse of Order, and "Ground Place Power"

The local spaces and places inhabited by the Kawelka have for long been invaded by the "outside" in ways that immediately became intimate, local, and "inside" in terms of the people's experience. Early patrol officers forced people to dig large holes that became temporary prison pens for persons arrested; they required rest houses to be built; they instituted road building, schools, and aid posts, causing entirely new centers of activity to emerge that brought people together in new ways. Markets sprang up around such facilities and later at Local Government Council headquarters. People went away on labor migration to the north and south coasts and to other parts of the Highlands. They brought back wages in shells and sometimes were accompanied by spouses from places to the west and east such as Enga and the Eastern Highlands. Clearly, the processes of multiethnicity began long ago, from the 1940s onward.

Nevertheless, these processes have accelerated and magnified in recent years. There is also a greater level of awareness that it is precisely these widened

contexts of interaction and their unpredictable and uncontrollable consequences that are producing ramified problems for the maintenance of locally co-
herent forms of activity. In the past, Hageners maintained an embracing attitude
toward the outside world, seen as a source of "good things," shells and later
money, as well as government services, and a plethora of Christian missions and
churches. Much of this had to do with the channeling of ambitions and productive action into moka and fertility cults, the enhancement of prestige and of the
earth's fertility on which all prestige depends. This channeling effect, however,
has now ceased. There is no unifying ideology. People are much less inclined to
decorate and dance, especially since the church condemns such displays of self-
expression as ungodly. This means that intergroup ties based on moka alliance
have foundered and have been replaced by violence on the one hand and political
patronage on the other, reverting in some sense to a pre-moka time when warfare
brought prestige but was also a source of danger and insecurity in people's lives.
The net result is a perception of the collapse or potential collapse of the order of
categories in the world.

Images of mixing and confusion that go with perceptions of hybridization are indications of such a sense of transgression and collapse. The image
projected in one interview of male angels that came from Heaven and lay with
human women who believed them to be "real men" (a theme derived from folktales) precisely reveals the underlying concerns here. Attempts are made both to
profit from and to straighten out the confusion of categories in an effort to grasp
an understanding of what is "concealed" versus what is "revealed" about a person. We witnessed and took part in an occasion in which one of our friends and
sponsors, R., organized a novel kind of affiliation payment for a grandson of his
(the product of a relationship between his son H. and a woman whose mother
was from Simbu and father was from Kerema), contracted in Port Moresby,
the capital city far from Hagen where H. works at the Public Service Training Institute as a manager of physical plant. In addition to this relationship in which
no brideprice was paid or any civil or church marriage conducted, H. also had
a sexual relationship with a woman from Mendi in the Southern Highlands
Province with whom he worked and who was *also* attempting to establish more
permanent ties with R.'s locality, thereby strengthening her ties to H. and his
family. The Mendi "wife," who also had not received a brideprice payment or
been united to H. in a civil or church ceremony, was jealous of the Simbu/
Kerema "wife" and was reported to have told some of her younger male relatives,
referred to as "rascals," to enter H.'s apartment in Port Moresby and "damage" it.
She reportedly requested this when she learned that the Simbu/Kerema "wife"
was traveling to Hagen. In the midst of these confusions, R. pursued his own

project of affiliating the boy to his group, the Kawelka, since he is short of patri-lineal male descendants. He attempted to convert the multiplicity of the situ-ation back into a unity by means of a wealth transaction. The speeches were made partly in Tok Pisin, the Simbu women represented themselves at the event without male kin, pork was given to them even though they belonged to the Sev-enth Day Adventist church (which condemns the eating of pork), and the main cooking of freezer meat was done in the style of Simbu and also Tambul south of Hagen because some of those helping on the occasion were immigrants from the Tambul area who live with the Kawelka. Multiplicity thus asserted itself at the heart of an attempt to obviate it (Strathern and Stewart n.d.c.).

The Kawelka themselves are an island in an area that otherwise belongs to a different council area and electoral constituency. They are immigrants, albeit back to their ancestral area. They themselves have taken in further immigrants. Their life consists equally of the mixing of categories and the attempt to unmix these and reestablish boundaries. Putting the name as a "contract" in the "gov-ernment book" as Kawelka is an act of unmixing that shows the attempt to deal with the hybridization of experience we have identified here. It mirrors the idea of having one's name changed as a result of baptism to a biblical name and this new name being written into the "Book of Life" controlled by God at the en-trance into Heaven (Stewart and Strathern 1998a).

Into this arena of ambivalence the concept of ground place power, articu-lated by Mande, enters poignantly. Everything has its good and bad side. The earth, seen before as good and fertile, now becomes in a new image the site of alien power. This is because of a semantic shift in which "earthly" is opposed to "heavenly." Similarly, indigenous magic is described as *möi kongon*, "earth work." The term *möi* here connotes both an indigenous, pagan sphere of action and an arena implicitly considered to be inferior. Both senses of the term are new and emerged in the 1970s when Christian rhetoric began to penetrate more deeply into people's lives. The bifurcation of epistemology that goes with such notions is an attempt to reorder the world and find a consistent ideology in it. But this re-ordering is also threatened by the prospect of world's end, when "the earth and the sky together will end." Meanwhile, multiethnicity is one aspect of the fact that a world, indeed several worlds, has already ended and a series of confusing worlds is in process of coming into being.

This inchoate process of gestation brings sharply into focus the general problem of boundaries, both conceptual and social, in contemporary social life. Indigenous social practices in Hagen, as in many other parts of New Guinea, are marked by a degree of flexibility that tends to work against the rigid application of rules, for example rules concerning group affiliation or marital eligibility. The flexible extension or modification of rules has been one of the mechanisms whereby Hageners have accommodated change into their lives and have tried to incorporate the outside world into their own, as when they easily introduced money into their moka exchanges and rapidly adopted various forms of Christianity. In this regard, they conformed to the picture of a people who were unconcerned with boundaries and more interested in extending their networks of relationship and influence. Yet this picture is also inadequate. In more recent times (the 1990s as opposed to the 1970s and 1980s) they have become sharply aware that they cannot contain the outside by simply taking it into their own institutions, and they cannot extend their networks without placing themselves greatly in dependency on forces well beyond their control. It is in this more recent and somber context that they have developed their own dichotomous "ethnodependency" theory in which they contrast a world of gifts with a world of commodities; rather than blurring the boundaries between these categories, as they have done in the past, they have now reached a point of structural nostalgia in which they develop their own reification of past and present as a tool for reforming history. As a part of this drive much of their struggle nowadays has to do with reasserting the local against the global, even if this is done in the borrowed garb of the global itself. The whole process and its intractable dilemmas is poignantly exemplified by the encircling of our field house. The young apprentice pastor who led the procession called out in English, "Let justice be done in the world! I rebuke you, Satan, and all your works! Praise be to the Lord Jesus! May he protect this area and all who live in it!" Using phrases that resonated with the rhetoric of Christian revivalist preachers from many times and places, he sought to hold at bay the outside and all its evil, summed up as Satan, and to make a boundary around the area of his immediate family and friends against the patent facts of its permeability and vulnerability. While the idiom and the concerns are new and urgent, the interplay between making boundaries and crossing boundaries is one that has a long history in Kawelka life, with its alternate moments of flux and stability. Christian rhetoric provides a novel tool for dealing with this dialectic on a scale far beyond that of the precolonial past while recapitulating the theme of importing power from the outside in order to deal with problems that arise from inside, as when spirit cults were brought in to cope with epidemics of sickness and infertility.

Conclusions

One of our basic standpoints in this study has been that to understand processes of change and expressions of experience in Hagen in 1990s, we need to break free from the remnants of the "Highlanders as secular pragmatists" picture that informed some of the earlier literature. The ethnography of "relational persons" that succeeded the "secular, individualist" ethnography of the 1960s itself, however, needs to be supplemented in two ways. First, Christianity has joined persons together into a new nexus of relationality and individuality. There is therefore a new religious dimension of life and a new propensity to seek Christian-based ritual solutions to the dilemmas of exchange versus consumption in social practice. Second, there is a drive toward individual consumption, which has to be counterbalanced in ritual terms by actions such as fasting. This drive is also not entirely new, since it had its place and its negative image before in the notion of kum (greed). Fasting is an attempt to make the body free from its own permeability through consumption, a way of coping with the permeable body that kum can enter.

The whole elaborate apparatus of symbolism that has built up around world's end can thus be seen as an attempt both to solve the problems of category collapse and to resolve the old tension between exchange and consumption, the difficulty here lying in the transformations of the old moka exchange economy. The "ropes of moka" no longer lie tangled on people's skins, and the old rope itself is unraveled (A. J. Strathern 1971:229). Yet the concerns and images of the exchange economy still haunt Hageners, and they seek to recreate a world of exchange in commodified versions of bridewealth and compensation that cannot quite serve this purpose. In classic vein they seek to overcome these contradictions by ritual practices such as fasting and most recently in communalistic projects of building new churches (Stewart and Strathern n.d.a., n.d.b.). There is also the "double take" that makes for a continuing puzzlement in their lives. Ritual and religion are the "answer" to the question of how to live in a commodified world; yet they also contain a message of the end of that world and its transcendence. In terms of their own symbols and paradigms, this in turn would mean a reversion to a world of morality and exchange, yet that is not how they portray Heaven. Indeed, Heaven itself remains an enigma, perhaps simply because if it is neither a world of exchange nor a world of commodity, it is in principle unthinkable.

TWELVE
▶ ▶ ▶ ▶ ▶

Resolutions and
Revolutions

As explained at the outset, we have defined this book as an historical ethnography but not as a chronological account of history. Moreover, while we have been concerned to point out major dimensions of historical changes, our purpose has not been to explain every aspect of history or to tackle directly all the major analytical issues that emerge from looking at the broad transformations of Hagen society over time. Rather, our discussions have had two purposes. First, we have explored certain themes that have developed in the field of synchronic ethnography since the 1960s, particularly the ideas of transaction and social personhood, and have set these into a diachronic framework, for example, by considering transformations in leadership through political change, in dispute settlement, exchange practices, conflict, and compensation. Second, in looking at these themes in this dual synchronic-diachronic way, we have stressed wherever possible the significance of rhetorical communication (hence "arrow talk") and of crosscutting topics such as gender relations and gender-based symbolism and the influence of Christianity throughout all the domains of contemporary life.

In terms of transaction and social personhood our main aim has been to suggest the advantages of our concept of the relational-individual, which enables us to take into account the two poles of behavior corresponding to this term, relationality and individuality. Further, we have argued that these two poles are in evidence in sequences of events and behavioral patterns and may be either harmoniously co-present or in disjunction with each other. The two poles are not to be seen as equated with the normative versus the deviant. Matters are more complicated. Both poles may encompass normative behavior, and action may in some instances instantiate both simultaneously, as when a big-man, acting in the "fractal" manner suggested by Roy Wagner (Wagner 1991; cf. Brown 1995:256), stands both for himself and for a group. We are interested, however, in cases where there is disjunction and we can see individual dimensions underlying re-

190

lational aspects of action and vice versa. Where there is a disjunction between these elements, people themselves may point this out, and are in fact quick to do so, looking for underlying aims in surface rhetorical statements in accordance with the practices of "veiled speech." Seen in structural terms, a disjunction between relational and individual components of action may also show a form of structural contradiction, as pointed out by Raymond Kelly (Kelly 1977:288) in his discussion of Etoro social structure. Contradictions of this kind may underlie the operation of competing principles in social life, leading among other things to an apparent discrepancy between norms and practice.

In his own study Kelly identified a contradiction between siblingship and descent, which in the arena of leviratic remarriage led to the rule that a widow should be remarried in her dead husband's lineage but not to his immediate brother being broken in 65 percent of a set of cases, the widow often marrying an immediate brother in this way (Kelly 1977:285). Kelly rules out demographic factors as the explanation of this. (We might add that the preferential choices and agency of the widows should also be taken into account here.) The contradiction has consequences because the empirical pattern conduces to lineage fission.

In this study we have been interested in the question of contradictions of this sort mostly in contexts of historical change and also in terms of people's own forms of historical consciousness. The tension we see as existing between relational and individual aspects of personhood has led to a gradually shifting distribution of emphases on these aspects, one which is commented on by the actors in various ways, and with some ironic implications.

Leaders, for example, who claimed both preeminence and individual prowess through their standing in moka exchanges, decry, as Ongka does, the individualism of today, in which people no longer care about each other. Following Kelly (1993:477) we can analyze this as follows. Big-men claimed inequality for themselves, but in a relational fashion, since moka activities contributed to group affairs and prestige, and they recognized an "egalitarian" context in which they could be challenged by others in the name of communal interests. Today, younger people are being accused of autonomous tendencies, seen as nonrelational and highly individualistic, in which they do not claim status through a communal activity but instead appropriate the right to do as they please, thereby converting the "egalitarian" society into one seen as anarchic. While, then, we need not see relationality and individuality as principles necessarily in contradiction, we can certainly see them as potentially in conflict and we can look at emergent social practices as attempts to control such conflict. The example of confession discussed in chapter 10 is a case in point. In general, older leaders in Hagen deplore the forms of individuality younger people adopt (spending money in town rather than helping with community enterprise at home, for instance), while arguing that their own forms of individuality practiced in the past (fighting prowess, preeminence in moka) were harmonious with relational ends, although this was not always so.

It is in the context of debates such as these that two aspects of change come strikingly to the fore: inter-generational tension and urgent reformations of morality. In 1999 we learned that older leaders were not only critical of younger men in their clan groups but were also apprehensive regarding possible physical attacks on themselves by youths inebriated from drinking illicit liquor or made insensible to ordinary forms of control through smoking marijuana. This conversion of disapproval into fear marked an endpoint in the loss of control over moral leadership or hegemony on the part of older people. The moka system provided a framework for such a control in the past, and younger leaders, such as pastors who advocate its wholesale adoption, clearly see Christianity as the replacement for the moka, while older men seek to inject communal patterns of effort and exchange into the Christian project itself by organizing the building of churches, for example.

Morality, in turn, has been based on such social values encapsulated in notions of shame, anger, pity, and sickness, all intertwined together, as we have discussed in chapter 10. Shame may be said to be central to this nexus of ideas and embodied practices, and it is exactly the lack of shame on the part of younger people that the older generation sees as the cause for alarm. Inebriated youths represent a great threat to an order based on a morality of shame and, correspondingly, of respect for others. Moreover, with their violence these youth are prepared to violate the rules of respect and compassion within their own clan group by physically stealing from and injuring their own kin, not just enemies or strangers. Kenneth Read's topic of "morality and the concept of the person," which he broached early on in the history of the ethnography of the Highlands (Read 1955) has become urgently relevant in today's social flux, not just to the anthropologists but to the people themselves.

An additional aspect of generational tensions is the rise of rape within and outside of communities. The moral code that historically included rape of women affiliated with enemy groups during warfare does not encompass this new form of aggression. Indeed, the complex psychology of "worth" and "self-worth" is clearly involved here.

A potential sphere of contradiction commented on since at least the early 1970s is identified as that between "law" and custom, as discussed in chapter 7 and following chapters. This is an indigenous formulation. The Kawelka leader,

Ongka, for example, in a speech at a moka where the Kawelka received money from a Kombukla group, argued that "law" and "custom" can coexist:

> As to law and custom, [in following law] we make fences for cattle projects, we buy cars, we build trade stores, we dig fishponds, all to get money. Custom means making moka, sacrificing pigs, paying bridewealth. These two things are in competition, they are like a husband and wife, each looks after the other, the law is like the man, and custom is like the woman. Law is for money, if we give it up we will be "rubbish" in terms of money; if we give up custom we will be "rubbish" in terms of our own ways. When the older men die, law will take over, people will wear foreign clothes, eat foreign foods, stop making moka, live in strange houses. But till then we will hold onto both of them. I [for example] know the talk of sacrificing pigs, I know all the old ways. Pearl shells, nassa shells, cowries have all been killed by law, we've forgotten them. But pigs and money will remain, in competition with each other.

Ongka went on to praise the values of work and to admonish young women not to be swayed by fine exteriors: "Some men work, they spoil their skin, and wear poor clothes. You girls see this and want to marry men with fine clothes, men who wash often, but these men have no business and no work to support them, and if you ask such a man for money or food he will have none to give you and you'll be 'rubbish' [korpa] and 'angry' [popokl] and in a bad way."

Ongka's speech neatly encapsulates his state of consciousness at a midpoint in historical change during his lifetime. He sees introduced and indigenous practices as coexisting but anticipates the former will prevail in coming generations. He compares the two to a married couple, and in his imagery if "law" is like the husband this means it is the more powerful; yet he himself identifies with custom, since that is what he knows. He mediates the domains by telling women that they must look for husbands who work, as in the past, so that they will avoid being rubbish (the nuim/korpa axis). This axis (that of success versus failure) accommodates both poles of the relational/individual model and hence mediates contradictions between them, and it is understandable that Ongka, a traditional nuim, should wish to subsume all discourse within it. We see him here attempting his own "resolutions" of a potentially major set of contradictions between old and new, while also anticipating a later set of "revolutions" in which custom would be swallowed by law and their collaborative but competitive "spousal" relationship brought to an end.

In chapter 11 we pulled together several themes pointing in the same direction as Ongka's own analysis. The combination of cash cropping and parliamentary politics and the ramifying uses of money have brought the society close to a revolution in ways of behaving. The contradictions between law and custom in Ongka's sense have become all too evident. Money's power is recognized, and its new leverage in the old context of the "you owe me" discourse (the discourse of debt) has derailed the wagons of custom in many ways, setting up new contradictions and conflicts (e.g., those of social class) in doing so.

In 1971, however, Ongka did not explicitly mention Christianity in the speech quoted. But by 1989 he himself had become baptized into the Catholic church, marking the beginnings of his withdrawal from the customary contexts of ceremonial and political life. This underscores the growing importance of the various churches in the process of historical change in Hagen, as everywhere and at every level throughout the wider nation. Although "law," in terms of secular activities, may have "won" over custom and the churches are themselves a part of "law," it is also evident both to Hageners themselves and to us as outside observers that this gradual victory has caused many problems. The decline of moka and the proud forms of symbolic self-decoration and communal cooperation that went with it has itself produced huge difficulties in mediating intergroup conflicts as well as denying an avenue of social expression and individual attainment. Cash cropping and wealth disparities produce land shortages and widespread resentments, and contradictions between communal land tenure and individual cropping ambitions have become very clear. Social solidarity overall is threatened. In this atmosphere of flux, as we have argued, the fervent turn to the churches that has broken into history in the 1990s has to be seen as a complex search for the recreation of order, the construction of a new or at least revised version of the relational-individual through the marking of new baselines for community participation.

In certain ways the Hagen forms of ideology resemble those described by Michael Smith for the Kragur villagers of Kairiru island on the north coast of Papua New Guinea. Smith points out the Kragur view of the world is personalistic, and "the natural world response to human emotion and expression. . . . The strength of this orientation in Kragur helps account for the tendency to see material well-being and social relations as closely interdependent" (Smith 1994:45). Smith goes on to discuss the Kragur concept of the Good Way in which success in development projects is seen as dependent on maintaining cooperative relations in the village. He relates this idea partly to the exigencies of difficult times in which success is hard to achieve and moral cooperation holds people together, and he wonders if the concept might vanish if times were easier and individuals were able to increase their monetary earnings. He notes that the ideology is malleable and that successful young migrants may be eager both to avoid the financial demands of relatives and to speak warmly of how supportive their kin have been (Smith 1994:230–231). We see here clearly the same tension between old and new ways of constructing the person that we have identified for Hagen, with two differences. First, Hagen ideas are inflected more toward the individual pole through the operation of the nuim/korpa axis (a "hierarchy of virtue" in the terms of Kelly 1993); and second, the Hageners have become richer than the people of Kairiru because of their fertile land and success in cash cropping. We might expect, then, that they both praise the acquisition of wealth which makes people nuim and at the same time feel keenly the deleterious effects of the results of wealth in the rise of individualism, not just individuality (Cohen 1994:168–192), the growth of crime, and the dissensions springing from jealousy in the community. As well, their concern for the cosmos, the nexus between material and social well-being which is shown so clearly in their indigenous cult activities such as the Female Spirit cult (Strathern and Stewart 1999d), is threatened when the one is out of joint with the other, when there is no longer a recursive positive feedback between the two forms of well-being, when wealth no longer benefits the group, or when an indvidual's prestige no longer benefits others in clear ways. It is just this feeling that "the times are out of joint" which has led them increasingly into forms of charismatic Christianity that offer to recreate harmony, peace, and hope, while also wielding the threat of world's end and disaster to the wicked. And as the charismatic churches have come to the fore, the established Catholic and Lutheran churches have either been forced to follow in similar directions to those the newer churches establish or to lose adherents. Charismatic Christianity therefore becomes pervasive.

The churches as a whole, then, offer the following resolutions to the problems of contemporary life in Hagen: they decry the pursuit of individual wealth except insofar as those who possess it give part of it, and their own allegiance, to the church; they oppose polygyny and the old big-man complex that went with it; they forbid alcohol consumption, or excess consumption, pointing out that it leads to violence and crime; they attempt to convert "rascals" who disturb community life; they emphasize prayer, fasting, and healing rituals as both individual and communal acts and elevate the status of pastors and preachers to that of the old-style big-men; and they argue against corruption and bribery in politics. In social terms, taken together, these stipulations certainly amount to something like a revolution, at least on the surface. Basically, the churches have been instrumental in the erosion of "custom" as Ongka defines it (moka, sacrifices, and the like). The newer churches do this more aggressively, to the point that in 1998 it seemed to us unlikely that the Kawelka would ever again be seen in decorations holding a moka. The churches have therefore stood mostly on the side of "law." But "law" includes individual economic enterprise and all the patterns that go with it. So the churches must also oppose what they see as bad that operates beyond the law/custom divide.

Against new versions of individualism, church leaders instigate intensive communal life focused on church activities. They offer new individual roles as pastors or as witnesses to experience in church services. Women can actively participate in church business and achieve roles as dreamers or dream-interpreters. The churches further prescribe taboos to be followed, as in the old cults; they offer outlets in song composition and performance; they attempt to constrain morality and to set up new bases of family life through prayers; and they have, as we argued in chapter 10, turned certain indigenous concepts around, for example with regard to anger and confession, so as to give them a Christian cast. Many people have turned to the solutions they offer, accepting the revolutions in behavior they demand.

With regard to personhood, relationality is reconstructed strongly in the context of the Christian congregation, built partly but not exclusively on group lines. Individuality appears in the responsibility of the person for sin and for saving one's own soul by acts of repentance and prayer, as well as confession. Individual prestige can be achieved in the new communal contexts by the use of verbal arts and skills and by conspicuous contributions to church concerns (gifts to God, as pointed out by Gregory 1982). Gender relations are both affirmed and modified. Women are in every way a part of the churches and their rituals and can hold prominent places; but pastors still tend to be men, and these are orators, whose arrow talk now pierces the hearts of people and makes them repent, mend their ways, and give money to the church.

In 1998 we observed a further twist on all these shifts. Many people declared that on the whole (pace Ongka's remonstrance that as far as he was concerned the moka was still alive in the form of compensation payments) the old moka system was dead and that young people would scornfully refuse to listen to their elders if asked to contribute to such an event; this also despite the fact that young people of both sexes commit violent acts that necessitate the disbursement of large amounts of wealth in unilateral payments of compensation. At the same time, coalitions of leaders were beginning to infuse into the Charismatic Christian ritual cycle elements of big-manship that were highly reminiscent of the past, planning that their own future baptisms would be public events demonstrating their own status, crucial events also bringing prestige to the church and causing many others to convert (a classic phenomenon in Pacific history), and marked above all by the building of expensive new churches (viz., cult houses), the slaughtering of pigs (viz., sacrifices), and the making of eloquent speeches to large crowds, as well as the necessary acquisition of vehicles to transport supporters. In such a vision, moka and charismatic Christianity become ouroboric and recursive as well as antithetical. The alterations in moka coincide with the birth of Christian ways, but these ways are then adapted so as to reproduce many of the essential patterns of the moka itself. The rope of moka is unraveled and then raveled again, and those who see themselves as holding its ropes are leaders cut from similar cloth as those in the past. In addition, political leaders were in 1999 planning to restart some moka exchanges as an integral part of their external political campaigns for national elections. This is not simply, however, a case of plus ça change. Change is real and overwhelming; but in the process of adjusting to it and interpreting it people turn the very instruments and institutions of change into devices for continuity, for resolving and transcending contradictions, and for making the new at least analogous to the old.

The historical span of this study has corresponded in good part to the period 1964 to 1998, which is coincident with the span of fieldwork that is the basis of the study itself. Although such a period is in some ways arbitrary, it does relate to two important historical moments in Hagen: the colonial efflorescence of moka exchanges in the 1960s and their postcolonial decline in the 1990s: not quite the birth and death of moka because the moka existed in precolonial times and, as we have seen, the values expressed in it are in the process of being partially recreated in a new institutional form; but certainly times of dramatic growth and equally dramatic decline in the life history of an institution that has played an important part both in defining the responses of the Hagen people to change and in forming anthropological models of what the Highlands societies of Papua New Guinea are all about. The transformation of moka means both that Hagen social life is being transformed and that the classic picture of the big-man society developed by anthropologists in the 1960s must now be matched by complex models of historical change. Our book has been intended as a step in that direction.

▶ ▶ ▶ REFERENCES ▶ ▶ ▶

Amarshi, Azeem, Kenneth Good, and Rex Mortimer

    1979   *Development and Dependency. The Political Economy of Papua New Guinea.* Oxford University Press, Melbourne.

Appadurai, Arjun

    1991   Global Ethnoscapes: Notes and Queries for a Transnational Anthropology. In *Recapturing Anthropology: Working in the Present,* pp. 191–210, edited by Richard G. Fox. School of American Research Press, Santa Fe.

Barker, John (editor)

    1990   *Christianity in Oceania.* Association for Social Anthropology in Oceania. Monograph no. 12. University Press of America, Lanham, MD.

Barth, Fredrik

    1966   *Models of Social Organization.* RAI Occasional papers no. 23, London.

Bercovitch, Eytan

    1998   Disembodiment and Concealment among the Atbalmin of Papua New Guinea. In *Bodies and Persons,* edited by M. Lambek and A. Strathern, pp. 210–231. Cambridge University Press, Cambridge.

Bieniek, Jan and Garry W. Trompf

    2000   The Millennium, Not the Cargo? In *Ethnohistory* 47(1), special issue on the Millennium, edited by Pamela J. Stewart and Andrew Strathern (forthcoming).

Boehm, Christopher

    1984   *Blood Revenge: The Enactment and Management of Conflict in Montenegro and other Tribal Societies.* University of Kansas Press, Lawrence.

Brown, Paula

    1978   *Highland Peoples of New Guinea.* Cambridge University Press, New York.

    1995   *Beyond a Mountain Valley. The Simbu of Papua New Guinea.* University of Hawaii Press, Honolulu.

Busby, Cecilia

    1997   Permeable and Partible Persons: A Comparative Analysis of Gender and Body in South India and Melanesia. *JRAI* 3(2): 261–278.

Carrier, James G. and Achsah Carrier

1991   *Structure and Process in Melanesian Society: Ponam's Progress.* Harwood, London.

Clark, Jeffrey

1991   Pearlshell Symbolism in Highlands Papua New Guinea, with Particular Reference to the Wiru People of Southern Highlands Province. *Oceania* 61: 309–339.

Cohen, Anthony P.

1994   *Self Consciousness. An Alternative Theory of Identity.* Routledge, London.

Connolly, Bob and Robin Anderson

1987   *First Contact.* Viking Penguin, New York.

Dinnen, S.

n.d.   Fighting and Votes—Violence, Security and the 1992 Papua New Guinean National Elections. Ms., National Research Institute, Port Moresby.

Douglas, Mary

1996   *Thought Styles. Critical Essays on Good Taste.* Sage, London.

Epstein, Arnold L.

n.d.   *Gunantuna: Aspects of the Person, Self, and Individual among the Tolai.* Crawford House, Bathurst, NSW (in press).

Errington, Frederick K. and Deborah B. Gewertz

1995   *Articulating Change in the "Last Unknown."* Westview Press, Boulder.

1997   the Wewak Rotary Club: the Middle Class in Melanesia. *Journal of the Royal Anthropological Institute* 3(2): 333–353.

Feil, Daryl

1978   Women and Men in the Enga Tee. *American Ethnologist* 5:263–279.

1982   From Pigs to Pearlshells: The Transformation of a New Guinea Highlands Exchange Economy. *American Ethnologist* 9:291–306.

1987   *The Evolution of Highland Papua New Guinea Societies.* Cambridge University Press, Cambridge.

Fernandez, J. W.

1986   *Persuasions and Performances. The Play of Tropes in Culture.* Indiana University Press, Bloomington.

Finney, Ben

1973   *Big-Men and Business: Entrepreneurship and Economic Growth in the New Guinea Highlands.* University of Hawaii Press, Honolulu.

1974   Pearl Shells in Goroka: from Valuables to Chickenfeed. *Yagl-Ambu* 1: 342–349.

1993   From the Stone Age to the Age of Corporate Takeovers. In *Contemporary Pacific Societies: Studies in Development and Change,* pp. 102–116, edited by Victoria S. Lockwood, Thomas G. Harding, and Ben J. Wallace. Prentice Hall, Englewood Cliffs, NJ.

Fortes, Meyer

1987   *Religion, Morality, and the Person. Essays on Tallensi Religion,* edited by Jack Goody. Cambridge University Press, Cambridge.

Foster, Robert. J. (editor)

    1995   *Nation-Making in Post-Colonial Melanesia.* University of Michigan Press, Ann Arbor.

Gell, Alfred

    1992   Inter-tribal Commodity Barter and Reproductive Gift-exchange in Old Melanesia. In *Barter, Exchange and Value,* edited by C. Humphrey and S. Hugh-Jones, pp. 142–168. Cambridge University Press, Cambridge.

Gewertz, Deborah and Frederick Errington

    1998   Why We Return to Papua New Guinea. *Anthropological Quarterly* 70(3): 127–136.

    1999   *Emerging Class in Papua New Guinea.* Cambridge University Press, Cambridge.

Godelier, Maurice

    1982   Social Hierarchies among the Baruya. In *Inequality in New Guinea Highlands Societies,* edited by A. J. Strathern. Cambridge University Press, Cambridge.

    1986   *The Making of Great Men: Male Domination and Power among the New Guinea Baruya.* Cambridge University Press, Cambridge.

Goffman, Erving

    1959   *The Presentation of Self in Everyday Life.* Doubleday, New York.

Goldman, Laurence

    1983   *Talk Never Dies.* Tavistock, London.

Greenhouse, Carol J.

    1992   Signs of Quality. *American Ethnologist.* 19(2): 233–254.

    1986   *Praying for Justice: Faith, Order, and Community in an American Town.* Cornell University Press, Ithaca.

Gregory, Christopher

    1982   *Gifts and Commodities.* Academic Press, London.

Harris, Grace G.

    1989   Concepts of Individual, Self, and Person in Description and Analysis. *American Anthropologist* 91(3): 599–612.

Hau'ofa, Epeli

    1975   Anthropology and Pacific Islanders. *Oceania* 45:283–290.

Healey C. J.

    1984   Trade and Sociability: Balanced Reciprocity as Generosity in the New Guinea Highlands. *American Ethnologist* 11:42–60.

    1990   *Maring Hunters and Traders. Production and Exchange in the Papua New Guinea Highlands.* University of California Press, Berkeley.

Hepworth, Michael, and Bryan S. Turner

    1982   *Confession: Studies in Deviance and Religion.* Routledge and Kegan Paul, London.

Herzfeld, Michael

    1992   *The Social Production of Indifference. Explaining the Symbolic Roots of Western Bureaucracy.* University of Chicago Press, Chicago.

Humphrey, Caroline and Stephen Hugh-Jones (editors)

1992 *Barter, Exchange and Value. An Anthropological Approach.* Cambridge University Press, Cambridge.

Iamo, Wari and Joseph Ketan

1992 *How Far Under the Influence?* National Research Institute, Port Moresby.

Jolly, Margaret

1987 The Chimera of Equality in Melanesia. *Mankind* 17 (2):168–183.

Jolly, Margaret, and Roger Keesing

1992 Epilogue. In *History and Tradition in Melanesian Anthropology,* edited by J. G. Carrier, pp. 224–247. University of California Press, Berkeley.

Kapferer, Bruce (editor)

1976 *Transaction and Meaning.* ISHI Publications, Philadelphia.

Keesing, Roger M.

1992 *Custom and Confrontation. The Kwaio Struggle for Cultural Autonomy.* University of Chicago Press, Chicago.

Kelly, Raymond C.

1968 Demographic Pressure and Descent Group Structure. *Oceania* 39:36–63.

1974 *Etoro Social Structure.* University of Michigan Press, Ann Arbor.

1993 *Constructing Inequality. The Fabrication of a Hierarchy of Virtue among the Etoro.* University of Michigan Press, Ann Arbor.

Ketan, Joseph

1996 Electoral Politics in Mount Hagen: The Dei Open Election. In *The 1992 PNG Election,* edited by Y. Saffu, pp. 240–265.

1998 "The Name Must Not Go Down." Ph.D. dissertation, University of Wollongong, Australia.

Knauft, Bruce

1993 *South Coast New Guinea Cultures.* Cambridge University Press, Cambridge.

1997 Gender Identity, Political Economy and Modernity in Melanesia and Amazonia. *Journal of the Royal Anthropological Institute* 3(2):233–259.

1999 *From Primitive to Postcolonial in Melanesia and Anthropology.* University of Michigan Press, Ann Arbor.

Lattas, Andrew

1998 *Cultures of Secrecy. Reinventing Race in Bush Kaliai Cargo Cults.* University of Wisconsin Press, Madison.

Lederman, Rena

1986 *What Gifts Engender: Social Relations and Politics in Mendi, Highland Papua New Guinea.* Cambridge University Press, Cambridge.

Lemonnier, Pierre

1986 *Guerres et Festins.:* Editions Maison des Sciences de l'Homme, Paris.

1991 From Great Men to Big Men. In *Big-men and Great Men,* edited by M. Godelier and M. Strathern, pp. 7–27. Cambridge University Press, Cambridge.

Levine, Hal. B.

1999   Reconstructing Ethnicity. *Journal of the Royal Anthropological Institute* 5(2): 165–180.

LiPuma, Edward

n.d.   *The Magic of Modernity.* University of Michigan Press, Ann Arbor (in press).

Malinowski, Bronislaw

1922   *Argonauts of the Western Pacific.* Routledge and Kegan Paul, London.

Mapusia, Mike

1987   Police Policy Towards Tribal Fighting in the Highlands. In *Law and Order in a Changing Society,* edited by L. Morauta, pp. 57–69. Australian National University, Canberra.

Marcus, George E.

1998   *Ethnography through Thick and Thin.* Princeton University Press, Princeton.

Marcus, George and Michael J. Fischer

1986   *Anthropology as Cultural Critique. An Experimental Moment in the Human Sciences.* University of Chicago Press, Chicago.

Mauss, Marcel

1925   (1967) *The Gift: Forms and Functions of Exchange in Archaic Societies.* Norton, New York.

May, Ronald J. and Matthew Spriggs (editors)

1990   *The Bougainville Crisis.* Crawford House Press, Bathhurst.

Mageo, Jeannette M.

1998   *Theorizing Self in Samoa. Emotions, Gender, and Sexualities.* University of Michigan Press, Ann Arbor.

1995   The Reconfiguring Self. *American Anthropologist* 97 (2): 282–296.

Meggitt, Mervyn J.

1962   Dream Interpretation among the Mae Enga of New Guinea. *Southwestern Journal of Anthropology* 18:216–229.

1977   *Blood Is Their Argument.* Mayfield Publishing, Palo Alto.

Meggitt, Mervyn J. and Robert Gordon

1985   *Law and Order in the New Guinea Highlands.* University Press of New England, Hanover.

Merlan, Francesca, and Alan Rumsey

1991   *Ku Waru. Language and Segmentary Politics in the Western Nebilyer Valley, Papua New Guinea.* Cambridge University Press, Cambridge.

Modjeska, Charles N.

1982   Production and Inequality: Perspectives from Central New Guinea. In *Inequality in New Guinea Highlands Societies,* edited by A. J. Strathern, pp. 50–108. Cambridge University Press, Cambridge.

Morris, Brian

1994   *Anthropology of the Self: The Individual in Cultural Perspective.* Pluto Press, London.

O'Hanlon, Michael

1989   *Reading the Skin: Adornment, Display and Society among the Wahgi.* Crawford House Press, Bathhurst.

Otterbein, Keith

1994   *Feuding and Warfare. Selected Works of Keith Otterbein.* Gordon and Breach Science Publishers, Langhorne, PA.

Otto, Ton, and Nicholas Thomas (editors)

1997   *Narratives of Nation in the South Pacific.* Harwood Academic Publishers, Amsterdam.

Parry, Jonathan, and Maurice Bloch (editors)

1989   *Money and the Morality of Exchange.* Cambridge University Press, Cambridge.

Rappaport, Roy A.

1968   *Pigs for the Ancestors.* Yale University Press, New Haven.

Read, Kenneth E.

1955   Morality and the Concept of the Person among the Gahuku-Gama. *Oceania* 25:233–282.

Riches, David (editor)

1988   *The Anthropology of Violence.* Basil Blackwell, Oxford.

Robbins, Joel L.

1997   666, or Why Is the Millennium on the Skin? Morality, the State and the Epistemology of Apocalypticism among the Urapmin of Papua New Guinea. In *Millennial Markers,* edited by P. J. Stewart and A. J. Strathern, pp. 35–58. JCU-Centre for Pacific Studies, Townsville.

1998   Becoming Sinners. Christian Transformations of Morality and Culture in a Papua New Guinea Society. Ph.D. dissertation, University of Virginia.

Rosenberger, Nancy R. (editor)

1992   *Japanese Sense of Self.* Cambridge University Press, Cambridge.

Saffu, Yaw (editor)

1996   *The 1992 PNG Election: Change and Continuity in Electoral Politics.* Australian National University, Canberra.

Sahlins, Marshall

1963   Poor Man, Rich Man, Big Man, Chief: Political Types in Melanesia and Polynesia. *Comparative Studies in Society and History.* 5:285–303.

1985   *Islands of History.* University of Chicago Press, Chicago.

Salisbury, Richard F

1962   *From Stone to Steel.* Oxford University Press, Melbourne.

Samuel, Geoffrey

1990   *Mind, Body, and Culture.* Cambridge University Press, Cambridge.

Shipton, Parker M.

1989   *Bitter Money: Cultural Economy and Some African Meanings of Forbidden Commodities.* American Anthropological Association, Washington, D.C.

Shweder, Richard A., and Edmund J. Bourne

    1984   Does the Concept of the Person Vary Cross-culturally? In *CultureTheory. Essays on Mind, Self, Emotion,* edited by Richard A. Shweder and Robert A. LeVine, pp. 158–199. Cambridge University Press, Cambridge.

Sillitoe, Paul

    1979a   Cosmetics from Trees, an Underrated Trade in Papua New Guinea. *Australian Natural History* 19 (9):292–297.

    1979b   *Give and Take. Exchange in Wola Society.* Canberra: Australian National University Press.

    1981   Some More on War: a Wola Perspective. In *Homicide Compensation in Papua New Guinea: Problems and Prospects,* edited by R. Scaglion, pp. 70–81. Law Reform Commission Monograph no. 1, Port Moresby.

    1985   Divide and No-One Rules: The Implications of Sexual Divisions of Labour in the Papua New Guinea Highlands. *Man* (n.s.) 20(3):494–522.

    1996   *A Place Against Time. Land and Environment in the Papua New Guinea Highlands.* Harwood Academic Publishers, Amsterdam.

Smith, Michael F.

    1994   *Hard Times on Kairiru Island: Poverty, Development, and Morality in a Papua New Guinea Village.* University of Hawaii Press, Honolulu.

Stephen, Michele

    1995   *A'aisa's Gifts. A Study of Magic and the Self.* University of California Press, Berkeley.

Stewart, Frank H.

    1998   *Honor.* University of Chicago Press, Chicago.

Stewart, Pamela J.

    1998   Ritual Trackways and Sacred Paths of Fertility. *In Perspectives on the Bird's Head of Irian Jaya, Indonesia, Proceedings of the Conference (Leiden 13–17 Oct. 1997),* edited by Jelle Miedema, Cecilia Odé, and Rien Dam, pp. 275–289. Rodopi, Amsterdam.

Stewart, Pamela J. and Andrew J. Strathern (editors)

    1997   *Millennial Markers.* JCU–Centre for Pacific Studies, Townsville.

    2000   *Identity Work: Constructing Pacific Lives.* ASAO Monograph Series No. 18. University of Pittsburgh Press, Pittsburgh.

Stewart, Pamela J. and Andrew J. Strathern

    1997a   Netbags Revisited: Cultural Narratives from Papua New Guinea. *Pacific Studies,* 20(2):1–30.

    1997b   Sorcery and Sickness: Spatial and Temporal Movements in Papua New Guinea and Australia. JCU-Centre for Pacific Studies Discussion Papers Series, No. 1, James Cook University, Townsville.

    1998a   Life at the End: Voices and Visions from Mt. Hagen, Papua New Guinea. *Zeitschrift für Missionswissenschaft und Religionswissenschaft,* 82, No. 4:227–244.

1998b Money, Politics, and Persons in Papua New Guinea. *Social Analysis* 42(2): 132–149.

1998c End Times Prophecies from Mount Hagen, Papua New Guinea: 1995–1997. *Journal of Millennial Studies* 1(1) [electronic journal].

1999a Female Spirit Cults as a Window on Gender Relations in the Highlands of Papua New Guinea. *The Journal of the Royal Anthropological Institute* 5(3): 345–360.

1999b Death on the Move: Landscape and Violence on the Highlands Highway, Papua New Guinea. *Anthropology and Humanism* 24(1):20–31.

2000 Introduction: Latencies and Realizations in Millennial Practices. In P. J. Stewart and A. Strathern (eds.) Millennial Countdown in New Guinea, *Ethnohistory* Special Issue 4:7(1).

n.d.a End Time Frustrations in Hagen: The Death of Moka and Polygamy: Is There a Better World? Paper presented at the 1998 American Anthropological Association's ninety-seventh annual meeting, Philadelphia, PA (Dec. 2–6, 1998).

n.d.b The Great Exchange: Moka with God. Paper presented at the 1999 Association for Social Anthropology conference in Hilo, Hawai'i (Feb. 2–7, 1999).

Strathern, Andrew

1969 Finance and Production. *Oceania* 40:42–67.

1970 To Choose a Strong Man. The House of Assembly Elections in Mul-Dei 1968. *Oceania* 41:136–147.

1971 *The Rope of Moka. Big-Men and Ceremonial Exchange in Mount Hagen, New Guinea.* Cambridge University Press, Cambridge.

1972a The Entrepreneurial Model of Social Change: from Norway to New Guinea. *Ethnology* 11:368–379.

1972b *One Father, One Blood.* Australian National University Press, Canberra.

1972c The Supreme Court: a Matter of Prestige and Power. *Melanesian Law Journal* 2:23–28.

1974 When Dispute Procedures Fail. In *Contention and Dispute,* edited by A. L. Epstein, pp. 240–270. Australian National University Press, Canberra.

1975 Veiled Speech in Mount Hagen. In *Political language and Oratory in Traditional Societies,* edited by M. Bloch, pp. 185–203. Academic Press, London.

1976 Seven Good Men: The Dei Open Electorate. In *Prelude to Self-Government,* edited by D. Stone, pp. 265–287. University of Papua New Guinea Press, Port Moresby.

1977a Melpa Food-names as an Expression of Ideas on Identity and Substance. *Journal of the Polynesian Society* 86:503–511.

1977b *Myths and Legends from Mount Hagen,* by Georg F. Vicedom. Institute of Papua New Guinea Studies, Port Moresby. Translated by Andrew Strathern.

1979 Gender, Ideology, and Money in Mount Hagen. *Man* (n.s.) 14:530–548.

1979–80   The Red Box Money Cult in Mount Hagen, 1968–71. *Oceania:* 50(1):88–102; 50(2):161–175.

1985   Digging out Causes: Health Care in Mount Hagen. In *Traditional Medicine and Primary Health Care in PNG,* edited by W. G. Jilek, pp. 26–32. WHO and University of Papua New Guinea Press, Port Moresby.

1987   Social Classes in Mount Hagen? The Early Evidence. *Ethnology* 26(4):245–260.

1989   Melpa Dream Interpretation and the Concept of Hidden Truth. *Ethnology* 28(4):301–316.

1992   Let the Bow Go Down. In *War in the Tribal Zone,* edited by R. B. Ferguson and N. Whitehead, pp. 229–250. School of American Research Press, Santa Fe.

1993a   Big-man, Great Man, Leader: The Link of Ritual Power. *Journal de la Société des Oceaniste* (2):145–158.

1993b   *Voices of Conflict.* Pittsburgh: Ethnology Monographs no 14.

1993c   Violence and Political Change in Mount Hagen. *Pacific Studies* 16(4):41–60.

1994   Keeping the Body in Mind. *Social Anthropology* 2 (1): 43–53.

1996a   *Body Thoughts.* University of Michigan Press, Ann Arbor.

1996b   Structures of Disjuncture. In *Work in Progress: Essays in New Guinea Highlands Ethnography in Honour of Paula Brown Glick,* pp. 258–268, edited by Hal Levine and Anton Ploeg. Peter Lang, Frankfurt am Main.

Strathern, Andrew (translator)

1979   *Ongka. A Self-Account by a New Guinea Big-man.* Gerald Duckworth, London.

1993   *Ru. Biography of a Western Highlander.* National Research Institute, Port Moresby.

Strathern, Andrew J., and Pamela J. Stewart

1997a   The Efficacy-Entertainment Braid Revisited: From Ritual to Commerce in Papua New Guinea. *Journal of Ritual Studies* 11(1):61–70.

1997b   The Problems of Peace-Makers in Papua New Guinea: Modalities of Negotiation and Settlement. *The Cornell International Law Journal* 30(3): 681–699.

1997c   Introduction: Millennial Markers in the Pacific. In *Millennial Markers,* edited by P. J. Stewart and A. J. Strathern, pp. 1–17. JCU–Centre for Pacific Studies, Townsville.

1998a   Embodiment and Communication. Two Frames for the Analysis of Ritual in Papua New Guinea. *Social Anthropology* 6(2):237–251.

1998b   *A Death to Pay for: Individual Voices.* Distributed by Penn State University Media Services. Pittsburgh: Department of Anthropology, University of Pittsburgh.

1998c   Seeking Personhood: Anthropological Accounts and Local Concepts in Mount Hagen, Papua New Guinea. *Oceania* 68(3):170–188.

1998d   Shifting Places, Contested Spaces: Land and Identity Politics in the Pacific. *The Australian Journal of Anthropology* 9(2):209–224.

1998e   The Embodiment of Responsibility: "Confession" and "Compensation" in Mount Hagen, Papua New Guinea. *Pacific Studies* 21 (1/2):41–62.

1999a   Objects, Relationships, and Meanings: Historical Switches in Currencies in Mount Hagen, Papua New Guinea. In *Money and Modernity: State and Local Currencies in Melanesia,* edited by David Akin and Joel Robbins, pp. 164–191. ASAO (Association for Social Anthropology in Oceania) Monograph Series No. 17. University of Pittsburgh Press, Pittsburgh.

1999b   *Collaborations and Conflicts. A Leader Through Time.* Harcourt Brace College Publishers, Fort Worth.

1999c   *Curing and Healing: Medical Anthropology in Global Perspective.* Carolina Academic Press, Durham.

1999d   *"The Spirit is Coming!" A Photographic-Textual Exposition of the Female Spirit Cult Performance in Mt. Hagen.* Ritual Studies Monograph Series, Monograph No. 1, Pittsburgh.

2000   *The Python's Back: Pathways of Comparison between Indonesia and Melanesia.* Bergin and Garvey, Greenwood Publishing Group, Westport, CT.

n.d.a   *Stories, Strength, and Self-Narration: Western Highlands, Papua New Guinea.* Crawford House Publishing, Bathhurst, Australia (forthcoming).

n.d.b   Mi les long yupela usim flag bilong mi: Symbols, Identity, and Desire in Papua New Guinea. *Pacific Studies* (in press).

n.d.c   Creating Difference: A Contemporary Affiliation Drama in the Highlands of New Guinea. *The Journal of the Royal Anthropological Institute* (in press).

Strathern, A. and Pamela J. Stewart (editors)

1998   *Kuk Heritage: Issues and Debates in Papua New Guinea.* The National Museum of PNG and the JCU–Centre for Pacific Studies and the Okari Research Group, Department of Anthropology, University of Pittsburgh, Pittsburgh.

Strathern, Marilyn

1988   *The Gender of the Gift.* University of California Press, Berkeley.

Strauss, H. and H. Tischner

1962   *Die Mi-Kultur der Hagenberg Stämme.* Hamburg: Cram de Gruyter & Co.

Taussig, Michael

1980   *The Devil and Commodity Fetishism in South America.* Chapel Hill: University of North Carolina Press.

1993   *Mimesis and Alterity.* Routledge, London and New York.

Toft, Susan (editor)

1997   *Compensation for Resource Development in Papua New Guinea.* Port Moresby: Law Reform Commission Monogr. No. 6.

Thomas, Nicholas

1989   *Out of Time. History and Evolution in Anthropological Discourse.* Cambridge University Press, Cambridge.

1991   *Entangled Objects. Exchange, Material Culture and Colonialism in the Pacific.* Cambridge: Cambridge Uniiversity Press.

Vicedom, G. F. and H. Tischner

1943–48   *Die Mbowamb* (3 vols.). Hamburg: Friederichsen, de Gruyter and Co.

Wagner, Roy

1991   The fractal person. In M. Godelier and M. Strathern (editors.) *Big Men and Great Men* pp. 159–173. Cambridge University Press, Cambridge.

Ward, R. G. and E. Kingdon (editors)

1995   Land, Custom and Practice in the South Pacific. Cambridge University Press, Cambridge.

Watson James B.

1983   *Tairora Culture: Contingency and Pragmatism.* University of Washington Press, Seattle.

Weiner, James F.

1988   *The Heart of the Pearl Shell. The Mythological Dimension of Foi Sociality.* Berkeley: University of California Press.

1993   To Be at Home with Others in an Empty Place: A Reply to Mimica. *The Australian Journal of Anthropology* 4: 233–244.

Wesley-Smith, T. and E. Ogan

1992   Copper, Class, and Crisis. Changing Relations of Production in Bougainville. *The Contemporary Pacific* 4(2):245–267.

Wiessner, Polly and Akii Tumu

1998   *Historical Vines. Enga Networks of Exchange, Ritual and Warfare in Papua New Guinea.* Washington: Smithsonian Institution Press.

White, Geoffrey

1990   Emotion Talk and Social Inference: Disentangling in Santa Isabel, Solomon Islands. In Watson-Gegeo, K. and G. White eds. *Disentangling. Conflict Discourse in Pacific Societies.* Stanford University Press, Stanford.

Wormsley, W. and M. Toke

n.d.   Final Report: The Enga Law and Order Project. Enga Provincial Government, Wabag, Papua New Guinea.

▶ ▶ ▶ INDEX ▶ ▶ ▶